OIL COMPANY

FINANCIAL ANALYSIS

IN NONTECHNICAL

LANGUAGE

OIL
COMPANY

FINANCIAL ANALYSIS

IN NONTECHNICAL

LANGUAGE

DANIEL JOHNSTON

PennWell Books

PENNWELL PUBLISHING COMPANY
TULSA, OKLAHOMA

Copyright © 1992 by

PennWell Publishing Company

1421 South Sheridan/P.O. Box 1260

Tulsa, Oklahoma 74101

Library of Congress Cataloging-in-Publication Data

Johnston, Daniel.

  Oil company financial analysis in nontechnical language / Daniel Johnston.

    p. cm.

  Includes index.

  ISBN 0-87814-374-2

  1. Petroleum industry and trade—Finance. 2. Stock-exchange.

  I. Title.

  HG6047.P47J64 1992

  622'.3382'0681—dc20

Printed in the United States of America

To my wife Jill and our children:
Erik, Lane, Jill Danielle,
Julianna, and David.

CONTENTS

TABLES

FIGURES

WORKSHEETS

ILLUSTRATIONS

ACKNOWLEDGEMENTS

This book reflects the efforts of a number of people. I would like to thank the following for their reviews, comments, and their helpful suggestions:

Carl Brown, Dr. Gary Cadenhead, Michael Flanigan, Marvin Gearhart, Jeff Gentry, David Johnston, Jill Johnston, William Kuhn, Jim Leonard, Hill Martin, Sue Rhodes Sesso, Selonna Stahle, Steve Weber, and Charles Woodard.

I would also like to thank my good friends and associates, Dr. Jimmie Aung Khin, Mitchel Hurwitz, and David Wengierski.

INTRODUCTION

There is a bit of magic in the stock market, especially when it comes to oil companies. When the oil industry and the stock market get together, the affair is usually dynamic and not always pleasant. This book is about the financial side of the petroleum industry.

Basic principles are widely understood in the financial industry, but the terminology and analytical techniques can vary greatly. This book is written for the nonfinancial shareholders, managers, and oil company employees interested in the forces that influence stock values.

The bottom line in any company is expressed in the language of finance. This book explains financial concepts in a nontechnical, practical way so that nonfinancial professionals and others may understand and appreciate this aspect of the business. Even 15 years ago, companies disclosed substantially less information than what is available now. This additional information allows a better understanding of the financial status and health of a company.

Many times management has been held hostage by corporate raiders. Employees get caught in the middle. From the employees' point of view, there is seldom such thing as a *friendly* takeover. Shareholders in some instances make substantial short-term gains and other times feel cheated by the actions of raiding companies. Added understanding of basic financial issues will hopefully limit the surprise, confusion and vulnerability.

Many groups of individuals are interested in the financial impact of a merger or a takeover. To each group the perspective is slightly different, but the objectives always center around the concept of *value*. What is the company worth? What is the common stock worth? These are primary issues that confront:

• company shareholders (owners)

- company preferred stock shareholders
- company directors
- company management
- company bondholders or lenders
- investment bankers and financial advisors
- outside security analysts
- arbitrageurs
- the Securities and Exchange Commission
- the Justice Department

Nonfinancial professionals must become more aware of financial issues. Many have an excellent foundation through their understanding of *discounted cash flow analysis* used extensively in this industry. The financial concepts are not complex, but simply obscured by the unique terminology of the financial world.

The focus of this book is on financial issues and the role of management and shareholders. The turbulent restructuring in the industry during the 1980s changed things. Technical professionals traditionally were not involved with financial matters. Now if they are concerned, they need not panic when faced with an income statement or a balance sheet.

Analysis of oil company assets, financial reports, and valuation of common stock is the subject of this text. Techniques and aspects of evaluating an oil and gas company are discussed in detail. The text addresses specifically the analytical techniques that are based on public information. It is essentially a book about how to read an oil company's annual report to shareholders and the 10-K report. The book provides worksheets and step-by-step explanations to encourage active participation in financial analysis.

Examples and guidelines are presented to help the reader arrive at and characterize the value of a company. Valuation techniques are discussed within the context of current mergers and acquisitions, corporate restructuring, and market performance.

Analytical techniques, yardsticks, and tools of the trade are presented from many different perspectives. Examples and case studies illustrate the way it is done. The book provides insight into the analytical process as well as useful data and information for reference.

Research of statistical standards and financial trends is summarized in tables and appendices. This information came from computer database searches, periodical literature, annual and 10-K reports, brokerage house publications, and regularly published energy   statistics.

While the chapter titles reflect the principal coverage of major topics, basic valuation factors arise in various sections of the text. Where this occurs, cross-references are provided.

Discussions of financial and accounting theory usually are not recreational reading. The section on accounting theory, however, takes a practical approach. It is the foundation for understanding the information found in financial statements. The accounting principles are straightforward, and the fog around financial statements begins to clear. This book uses equations as sparingly as possible. The focus is on common sense and practical application, not details.

Chapter 5 is devoted to an extensive coverage of the driving forces behind the value of common stock.

Peer group analysis, comparing a company with its peers, can be interesting. It has practical value from a corporate strategy point of view as well as worthwhile analytical value.

Estimating the value of oil and gas reserves without detailed cash flow analysis is an unfortunate fact of life for many shareholders. Chapter 5 should help this situation. This chapter also provides insight into the downstream end of the industry. It should be interesting for those who are curious about the value of a refinery or a network of gas stations.

The chapter on corporate restructuring is a straightforward approach to the arithmetic of mergers, acquisitions, and other types of corporate restructuring.

This is not a book about how to make a fortune as an energy stock analyst or how to "beat the market." This book should clear up some of the myths and misconceptions of the investment world. The information about financial theory and the dynamics of the stock market hopefully will encourage people to participate and learn more. In knowledge there is strength.

FUNDAMENTALS OF VALUATION

The concept of value can be viewed many different ways. The perspective is different for bankers, accountants, shareholders, management, regulatory agencies, and for buyers and sellers. Most analysts and shareholders focus on two general concepts of value: *market value* and *fair market value.*

Market Value

Usually, the stock market determines the market value (MV) of a company as though it will conduct business indefinitely as *a going concern.* The terms *going concern* and *ongoing concern* indicate this view of a company that will continue its business functions into the future. The opposite of this would be the *breakup* value of a business. The market will take a different view of a company if it is expected to be acquired and then perhaps liquidated. At times like this the market will respond to the expectations of the ultimate acquisition price for the company. This will often reflect more than the value of the company as a going concern. The market will look deeper into the potential breakup value of the company. Sometimes privately held or closely held stocks will not have enough trading volume to allow the market to define a reasonable level of value. These exceptions can be ignored for the moment as the general concept of market value is explored.

The objective for most people is to determine not what market value is, but what it might be at a point in the future. By making an accurate estimate of the future market value of a stock, an intelligent investment decision can be made. This concept of value is the one most familiar. Analysts worldwide spend their time trying to estimate what will happen to the market price of a particular stock or a group of stocks. But market value is only one side of the coin. The other is fair market value.

Fair Market Value

Fair Market Value (FMV) is the price at which an asset would pass from a willing seller to a willing buyer after exposure to the market for a reasonable period of time. It is further assumed that both buyer and seller are competent and have a reasonable knowledge of the relevant facts and that neither party is under any undue compunction to buy or sell. This might sound like the description of the trading price of a stock on any given day. Fair market value in some situations is synonymous with market value. But when it comes to the value of common stock, there is often a difference between MV and FMV. This difference is evident in the *premiums* over market value that have been paid for stocks in takeovers.

The saying "The company is worth more dead than alive" is based on the difference between the liquidation value and going concern value. The view that the sum of the parts is worth more than the whole is still a common view. The more parts (or business segments), the more the difference in value between the market trading price of the stock and the underlying asset values that are part of FMV determination. The margin of difference between stock value and FMV usually increases with the more segments and business interests a company has.

Companies that integrated, diversified, or conglomerated always paid a price for adding diverse business segments. It appears that the market does not appreciate the additional complexity. This curse appears to be somewhat universal, particularly with companies that diversified into areas outside the energy industry. The margins have narrowed since the mid-1980s, but the market penalty for integration or diversification in the petroleum industry persists.

FMV is not a valuation technique. It is a concept, based on value, that can be derived by several techniques. The relationship between *value* and *price* can be quite complex when it comes to common stock. Regulatory agencies have had to establish guidelines and procedures to ensure that shareholders receive FMV for their stock in takeovers and other transactions. The relationship between market value of an asset and market value of a stock is different.

In the business of analyzing companies and predicting stock prices, there are two approaches: *fundamental analysis* and *technical analysis*. Furthermore, fundamentalists use two approaches to evaluate a corporate stock: *asset-based* and *income-based analysis*. The diagram in Figure 2–1 illustrates these relationships.

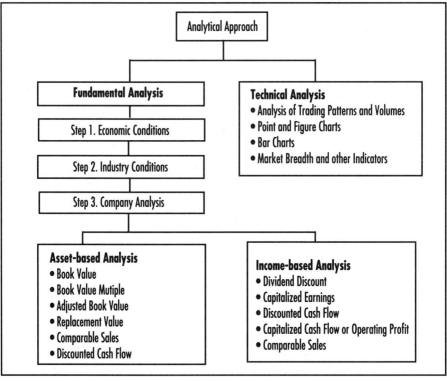

Fig. 2–1 Valuation Hierarchy

The analogy between astronomers and astrologers is sometimes used to compare these two schools of thought. This analogy is usually put forth by the fundamentalists (astronomers) to portray the approach taken by *technical analysts* (astrologers). Perhaps sometimes the analogy is apt, but most technical analysts use a proper sense of proportion. Many of them have a good understanding of fundamental analysis. The technical approach, however, gets lots of criticism. One of the strongest arguments is that "If they are right, they are right for the wrong reasons."

This book promotes the fundamental approach, but it is important to understand the differences. Fundamentalists use some techniques that verge on technical analysis. When a financial analyst looks at past sales or earnings performance of a company to predict future growth potential, he has one foot in *technical* territory.

TECHNICAL ANALYSIS

Technical analysis predicts stock prices based on past prices, trading volumes, and other factors such as trading highs, lows, and the breadth of the market (advances versus declines).

Technical analysts are referred to (sometimes disparagingly) as *chartists* because of their use of bar charts and graphs to depict historical stock price trends. The purpose of the charts and graphs is to interpret and predict stock performance. The analyst still uses charts and graphs, but now they are computer generated instead of hand plotted. The advent of the computer and increased availability of information has considerably elevated and expanded the tools available to the technical analyst and the fundamentalist.

DOW THEORY

The technical system was either started or at least formalized by Charles H. Dow, the father of technical analysis. Dow, in what is called the Dow Theory, described the overall market as having three cycles of movement, similar to the movement of the sea:

Narrow	day-to-day movements	(ripples)
Short swing	2 to 4 weeks or more	(waves)
Main movement	4 years or more	(tide)

While the day-to-day movements are of little value, analysts watch the short-swing movements closely. The main movement, or *primary trend,* is called either a *bull* or *bear* market. An example of a bull market trend is shown in Figure 2–2.

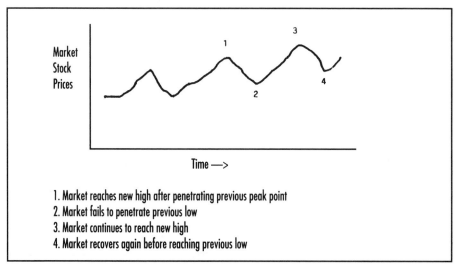

1. Market reaches new high after penetrating previous peak point
2. Market fails to penetrate previous low
3. Market continues to reach new high
4. Market recovers again before reaching previous low

Fig. 2–2 Example of Dow Theory Bull Market Signal

Dow theorists believe that the signals of *ascending tops and bottoms* described above must occur in both the industrial and transportation sectors of the market to confirm the signal of a bull market. The conclusion that a bull market had begun might have been reached between Point 2 and Point 3 as the market penetrated the previous peak the second time — the first time was at Point 1.

The Dow Theory was developed to explain the whole market. Pure technical analysis, on the other hand, is used for market segments, industry groups, or for the stock of a particular company.

The language of technical analysis used to describe trading patterns is colorful and exotic. Figure 2–3 illustrates an example of a familiar stock price pattern.

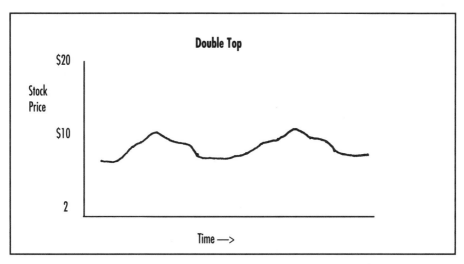

Fig. 2–3 Example of Technical Analysis

Stock price behavior like this is called a double-top pattern. Classical technical analysis interprets this as an indication the stock is encountering resistance to move higher than the high prices defined by the two peaks.

Other patterns have names like ascending triangle, double-bottom reversal, rounding-top reversal, and breakaway gap, each with a different interpretation.

Fundamentalists point out that given a particular trading pattern, technical analysts give different interpretations, and a unanimous opinion of stock price direction would be unlikely. This argument cuts both ways: fundamental analysts also disagree over matters of value.

Technical analysts theoretically are not concerned with the financial information about a company. From a practical point of view, technical analysts will find a stock that looks interesting on technical merits, and then often will look into its fundamentals.

If a fundamentalist evaluated a stock that looked interesting, he would not want to ignore the fact that the stock had been ratcheting downward for six straight months, regularly penetrating previous lows (if that were the case).

FUNDAMENTAL ANALYSIS

Fundamental analysis is the interpretation of financial data to estimate stock value and forecast future price movements. It is sometimes called *intrinsic value analysis*. Fundamental analysts consider many factors when evaluating a stock.

Fundamental analysis is a three-step exercise that encompasses the entire economic context in which an industry and company exist.

The First Step — Economic Conditions

Analysis begins with the aggregate state of the economy and the industry environment. Analysts must consider the macro conditions of the global economy and the geopolitical influences on supply of materials and product demand. Table 2-1 provides the kind of foundation material used in the first stage of analysis.

Table 2-1 United States Energy Consumption

	1980	1985	1990
Natural Gas	26.8%	24.2%	23.9%
Crude Oil Products	45.0	41.2	42.1
Coal	20.3	23.7	23.1
Hydroelectric	4.1	4.6	3.5
Nuclear and Other	3.8	6.3	7.4
	100.0%	100.0%	100.0%
Total Energy Consumption Quadrillion BTU	75.9	73.7	83.7

Source: U.S. Department of Energy

At this stage in the process, economic forces and problems that face an industry are translated into price projections. The primary objective of the first stage of the fundamental approach is the forecast of oil and gas prices. Appendix 6 summarizes wholesale oil and gas prices in the United States since 1935.

The key elements of this stage of analysis are:
- macroeconomics
- geopolitics
- industry structure
- supply and demand
- price projections

The Second Step — Industry Analysis

The next step is industry analysis. Industry is always at the mercy of interest rates, costs, competition, capital markets, and product prices. Analysis at this stage focuses on industry reaction and the competitive response by companies to various expected conditions. In addition, oil industry analysis monitors competing sources of energy and the response of consumers and government regulatory agencies.

Industry risk is influenced by stability of demand for products and raw material supply. For the past 20 years, the industry has observed a relatively stable environment on the demand side. Yet when prices peaked in 1981, conservation made a difference. The upstream sector has had to cope with dramatic changes in crude oil production levels that create a volatile and unstable investment environment.

Several characteristics distinguish the oil industry. As an extractive industry, the upstream sector is a highly specialized business environment with many implications that require special consideration. The industry is capital intensive, and invested capital is exposed to substantial risk. Unlike many commodity-based industries, the rewards can be spectacular. Yet the results of an exploration project may range from total failure to varying degrees of success.

The lead time from discovery to the point when production may begin can, in many cases, extend beyond several accounting periods. Considering that wells or fields produce for many years, the ultimate profitability of a property may not be certain until long after discovery.

The industry is fundamentally controlled by the Organization of Petroleum Exporting Countries (OPEC). At times, the OPEC cartel has had limited success at times attaining its goals of production quotas and price levels. However, given its vast reserve base, the influence of OPEC will continue to dominate the industry for many years. Standard supply and demand equations used for econometric analysis take a back seat to the efforts to second guess OPEC and the Middle Eastern problems. Many of the problems that face the industry are depicted in Figure 2–4.

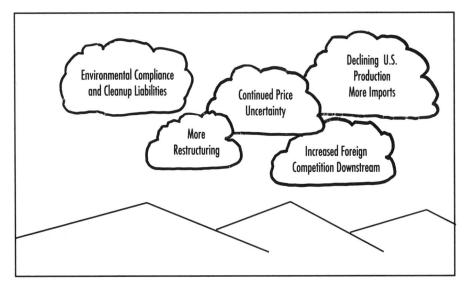

Fig. 2–4 Petroleum Industry — Clouds on the Horizon

The Third Step — Company Analysis

The final step deals with the analysis of a specific company. This is the focus of this book.

There are many reasons for evaluating an oil and gas company. The objective of an evaluation will usually determine the analytical techniques used and the amount of information available. Some of the reasons for performing an evaluation are:

- acquisition of a company
- merger of companies
- sale of a company or a subsidiary
- due diligence
- fairness opinion
- investment in the stock of a company
- share repurchase programs
- determination of capital structure
- debt collateralization
- initial public stock offering
- fair market valuation for tax purposes

Preliminary evaluations for merger/acquisition and many stock purchases are based solely on public information contained in annual reports, 10-K reports, and quarterly reports (see Chapter 4). Substantial investments are based on this information.

The *price* of an oil company common stock on a securities exchange like the NYSE is determined by:

- earnings and earnings history
- dividend yield
- cash flow
- present value of oil and gas reserves
- undeveloped acreage
- corporate track record
- opportunities available to the company
- environmental and legal contingencies
- other assets
- debt
- quality of management

Analysts know that the *value* of a company may be based on more than these factors. Analysis of a company can be viewed from a number of perspectives. There are, however, two main directions from which to approach an analysis. There is a fundamental difference between valuation techniques that address net asset value and those that evaluate a company as a going concern. This is due to the difference in the value of a company's assets and the company's income generating capability as viewed by the market.

ASSET- VS. INCOME-BASED TECHNIQUES

Techniques for estimating liquidation or breakup value are called asset-based techniques. Estimating value of a business entity as a going concern is done through analysis of income and cash flow. Because of this, the term income-based analysis is used.

Both asset- and income-based valuation techniques are based on present value theory. The difference between the two approaches is more in the view of how the assets will be treated. An income-based approach assumes the company will survive. The liquidation approach looks at individual assets and business segments as though they may no longer be part of the business.

Regardless of the reason for performing an evaluation, each applicable method should be used. In this way, the various results, when contrasted with each other, give a deeper insight into the value of an enterprise. The elements that make up the value of a company come to life.

ASSET-BASED VALUATION CONCEPTS

Asset-based analysis focuses on the individual values of a company's assets and liabilities. It begins with the balance sheet. Each asset and liability is viewed for its stand-alone market value. Sometimes major assets and even substantial liabilities are not accurately represented on the balance sheet, or may not be represented at all. This is particularly true of the oil industry. The analyst considers the value of each balance sheet item or asset group individually.

This concept of value is similar to the way individuals would estimate their net worth. The asset value of the home and furnishings is considered. Added to that would be other assets, such as cars, boats, investments in stocks and bonds, and cash. The home mortgage and any other debts such as credit card debt or car loans, are subtracted. The result is net worth. The asset-based approach to valuation of a business follows the same logic.

The net worth of a person or a business is often a bit abstract. Individuals do not want to liquidate and neither do businesses. Nevertheless, the calculations are performed regardless of how remote the possibility may be.

Liquidation value is only one perspective. Suppose that a busboy and a young doctor both have the same net worth. Are they really worth the same thing? The answer is, "Not for long!" Asset-based techniques miss one important dimension. That dimension is the potential for increase or decrease in net worth. If a choice had to be made between the busboy and the doctor for old age financial assistance, the choice would not depend on current net worth alone. Take the doctor.

CONTROL PREMIUM

There is often a greater price paid for a company's stock in a takeover. This is based on the difference between the market perception of value and the potential value in liquidation or under restructuring. The premiums paid in takeovers also represent the price a buyer is willing to pay for control of a company. With that control, the buyer has the ability to strip off assets and attempt to realize the underlying asset values that were perhaps not represented by income or cash flow.

INCOME-BASED VALUATION CONCEPTS

Income-based valuation concepts look at the income or cash generating capability of an entity. The income statement and the statement of cash flows are the focus of income-based valuation techniques. The estimate of growth is fundamental to income valuation techniques that are concerned with the earnings, dividends, and cash flow of a business entity. These techniques either directly or indirectly use present value theory as the basis of valuation.

In the preceding example, it is likely the busboy will not generate as much income as the doctor. Therefore, with time, the net worth of the doctor would be greater. This way of looking at value is the essence of income-based analysis.

The income approach assumes that a business enterprise will continue as a going concern; that is, it will continue to conduct business as usual and attempt to grow and profit as it has in the past. There are exceptions to this basic assumption. There is a gray area between pure liquidation and the ongoing business enterprise.

A company may choose a form of partial liquidation by gradual discontinuation of a product line, or by spinning off assets of a subsidiary (see Chapter 8). Income-based valuation techniques still apply. *Discounted cash flow analysis* can be used when evaluating a company as a going concern, or for evaluation of breakup value. Some of the assumptions will be different, but the technique works for both situations. The different valuation concepts are summarized in Table 2–2.

Figure 2–5 illustrates an example of the spectrum of value that might be represented by various valuation techniques. Analysts will use numerous methods to bracket and characterize value. Some methods can be used for determination of fair market value, as well as estimating reasonable trading value or market value for a stock. Analysts will use different factors depending on the objective. Standard multiples and factors are used for MV as well as FMV, and they are often different in each case.

While market value can sometimes exceed what might be judged to be FMV, it is an unusual situation. The relationship shown here, where FMV is greater than MV, is more typical. Stock prices trade primarily on earnings and cash flow, with some consideration for underlying asset values. Fair market value usually gives greater consideration to a company's asset values.

Table 2-2 Comparison of Valuation Concepts and Techniques

Corporate Valuation Concept	Valuation Basis	Remarks
Book Value	Assets	Based on accounting convention — usually not practical for an oil company. Depends on the business entity or particular asset.
Book Value Multiple	Assets	Based on *comparable sales* that establish a trend in multiples of book value paid.
Adjusted Book Value	Assets	Pure liquidation/breakup value approach. Individual assets will often be evaluated using income-based techniques.
Replacement Value	Assets	Useful for associated businesses or assets, often defines upper limit of value.
Comparable Sales	Both	Difficult to find truly comparable companies and situations — comparisons are sometimes made on basis of capitalized cash flow, earnings ratios, or other valuation concepts.
Dividend Discount	Income	Theoretical — not always practical.
Capitalized Earnings	Income	Common approach — indirectly estimates present value.
Discounted Cash Flow	Both	Best approach for analysis of a going concern or income - generating entities or assets.
Capitalized Cash Flow	Income	Inverse of Cash Flow Multiple. Proxy for detailed cash flow analysis — is useful for comparison and quick-look.
Capitalized Operating Income	Income	Similar to Cash Flow Multiple approach — proxy for cash flow analysis.

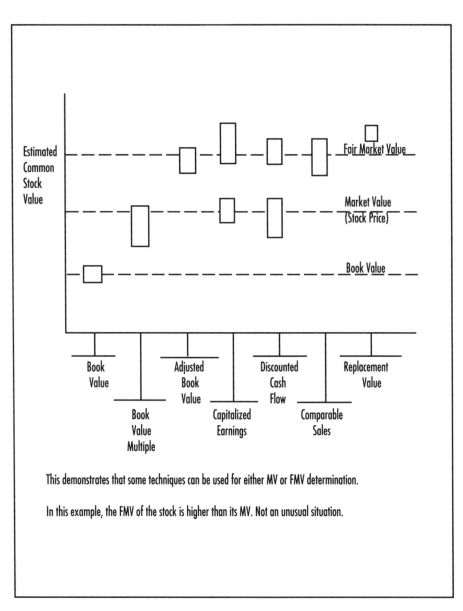

Fig. 2–5 Valuation Spectrum

Efficient Market Hypothesis

It is important before embarking on a discussion of investment theory and valuation techniques to address the concept of *market efficiency*. The notion of market efficiency deals with the availability of information about an asset (stock) and the market response to that information.

The Efficient Market Hypothesis (EMH) assumes that market prices reflect the knowledge and the expectations of all investors. EMH proponents believe that it is not possible to beat the market consistently. Put another way, it is not possible to generate returns above the average market rate of return without inside information.

The theory outlines three degrees of market efficiency.

Weak-form Efficiency. If the market value of stock reflects only historical information, market efficiency is weak. There is supposedly no virtue in estimating stock price trends based on past performance in a market that is weak-form efficient.

Semistrong. A market that is semistrong reflects all historical and publicly available information. When a market is this efficient, stock prices quickly respond to information found in annual and quarterly reports. The consensus among most EMH theorists is that the U.S. markets are semistrong.

Strong-form Efficiency. In a strong-form market, stock prices reflect all public information and inside information. The U.S. markets are supposedly not this efficient, but there are exceptions. Due to insider trading, there have been situations where stock prices of companies have risen prior to the announcement of a *tender offer*. This is perhaps a morbid sign of added efficiency.

The implications of the EMH disturb some people. The hypothesis concludes that stock prices cannot be predicted. This means that advice provided by many financial analysts is useless. If neither technical nor fundamental analysis can accurately predict stock prices, then it is time to throw darts. To support this, many argue that there is no evidence that, over the long term, the market has been beaten by anyone. The evidence for both sides of this argument is voluminous.

The EMH is not universally accepted. It is the focus of substantial controversy, and for good reason. A basic assumption of the EMH is that dissemination of information is instantaneous. While information transfer is fast in this electronic age, there are some who can react to information more quickly than the full-market response.

RANDOM WALK THEORY

The efficient market hypothesis is sometimes called the *Random Walk Theory*. This may not be completely appropriate, yet it is done frequently, and the theories go hand in hand. The Random Walk theory was introduced in 1900 by a French mathematician, Louis Bachelier. He stated that stock prices respond in various degrees of efficiency to information and influences as they become known. These influences enter the picture in a random fashion.

According to this theory, the U.S. market is at least moderately (weak-form) efficient. Stock prices reflect the reactions to information that becomes available in a random and unpredictable manner. Thus, past prices and price trends are of no use in forecasting future price movements.

Both theories flatly contradict the assumptions that are the foundation of technical analysis. This is a sore point with the technical analysts and they have many success stories to dispute the theories.

CATCH 22

How can fundamentalists argue that price trends have no influence on future prices when there are still technical analysts alive out there? Because technical analysts make investment decisions based on these trends, past prices must have an influence on market behavior. It is difficult to argue with that, and even more difficult to determine just how much of an influence past trends actually have.

NIELS BOHR — EARLY EMH PROPONENT

The Danish physicist Niels Bohr had an interesting view of the stock market. He considered a case where one class of investors chose invest-ments completely at random. They were, therefore, equally likely to win or lose when competing with the market rate of return. The aggregate performance of their investments would emulate the market itself.

He described another group of investors with inside information who would reap excess returns. But who would the losers be that would subsidize the inside traders? Those who bought and sold at random would neither win nor lose. They couldn't be the losers that provided the excess returns for the inside traders. The source, he proposed, would be from the investors who get limited historical and published information. Those who make investment decisions based on limited information then would do worse than those who buy and sell at random.

BACK TO THE DART BOARD?

The market exhibits a certain degree of efficiency. By the time the average shareholder receives his quarterly or annual report, the market has already responded, whether the report holds good or bad news. Large traders and institutional investors have access to financial information that does not wait for the mail.

Big news is delivered to the electronic news services long before the average shareholder finds out what is happening. Furthermore, when company management wants to make a pitch to institutional investors and brokerage house analysts, it is usually done through formal meet-ings and informal conversations that the average shareholder never attends.

Therefore, efficient market advocates believe that by the time the stock broker calls to say "Have you heard the good news?" it is too late to capitalize on that news.

From the point of view of the average individual shareholder, the market is plenty efficient and a security is worth its market price. Any attempt to beat the market is futile. The only realistic investment strategy would be to buy and hold a diversified portfolio of stock and simply try to achieve the market rate of return.

But if a stock is worth what the market is willing to pay for it, then why do most takeovers end up paying a premium over *market value* of around 40 – 50%? Where did that extra value come from? It usually comes from the willingness of a buyer to pay more for control of a company. Ownership of 51% of a company's stock can be substantially more valuable than 49% minority ownership.

Unfortunately, the subject of market efficiency is not simple. For example, efficient market theory has a hard time explaining market crashes like the one that occurred on October 19, 1987. It is one thing for the market to have timely information, and quite another for the market to establish the right price.

WHO CAN YOU TRUST?

Research reports published by the brokerage houses about a company are usually informative and well organized. The analyst has access to information and direct contact with management that the average shareholder will never have. Most analysts follow about a dozen companies and generate 10 to 15 reports every month. Usually, the reports support a *buy*, *hold*, or *sell* recommendation. The important thing to keep in mind is that the analysts are not totally free to issue just any opinion. There is tremendous pressure to avoid publishing *sell* recommendations.

Companies are sensitive to the conclusions in these research reports, and they can have substantial leverage with analysts. Sometimes the analyst's firm provides investment banking services for the company. In other cases, the analyst simply risks jeopardizing the good relationship he has with management from whom he obtains important information long before anybody else does. These research reports should (and usually do) disclose any special relationship between the analyst or brokerage house and the company being researched.

Many of these reports will have *buy* and *hold* recommendations, but few, if any, *sell* recommendations. Even a *hold* recommendation can come with some anxiety.

Buy and hold strategy is often discussed when this subject comes up. Many studies of the market suggest that an investor may be better off buying a diversified stock portfolio and simply holding it, rather than trying to beat the market by buying and selling regularly.

STOCK QUOTATIONS

Daily newspapers provide basic trading information for stocks in a standard format. Table 2–3 is a typical example from a November 6, 1990, newspaper showing the results of the previous day's trading for Maxus common and preferred stock.

Table 2–3 Standard Stock Quotation Format

Monday, November 5, 1990

52-Week High-Low		Div	Yield	PE	Sales hds	High	Low	Close	Chg.
13 9	Maxus	–	–	–	1286	$11^1/_8$	$10^3/_4$	$11^1/_8$	$+^1/_8$
41 $37^1/_4$	Maxus pf 4.0		10.3	–	6	39	$38^3/_4$	39	$+1^1/_8$

52-Week High-Low

The highest and lowest trading values within the past 52 weeks are listed as a source of comparison to the current day trading values. In the case of both the Maxus common and preferred shares, the current market value was half-way between the 52-week trading range.

Dividend Rate (Div.)

The dividend rate is listed in dollars per share per year, even though dividends are usually paid quarterly. The Maxus common stock pays no dividend, and the preferred stock pays $4 per share.

Yield

Yield is equal to the dividend rate divided by the current stock price.

With the Maxus preferred stock, the yield is $4 divided by the $39 closing price of the stock. This is a 10.3% yield.

Price Earning Ratio (PE)

PE stands for the *price earnings ratio* of the stock. Sometimes it is shown as *P/E*. The P/E is the ratio of the stock price divided by the company's per-share earnings for the most recent four quarters. Whenever a company has negative earnings, the ratio is meaningless and no quote is given. Maxus reported negative earnings during this period. If Maxus had $2 per share in earnings, then a P/E of 5.6 would have been reported.

Sales in Hundreds (Sales Hds.) — Trading Volume

The sales in hundreds represents the number of shares purchased/sold during the day. This is the *trading volume*. On November 5, 1990, 128,600 shares of Maxus common stock traded hands. Out of 90.7 million shares, this represents a small percentage of the stock. If this many shares sold every trading day, it would represent roughly 35% of the stock. This is not an unusually high trading volume. However, it may not represent 35% of the freely traded stock. For example, if a company had 80% of its stock held by insiders that did not buy or sell, and the 20% available on the market turned over twice during the year, then it would appear that 40% of the stock had traded hands.

On the American and New York Stock Exchanges, the *turnover*, or annual trading volume, is around 50%. That is, half the shares appear to trade hands during the year. With 50 weeks of trading per year, a typical volume for a stock should range around 1% of the stock per week.

Closely held companies have a large percentage of their common stock held by a few inside shareholders. Sometimes the definition includes institutional shareholders. Closely held companies can have annual volume turnover around 20% or as low as 10%. Professional investors will refer to the stock as being *thinly traded* because of the low volumes. The reason is usually that the stock has a small *float*. Float is the amount of freely traded shares a stock has. An example calculation of float is shown in Table 2–4.

Table 2–4 Calculation of Float

Shares Outstanding	20,000,000
Shares Owned by Insiders	–8,000,000
Shares Held by Institutions	–5,000,000
Float – Freely Traded Shares	7,000,000

In the above example, the company has 35% float. The classical definition of float includes shares held by institutions such as pension funds, university endowment funds, insurance companies, and labor unions. Institutions were once thought of as stable shareholders who did not actively trade in and out of stocks. That is no longer the case. Institutions can be very active traders. Institutions own nearly half of all public companies, and typically more than 50% of daily trading volume in the major stock exchanges is done by or on behalf of institutional investors.

High-Low Close Change (Chg.)

Quotations show the highest and lowest prices paid for a stock during a given trading period. During trading on November 5, 1990, Maxus common stock traded between $10¾ and $11⅛ and per share. The stock closed *up* at $11⅛, or would be said to have *advanced* an eighth of a point. This is where Maxus common stock started trading the following day. The last column shows how much the price changed during the day's trading. It was up $⅛ per share. Evidently, trading on that day started at $11 per share.

News reports quote stock price changes in *points*. A point is a change of one dollar in the stock price. The trading of Maxus common closed up an eighth of a point. The relative amount of change is a more dynamic measure. If Maxus stock were to increase by 1 point, that would be a 9% increase. If another stock trading at $100 per share were to change by a point, the result would be a 1% change.

While the market value can be volatile, it establishes a *minimum* acceptable stock price to shareholders. Market value is based on current trends in trading value. It may be expressed as the average closing price of the stock during the past month or quarter.

Table 2–5 shows the typical point system criteria used by many investment managers. These are common factors used by investment houses.

Table 2–5 Portfolio Managers' Equity Investment Policy
(sample point system)

The criteria and relative weights used are:

1. Current Reinvestment Rate divided by Current P/E is greater than 1	= 1 Point
2. Current Reinvestment Rate is greater than market reinvestment rate	= 1 Point
3. Return on Equity is greater than market	= 1 Point
4. Return on assets is greater than market	= 1 Point
5. Total Debt is less than 40%	= 1 Point
6. Current P/E is less than market P/E	= 1 Point
7. Price/Cash Flow ratio is less than Market Price/Cash Flow ratio	= 1 Point
8. Price/Book Value ratio is less than 1.20	= 2 Point
9. Current Yield is greater than market	= 1 Point
10. Five-year Earnings growth is greater than 10%	= 2 Point

P/E = Price Earnings Ratio

A system like this is easily computerized. This is typical screening and investment criteria for portfolio managers and institutional investors. For example, the rating system might be designed to exclude any stocks that do not get a score of 6 or more. Earnings are a prime factor in 7 of the 10 criteria. The *reinvestment rate* is another focus of this point system. The reinvestment rate is the return on equity times the percentage of *retained earnings*.

The market mentioned in Table 2–5 could be the *Dow Jones Industrial* (Dow) Averages, the *Standard and Poor's 500*, or perhaps a universe of stocks used by the particular investment manager. There are better standards than the Dow for comparing financial ratios.

Analytical systems like the one in Table 2–5 are why management pays so much attention to company earnings. Earnings still have a strong influence on market price, and, because of that, many business decisions are influenced by the perceived impact on reported earnings.

ACCOUNTING VALUE VS. ECONOMIC VALUE

Corporate management is often criticized for paying too much attention to earnings (accounting profits). Management argues that the market responds primarily to reported earnings. They cannot ignore this.

Financial analysts generally believe that the real measure of corporate profitability is not earnings, but *cash flow.* Analysis of the cash generating capability of a company is the basis of *economic value.* The subject of cash flow is discussed further in Chapters 4 and 5. While earnings are regularly followed by the market, investors are sophisticated enough to know that profitability goes beyond reported earnings. But how far beyond that does the market go? This is an important issue. Does the market look enough beyond earnings to consider the underlying assets of a company?

Table 2-6 provides a comparison of energy investments that were representative during the mid- and late 1980s. The large integrated oil companies were trading at substantial discounts to their appraised asset values, while the MLPs and royalty trusts were trading close to, and sometimes above, their appraised values.

Table 2-6   Comparison of Energy Investments

	P/CF	Ratio [1]	Typical Market Discount From Appraised Value	
Investment Vehicle	1984	1989	1984	1989
Small MLP [2]	4	5	20%	10%
Large MLP [3]	6	7	1%	2%
Royalty Trust	8	8	10%	5%
Independent Oil Company	4	5.5	35%	20%
Integrated Major Oil Company	3	4.5	50%	30%

[1] P/CF = price to cash flow ratio
[2] Under $200 million market capitalization
[3] Over $200 million market capitalization

Market capitalization is the market price per share times the number of shares of stock.

The *market discount from appraised value* is the difference between the stock trading value established by the market and the appraised value of company assets. It represents the difference between the income-based and asset-based perspectives of value. This table shows the market penalty for integration in the mid-1980s was a 50% discount. Companies with margins like that were vulnerable to hostile takeover bids.

By the end of the 1980s, the margins had narrowed but there were still discounts. Oil stocks usually trade at less than their net asset value. Cash flow multiples had also increased towards the end of the 1980s. This was due to a 3% drop in interest rates from 1984 to 1989. It was also due to the restructuring of the industry during the 1980s. The companies that had been undervalued the greatest had either been taken over or restructured.

THE FAR SIDE   By GARY LARSON

"Einstein discovers that time is actually money."

Illustr. 2–1

Present Value Theory

The most fundamental financial concept is the *time value of money*. The *Far Side* cartoon (Illustration 2–1) captures the moment nicely with Einstein's discovery of the relationship between time and money. The old adage is true, "A dollar today is worth more than a dollar tomorrow." The difference between the value of a dollar today and a dollar tomorrow depends on interest rates.

Most people are familiar with the *future value* concept. For example, $100 placed in a bank account bearing 7% interest, would be worth $107 at the end of one year. Therefore, the future value is $107. It is because of the potential to earn interest that money has a *time value.*

If a person can invest money at 7%, then the *present value* of $107 receivedone year from now is $100. The formula for present value is the inverse of the formula for future value.

FUTURE VALUE

The formula for the future value of a single payment P is:

$$F = P(1 + i)^n$$

Where:
F = the future value of a payment
P = the principal, or present value of a sum
i = the rate of interest or discount rate
n = the number of time periods

For example, as depicted in Figure 2–6, $1,000 invested at 10% for five years would be equal to:

$$F = \$1,000(1 + .10)^5$$

$$F = \$1,611$$

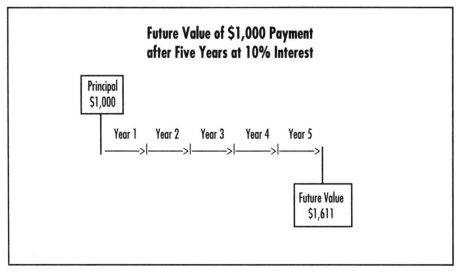

Fig. 2-6. Future Value Diagram

PRESENT VALUE

The formula for the present value of a single payment is:

$$P = \frac{F}{(1 + i)^n}$$

Where:
F = the future value of a payment
P = the principal, or the present value of a sum
i = the rate of interest or discount rate
n = the number of time periods

$$\frac{1}{(1 + i)^n} = \text{the } \textit{discount factor}$$

Part of this formula $[1/(1 + i)^n]$ is referred to as the discount factor. It is multiplied times the future payment F to arrive at its present value. F is said to be *discounted* by that factor. This is why the terms *discount rate* and *interest rate* are used interchangeably.

Assume that after five years a payment of $1,000 will be made. This is illustrated in Figure 2–7. The present value of that payment discounted at 10% for five years is equal to:

$$P = \frac{\$1,000}{(1+.10)^5}$$

$$P = \frac{\$1,000}{1.6105}$$

$$P = \$621$$

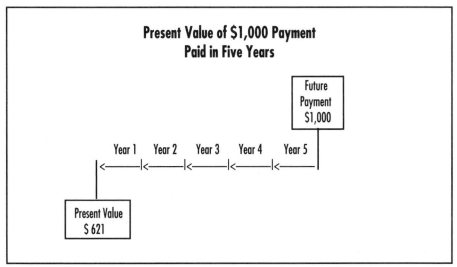

Fig. 2–7 Present Value Diagram

The analysis of a stream of payments or cash flows is based on *discounting* each future payment *F* back to the present, hence present value.

The financial analysis of an oil company, or even a single oil well, is based on the present value of the expected stream of cash flow. These payments come in regularly, not just once a year. Because it is easier to make estimates based on annual figures, *midyear* discounting is normally used to emulate the nearly continuous income stream.

The formula for present value using midyear discounting is:

$$P = \frac{F}{(1 + i)^{n - .5}}$$

Assume that a company expects $1 million in cash flow over the course of a one-year period, starting two years from now. The present value, assuming a rate of interest of 10%, would be:

$$P = \frac{\$1,000,000}{(1.1)^{3 - .5}}$$

= $788 thousand

Here the *discount rate* is 10%, and the discount factor is:

$$\text{Discount Factor} = \frac{1}{(1 + .1)^{3 - .5}}$$

$$= \frac{1}{1.269}$$

$$= .788$$

DIFFERENT DISCOUNTING METHODS COMPARED

Three discounting methods are compared in Table 2–7. Each method is used to estimate the present value of 12 monthly payments totaling $1 million expected to begin two years hence.

The most realistic technique is the monthly midmonth discounting, but it is usually not practical. Most evaluation work uses midyear discounting, which is slightly optimistic, but easier to use. Many spreadsheet programs default to end-of-year discounting. It is something to be aware of. Again, the difference between midyear and end-of-year discounting is small, but it helps to know the distinction.

Table 2–7 Comparison of Discounting Techniques

	End-of-year discounting	Midyear discounting	Monthly Midmonth discounting
Formula $P =$	$\dfrac{F}{(1 + i)^n}$	$\dfrac{F}{(1 + i)^{n-.5}}$	$\dfrac{F}{(1 + i)^{n-.5}}$
$i =$	10%	10%	.8333%
$n =$	3	3	25 – 36
$F =$	$1,000,000 paid at end-of-year	$1,000,000 paid at midyear	$83,333 12 monthly payments
Discount Factor (rounded)	.751	.788	.816 – .745
Present Value	$751,315	$787,986	$779,916

Where:
F = the future value of a payment
P = the principal, or the present value
i = the rate of interest
n = the number of time periods

ANNUITIES

An annuity is a fixed amount to be received or paid in each of a given number of time periods. Mortgage payments, salaries, wages, and dividends are examples of annuities.

The formula for the present value of an annuity is:

$$P = F \frac{1 - \left[\dfrac{1}{(1 + i)^n}\right]}{i}$$

Where:

P = the present value of an annuity
F = the annuity or future value of annual payments
i = the rate of interest
n = the number of time periods

If an annuity of \$7,000 per year for 10 years is evaluated using a 12% discount rate, the present value is:

$$P = \$7,000 \; \frac{1 - \left[\dfrac{1}{(1.12)^{10}}\right]}{.12}$$

$$= \$39,552$$

This means that an investor willing to accept a 12% rate of return would be willing to pay \$39,552 for the ten, \$7,000 annual payments. This formula treats the payments as though they will occur at the end of each year.

PERPETUITY

A perpetuity is an annuity that continues forever. In 1815, the British government consolidated various war debts through a bond issue that promised to pay interest forever. These bonds were called *consols*. Dividends for preferred and common stock can be viewed this way because the dividend stream, like the corporation, theoretically continues forever. The formula for the present value of a perpetuity is identical to the formula for an annuity, but n is equal to infinity. With n equal to infinity, the present value formula simplifies to:

$$P = \frac{F}{i}$$

Where:
   P = the present value of an annuity
   F = the annuity or future value of annual payments
   i = the rate of interest

Maxus preferred stock (Table 2–3) pays a $4 dividend. Using a discount rate of 10% to estimate the value of the stock yields:

$$P = \frac{\$4}{.10}$$

$$= \$40$$

The value of the preferred stock dividend stream, discounted at 10%, is $40. In financial language, the dividend was *capitalized* at 10%. In fact, the stock was trading quite close to this value. Notice the capitalization rate for the preferred is equal to the yield. This approach to capitalization of an income stream is a fundamental concept and is discussed further in Chapter 4.

PRESENT VALUE TABLES

Present value tables are provided in Appendices 8 and 9 for single payments or annuities.

Assume for example, a five-year cash flow stream that starts at $10,000 the first year and is expected to decline at a rate of 10% per year. The present value can be estimated by using the discount factors from Appendix 8. What would be the present value discounted at 15%? The example below shows the calculated present value of the declining cash flow stream using a midyear discount rate of 15%.

Year (n)	Declining Cash Flow (F)	Midyear Discount Factor* (i=15%)	Present Value (P)
1	$10,000	.933	$9,330
2	9,000	.811	7,299
3	8,100	.705	5,710
4	7,290	.613	4,469
5	6,561	.533	3,497
			$30,305

*From Appendix 8

The present value of the cash flow stream is $30,305.

Appendix 9 shows the present value for a series of equal payments — an annuity. For example, a five-year stream of cash flow, discounted at 15%, would have a present value of 3.329 times the annual payment. Thus a cash flow stream of $10,000 per year for five years would have a present value (discounted at a rate of 15%) of $33,290.

INTERNAL RATE OF RETURN

Much of the business of financial analysis is the determination of present value based on a specific discount rate. Sometimes the objective is essentially to work backwards and calculate the discount rate. What discount factor would yield a present value of $25,000 for an annuity of $10,000 per year for five years? This would be a natural question if the annuity was for sale for $25,000. The answer to that question would be called the *internal rate of return* (IRR).

The IRR is the discount rate at which the present value of a cash flow stream of an investment would equal the cost of the investment.

Assume than an investor was interested in buying a business that would provide $10,000 per year for five years. Income is relatively continuous, so a midyear discount rate is used. For this example the investor uses a discount rate of 20%.

Year (n)	Cash Flow (F)	Midyear Discount Factor* (i=20%)	Present Value (P)
1	$10,000	.913	$9,130
2	10,000	.761	7,610
3	10,000	.634	6,340
4	10,000	.528	5,280
5	10,000	.440	4,400
			$32,760

From Appendix 8

The present value of the income stream could also have been estimated by using the table in Appendix 9. The multiplication factor for a 5-year stream of income discounted at 20% (midyear) is 3.276.

If the investor paid $32,760 for the business, then the internal rate of return on that investment would be 20%. If he paid less than that, the IRR would be greater. A payment greater than $32,760 would yield an IRR of less than 20%.

What if he paid $35,000 for the enterprise? The IRR then would be whatever discount rate (i) it would take to produce a present value of $35,000. This calculation requires a trial-and-error procedure. The IRR will be less than 20%, but by how much? Computers try alternative discount rates to close in on the answer. This is called an iterative approach. The answer is approximately 16.4%. That is, the IRR of the investment would be 16.4% if the purchase price is $35,000. Another way of putting it would be that the present value of the five-year- stream of $10,000 payments discounted at 16.4% is $35,000.

Two rules of thumb are used to estimate the internal rate return (IRR) of a potential acquisition: *payout* and the *cash flow multiple*. For production acquisitions where a decline rate is usually a fact of life, payout is used more frequently. The IRR is estimated by dividing the payout (in years) into 100. If an acquisition had an expected payout of five years, then the IRR would be estimated at 20%.

Estimate of Internal Rate of Return
for Production Acquisitions

$$\text{Estimate of Internal Rate of Return} = \frac{100}{\text{Payout (in years)}}$$

For properties with substantial decline rates, this estimate is less helpful.

In a corporate acquisition where growth might be expected instead of a decline rate, the cash flow multiple is used. This is rough, but it is handy.

Estimate of Internal Rate of Return
for Corporate Acquisitions

$$\text{Estimate of Internal Rate of Return} = \frac{100}{\text{Cash Flow Multiple}}$$

REINVESTMENT ASSUMPTION

Some people insist that the IRR method has a weakness because proceeds might not be reinvested at the same rate as the project rate of return. This is the basis for the *reinvestment assumption controversy*. The controversy arises with the desire by many to treat the IRR as though it represented the actual earning power of the capital invested. The IRR is not the same as a bank deposit interest rate. A bank account will accrue and compound interest if the investor/depositor chooses to leave the funds in the account. Many investment opportunities generate cash disbursements that cannot be reinvested at the same IRR as the original investment.

The argument is that the IRR is too optimistic a measure of profitability unless the cash flows generated from an investment can be reinvested at that same rate of return. Therefore, a *growth rate of return* should be used for comparative purposes.

GROWTH RATE OF RETURN

The growth rate of return (GRR) concept is almost always brought up in the same breath as the discussion of IRR. The concept, sometimes called the Baldwin Method, or the *modified rate of return,* assumes that cash flow generated by an investment is reinvested at a different rate than the IRR of the investment. Assume that the investor in the example above can normally invest funds at 12%. The GRR calculation then is based on the present value of the revenue stream ($10,000 per year) that is reinvested at 12% until the end of the fifth year.

Year (n)	Cash Flow (F)	Midyear Compound Interest Factor (i=12%)	Future Value Year 5 (P)
1	$10,000	1.665	$16,650
2	10,000	1.487	14,870
3	10,000	1.328	13,280
4	10,000	1.185	11,850
5	10,000	1.058	10,580
			$67,230 Terminal Value

The value at the end of Year 5 of the $10,000 per year revenue stream reinvested at 12% is, therefore, $67,230. This is called the *terminal* value. The next step is to calculate the discount rate that would yield a present value of the $67,230 equal to the $35,000 investment. This formula then is simply the present value formula for a one-time payment where the equation is solved for i. This is the GRR.

$$P = \frac{F}{(1 + i)^n}$$

$$\$35{,}000 = \frac{67{,}230}{(1 + i)^5}$$

In this example, i is equal to 13.9%. This is the growth rate of return and would be equivalent to a compound interest rate of 13.9%. That is, if the $35,000 were invested at this rate, it would be worth $67,230 at the end of five years.

The IRR was 16.4%. When a GRR is calculated, it will usually lie somewhere between the IRR and the reinvestment rate.

COST OF CAPITAL

Cost of capital is the realm where corporate management establishes investment guidelines based on how much it costs the company to finance its activities. The cost of capital depends on the cost of debt, the cost of equity, and the corporate *capitalization structure*. The capitalization structure of a company is essentially the corporate balance of equity (common stock) and debt financing. When financial analysts talk about *financial leverage,* they are referring to the amount of debt financing a company uses. Theoretically, there should be some ideal capital structure, perhaps 40% debt for a particular company or even for a given industry.

Part of the determination of the financial structure deals with the cost of debt financing and the cost of equity financing. A typical oil company may be paying 10% interest on its bonds, but paying only a 5% dividend on common stock. The debt sounds more expensive at first.

Cost of Debt

The cost of corporate debt is usually 1.5–2.5% above long-term government bond rates. Interest payments are deductible, so if a company is paying 34% tax, the actual cost of debt financing (after tax) is 66% of the 10% interest rate, or 6.6%. This is still higher than the dividend payment.

Cost of Preferred Stock

There is no tax benefit for preferred dividends from the perspective of the issuing company. Preferred dividends are not tax deductible like interest rates. The cost of preferred stock capital is the dividend per share divided by the price per share, less the cost of issuing the stock. The costs of issuing or *floating* preferred stock can range 2–4%. For example, the dividend to price ratio for most preferred stocks is around 9%. If the issuing or underwriting costs are 4%, the cost is calculated at 9.37%.

$$\text{Cost of Preferred Stock} \ = \ \frac{\text{Dividend}}{\text{Stock price} - \text{Cost of issuing}}$$

$$\text{Cost of Preferred Stock} \ = \ \frac{9\%}{100\% - 4\%}$$

$$= \ 9.37\%$$

Cost of Equity

Equity capital is usually more expensive than debt. In some overleveraged companies, debt is such a burden that the cost of debt approaches the cost of equity. Junk bonds would be one example. This is an exception that can be ignored here. Cost of equity can be viewed a couple of different ways.

Some analysts take the dividend yield of a stock and add to that the expected growth rate of the dividend stream. A company paying a 5% dividend that is expected to grow at 5% would have a cost of equity of 10%. Some stocks do not pay a dividend, and a measure of the cost of equity based on earnings is usually preferred.

Earnings per share is divided by the stock price and added to the expected growth rate of the stock:

$$\text{Cost of Equity} = \frac{\text{Earnings per Share}}{\text{Stock Price}} + \text{Growth rate}$$

A stock that is expected to grow at a rate 5% per year, trading at 12 times earnings, would have a cost of equity equal to the earnings yield of 8.3% plus the 5% growth rate. This gives a cost of equity of 13.3%. This is over twice as costly as the 6.6% debt financing under these assumptions.

CAPITAL ASSET PRICING MODEL

The Capital Asset Pricing Model (CAPM) is a more sophisticated method for estimating the cost of equity. It is also used to determine the discount rate that should be used to evaluate a stock. It is based on the assumption that investors must aim for higher returns when dealing with the higher risks in the stock market. The CAPM calculates the cost of equity based on a risk-free return such as a U.S. government bond, plus an adjusted risk premium for the particular stock. The adjusted risk premium is based on the *market rate of interest* and the *beta* of the stock.

Market Rate of Interest

Two basic elements make up the market rate of interest, or the market rate of return. The first is the relatively risk-free rate of interest of a U.S. government bond—about 8.5%—which is composed of a *real* interest rate component and an inflation component. The real rate of interest is calculated by subtracting the inflation rate from the quoted *nominal* interest rate. The second element is the risk premium investors require to justify being involved with equity securities. Historically, market premiums have ranged 4–7%. The relationships are shown in Table 2–8.

Table 2–8 Components of the Market Rate of Interest

Risk-free rate		
Real interest rate	3.5%	
Inflation component	5.0%	
Government bond	8.5%	Nominal rate
Risk premium	5.5%	
Market rate of interest	14.0%	

Beta

The beta of a stock measures its trading price volatility relative to either a stock market index or an industry-related index of stocks. If a stock's price tends to follow its industry group up or down in synchronization, the stock will have a beta of 1. A stock that rises more than other stocks in a bull market and falls faster in a bear market will have a beta greater than 1. A high-beta stock will exhibit a more volatile performance during market fluctuations. If the stock price for a company went up by 12% whenever the market went up by 10%, then the beta for the company relative to the market would be 120% or 1.2. The beta, the market rate of interest, and the risk-free rate of interest are used to calculate the cost of equity capital for a company. An investor would use the same information to calculate his *required rate of return* for investing in a stock with the same parameters.

Capital Asset Pricing Model

$$RRR = Rf + Bi(Rm - Rf)$$

Where:

RRR = required rate of return from investor point of view, or cost of equity capital

Rf = risk-free rate of return (U.S. Government Bond)

Rm = market rate of return

Bi = beta of the investment

Bi(Rm - Rf) = risk premium for a particular stock with a beta equal to *Bi*.

$$RRR = 8.5\% + 1.2(14.0\% - 8.5\%)$$

$$RRR = 8.5\% + 6.6\%$$

$$RRR = 15.1\%$$

WEIGHTED AVERAGE COST OF CAPITAL

Many analysts prefer to determine discount rates, reinvestment rates, and company cost of capital by using the *weighted average cost of capital*. The cost of each component of corporate financing is weighted according to its percentage of the capital structure.

The example here is Company X with a beta of 1.2. The company has a capital structure that consists of 30% debt and 10% preferred stock. The after-tax cost of debt is 6.6%, and the 10% of capital provided by preferred stock has a cost of 9.4%. The CAPM calculates the cost of equity at 15.1%. The overall cost of capital is summarized below using the weighted average cost of capital (WACC) approach. Each form of corporate financing is weighted according to its market value percentage relative to the total market capitalization of the company. An example is illustrated in Table 2-9.

Table 2–9 Weighted Average Cost of Capital

Source of Capital	Cost %	Weight %	
Debt Financing	6.6%	30%	1.98%
Preferred Stock	9.4%	10%	.94%
Equity Financing	15.1%	60%	9.06%
Weighted Average			11.98%

The weighted average of 11.98% represents the cost of capital for Company X. The company theoretically would not invest in any venture that yielded an after-tax internal rate of return (IRR) of less than 12%. For growth rate of return (GRR) calculations, the company would probably use a reinvestment rate of 12%. There are other considerations, of course, but this is the benchmark for determining the boundary conditions for corporate financing and investment policy.

The example here is the common example always used in presenting the concept of cost of capital, but determining the cost of capital has elements of scientific procedure and art. Estimating the market rate of interest, for example, can be quite subjective, and the Beta for a company often changes from one period to the next. Furthermore, the position held by deferred taxes in the corporate capital structure can be fairly abstract. Discussion of deferred taxes, however, must wait for now. They are examined further in Chapters 4 and 7.

Industry Discount Rates

The concept of a reasonable discount rate for valuing oil and gas properties is usually shaped within the context of fair market value, which for production acquisitions is equal to market value as established by transactions. A common measure used by analysts is to discount future net revenues at a rate of 1–2% above the prime rate of interest. FMV would be equal to 66–75% of this value.

Another common benchmark for the oil industry that has withstood many changes in interest and tax rates is an after-tax discount rate of around 15% for mature production portfolios in the United States. This figure usually allows for some price escalation assumptions.

Another discount rate for FMV determinations is a before-tax rate of 18–20%. This is a general consensus of a fair rate of return consistent with interest rates and market conditions of the late 1980s and early 1990s.

GROWTH RATE

In all the equations for present value, the key factors are interest or discount rates and growth. Analysts have many ways of estimating earnings or cash flow growth. One of the most common is to calculate the growth rate of earnings or cash flow over a period of time. If earnings appear to increase consistently at a rate of 10% per year, then an analyst might be able to start with that and make some projections. Anyone in the oil industry knows that this is less realistic for oil companies than for other industries. The oil industry lives with volatile prices.

One calculation of the rate of growth for a company is based on the following formula:

$$\text{Growth Rate} = \frac{\text{Net Income} - \text{Dividends}}{\text{Shareholder Equity}}$$

Companies that pay out a larger share of net income in dividends would theoretically have a relatively smaller growth rate. One reason why growth companies characteristically pay no dividends can be seen in this formula. The lower the dividend rate, the higher the growth rate.

From a financial point of view, this would be considered a measure of *accounting growth* rather than *economic growth*. The formula must rely on accounting measures of corporate value (shareholder equity) and the increase in corporate wealth (net income after dividends). This approach is considerably less appropriate in the oil industry than in many other industries. The differences between economic value and accounting value is greater in the oil industry than in most other industries.

SUMMARY

The equations for estimating present value are constantly used by financial analysts and investors. Present value theory provides an important part of the foundation for financial analysis. As a rule, accountants are quite familiar with financial theory, but they seldom use present value techniques when reporting financial results. Because of this, the values found on financial statements seldom represent true economic value. This is particularly true of much of the oil industry.

Financial analysts are constantly examining financial reports to determine economic value which flows directly from present value theory. The financial reports, though, use accounting values that conform to accounting principles. Accounting principles follow guidelines which often diverge from economic value. An understanding of the accounting principles goes hand-in-hand with financial theory. With an understanding of the constraints placed on the accounting profession, the analyst can begin to make adjustments to financial statement accounting entries in an effort to assess economic value.

Analysis of financial statements requires an understanding of both present value theory and accounting theory.

ACCOUNTING SYSTEMS FOR OIL AND GAS

An understanding of basic accounting concepts and principles is enough to go a long way in the financial analysis of a company. The basic issues that govern the treatment of financial statement entries are straightforward and usually based on common sense. Knowing the reasoning behind accounting convention can breathe life into financial statement analysis.

The practice of accounting dates back hundreds of years. In 1494, Luca Pacioli first published the double-entry system of accounting in Venice. Fortunately, there is no need to mention debits or credits to explain basic principles.

Generally Accepted Accounting Principles

The organizations that govern the accounting industry and monitor financial reporting practices in the United States are: the American Institute of Certified Public Accountants (AICPA), superseded in 1973 by the Financial Accounting Standards Board (FASB), the Securities and Exchange Commission (SEC), and the American Accounting Association (AAA).

The Financial Accounting Standards Board (FASB) is an independent self-regulating organization. It establishes the standards for the industry known as the generally accepted accounting principles (GAAP). The FASB outlines procedures and rules that define accepted accounting practices for financial reporting. The FASB publishes broad guidelines and detailed procedures for financial accounting practices. These principles govern the auditor's report or opinion letter that is published with corporate financial statements.

It is well understood that financial statements based on GAAP do not provide the petrified truth as far as value is concerned, but they do provide a place to start.

Accounting theory is founded in economic and financial theory, yet different opinions exist as to what constitutes GAAP in different situations. There are some strict rules that provide some consistency, but accountants must exercise their professional judgment on many issues.

Accounting Concepts

Eleven basic accounting concepts provide the foundation of accounting theory. These principles are fundamental to the understanding of financial statements. They may not be perfect. In nearly every case where there is a weakness in a particular principle or accounting practice, it is easy to point out, but not so easy to find a better solution.

ACCOUNTING CONCEPTS
1. Money Measurement
2. Entity
3. Going Concern
4. Dual-aspect
5. Accounting Period
6. Materiality
7. Conservatism
8. Consistency
*9. Realization
*10. Matching
*11. Cost

* These concepts are of prime importance in understanding financial reporting in the oil industry.

The Money Measurement Concept. Financial information is expressed in monetary terms. It would not be practical to record on the balance sheet the number of barrels of oil or acres a company owns. Money is the common denominator. Fortunately, the number of barrels and acres can be found elsewhere.

The Entity Concept. Accounts are kept for business entities. The answer to any accounting issue must address the question: "How does it affect the business?" According to the entity concept, accountants are not concerned with persons who own or operate the business, but with the business itself.

The Going Concern Concept. Accounting assumes that a business will continue forever. If there is evidence to the contrary that the entity is going to liquidate, the accounting function might need to assess what the entity is *worth* to a potential buyer. Under the going concern assumption, current resale value or economic value of balance sheet items is usually irrelevant.

The Dual-aspect Concept. The resources owned by a business or entity are called *assets*. The claims against these assets are called *equities*. The two types of equities are: (1) *Liabilities* that represent the claims of creditors and (2) the *owners' equity*. The total claims on the assets are equal to the assets.

> **Assets = Equities**
> **Assets = Liabilities + Stockholders' Equity**

This is why both sides of the balance sheet balance. The essential concept is that for every resource available to a company, somebody has a claim on it.

The Accounting Period Concept. Accounting practices are based on the need to report periodically the status of a business entity. The basic time period is the fiscal year (12 months). Many companies use interim (usually quarterly and/or monthly) reports.

Materiality Concept. Insignificant items do not require attention. To a small company, a $5 million asset may be a very important item, but to Exxon it may not be sufficiently *material* to deserve a separate balance sheet entry or even a footnote. The Exxon 1989 balance sheet listed $1,941 million worth of odds and ends under "other assets, including intangibles."

The Conservatism Concept. This principle dictates that given a choice, an asset will be recorded at the lowest or most conservative value. As far as the income statement is concerned, this principle provides that potential losses be accounted for, and yet potential gains or profits are not registered until they are realized. The result theoretically is that financial statements will provide a conservative view of the business.

Consistency Concept. The consistency concept stipulates that once an entity embarks on an accounting methodology, it must be consistent in its treatment of accounting issues unless it has good reason to do otherwise. At times, companies decide to make changes in accounting policies. These changes are explained in the footnotes.

The Realization Concept. The realization principle dictates that revenue should be recognized only at the time a transaction is completed with a third party, or when the value is reasonably certain. One common concern centers on the applicability of the realization principle to the petroleum industry. Some feel this principle should not be applicable because the major asset of an oil and gas company is its reserves, and the value of a company's reserves is not directly reflected on the balance sheet.

Neither the balance sheet nor the income statement allow appropriate recognition for important oil and gas discoveries in the accounting period in which a discovery is made. When a company makes a major discovery, there is no mechanism for reporting the results from an accounting point of view. The impact on the income statement comes when the discovery begins to produce, yet economic value was realized the moment the discovery was made. But just how much economic value? This is the first natural question posed by the accountant. It is a fair question, too, because at the point of discovery, the uncertainty as to the quantity and value of reserves is greatest. Fortunately, the analysis of a company does not end with the financial statements.

ACCRUAL VS. CASH

Another aspect of the realization concept is the *accrual method* of accounting for revenue and expenses. Under this method, revenue is recorded as it is earned, or is said to have accrued, and does not necessarily correspond to the actual receipt of cash. This concept is important for the understanding of the Statement of Cash Flows and the concept of cash flow. For example, assume that a company sold 1,000 barrels of oil for $20 per barrel, but had only received $17,000 by the end of the accounting period. From an accrual accounting point of view, revenues are recorded as $20,000.

Revenues	$20,000
Beginning Receivables	1,000
Cash Flow Potential	21,000
Ending Receivables	– 4,000
Realized Cash Flow	$17,000 = Sales less increase in receivables

The income statement would reflect $20,000 because the accrual method of accounting realized the income at the point of sale, not at the point of actual cash exchange. The balance sheet would show the $17,000 increase in cash as well as an increase in accounts receivable for the $3,000 not yet received.

However, the actual cash received is $17,000. This is why the statement of cash flows treats increases in the working capital account as a reduction in cash flows. As a business grows, the required amount of working capital also increases, and therefore, most detailed cash flow analyses include a negative adjustment for increases in working capital. This is discussed further in Chapter 4.

The Matching Concept. The matching principle provides that revenues should be matched with the corresponding costs of producing such revenues. A serious accounting issue in the oil and gas industry deals with the matching principle because it is so difficult to match the costs of finding oil and gas with the revenues from production. Under GAAP, assets reported on the balance sheet consist of capitalized historical costs. Earnings are recognized as reserves are produced, rather than when they are discovered or revised.

Two separate systems of accounting in the industry are based primarily on this issue as it pertains to the treatment of exploration costs. The two systems are called Full Cost and Successful Efforts accounting. While revenues are typically recognized when oil or gas are sold, the fundamental difference between the FC and SE accounting systems lies in how the corresponding costs of finding those reserves match those revenues.

The Cost Concept. In accounting, an asset is recorded at its original cost. This cost is the basis for all subsequent accounting for the asset. The primary rationale behind the cost principle is that the value of an item may change with the passage of time, and determination of value is subjective. There is no subjectivity associated with the actual cost of an item.

Because of the cost principle, the accounting entry on the balance sheet for oil and gas assets usually has little to do with the actual value of the assets. For instance, if a company were to obtain a lease and then discover a million barrels of oil, the accounting entry would not change because of the discovery. It would never reflect anything other than the associated costs less depreciation. Only the net tangible costs would represent all that oil.

In this example, there is substantial appreciation in value that is ignored by GAAP. However, accountants do not ignore economic value completely. The cost principle provides that assets should be reflected on the balance sheet at cost, unless there has been a decline in their utility or economic value. Accountants do not mind an asset on the books at less than its true market value, but they are careful to keep accounting entries from exceeding economic value.

RESERVE RECOGNITION ACCOUNTING

Many methods have been considered in an effort to find a way to adequately represent the actual value of oil and gas assets. In 1978, in response to a request from the SEC, the FASB announced a program of financial reporting, *FASB Statement No. 19*, termed *Reserve Recognition Accounting (RRA)*. Here the value of a company's reserves could be recognized as an asset. Also, additions to proved reserves could be recognized as assets, and the additions could be included in earnings.

The SEC originally intended RRA to replace FC and SE accounting methods. But RRA was only required as supplemental information during a trial period from January 1979 to November 1982. The FASB issued *Statement No. 25* in February 1979, suspending all but the disclosure requirements of *FASB Statement No. 19*. It was determined that RRA could not replace FC and SE accounting due the inaccuracies of reserve reporting. In response to a request from the SEC, the FASB then developed disclosure requirements that were issued in November 1982 in *Statement No. 69, Disclosures About Oil and Gas Producing Activities.*

These disclosure requirements provide a substantial amount of information. The basic information is summarized as follows:

1. Quantification of proved oil and gas reserves. Reserves are further categorized as *developed* or *undeveloped.*
2. Annual production information and results of exploratory and development drilling, production acquisitions, and revisions to previous reserve estimates.
3. Capitalized costs associated with producing properties and costs incurred for lease acquisition exploration and development activities.
4. Standard Measure (SEC Value of Reserves) based on standardized discounted cash flow analysis of proved reserves.

The SEC requirements that provide the basis of standardization are as follows:
- prices received at fiscal year end for products (oil, gas, coal, sulfur) sold
- prices are held constant, no escalation
- costs are not escalated
- a 10% discount rate is used

5. Changes in Standard Measure and reasons for change are reported.
6. Accounting method used must be disclosed as well as the manner of disposing of capitalized costs.

Costs associated with oil and gas exploration and production fall into four fundamental categories:

Lease Acquisition Costs. Costs associated with obtaining a lease or concession and rights to explore for and produce oil and gas.

Exploration Costs. Costs incurred in the exploration for oil and gas such as geological and geophysical costs (G&G), exploratory drilling, etc.

Development Costs. Costs associated with development of oil and gas reserves. Drilling costs, storage and treatment facilities, etc.

Operating Costs. Costs required for lifting oil and gas to the surface, processing, transporting, etc.

Treatment of these costs is fairly straightforward. The one exception is the way that exploration costs are treated. This provides the basis for the two different accounting practices that are used in the industry.

Full Cost and Successful Efforts Accounting

These two accounting methods, Full Cost (FC) and Successful Efforts (SE) can give very different results on earnings, return on equity, and book value. Both systems follow as best they can the accounting principles of matching, realization, and cost, yet there is debate about which system is most appropriate. Primarily, the two systems differ on how capital costs associated with exploration drilling are treated. The main difference is that drilling costs of unsuccessful exploration wells are capitalized under FC accounting and expensed under the SE accounting system.

SUCCESSFUL EFFORTS ACCOUNTING

Prior to the 1950s, virtually all oil companies used some form of Successful Efforts (SE) accounting. The rationale behind SE is that expenditures providing no future economic benefit should be expensed at the time incurred. The SE approach will expense or write off exploratory dry-hole costs in the accounting period in which they are incurred. This is similar to many other businesses that will write off business failures. Proponents of SE agree that only expenditures directly associated with the discovery of hydrocarbons should be capitalized. SE companies treat exploration expenditures like other companies would treat research and development. If a research project results in a viable product, then capital expenditures are capitalized, otherwise, the costs are expensed.

In 1969, the American Institute of Certified Public Accountants published *Accounting Research Study No. 11*, "Financial Reporting in the Extractive Industry." The basic thesis of the report was to promote the use of the SE method.

COST CENTERS

One of the main differences between the two systems results from the choice of size and use of *cost centers*. It is this difference that makes the largest financial impact. With SE, costs for a cost center can be held in suspense until it is determined if commercial quantities of oil or gas are present. With a well or lease as the cost center, costs are expensed if the well is dry and capitalized if it is a discovery. This can be a very subjective decision. Sometimes the decision to drill a well may be held up because of the perceived impact on the financial statements during a specific accounting period, should the well turn out to be unsuccessful.

FULL COST ACCOUNTING

Full Cost (FC) accounting was developed in the 1950s. The first corporation to use FC accounting was Belco Petroleum in 1957, which at that time was just going public. FC allowed smaller companies and especially startup companies to access the capital markets more easily. These companies believe that the system is more fair and reported earnings are less volatile.

The philosophy behind FC accounting is that costs of acquisition, exploration, and development are necessary for the production of oil and gas. This rationale acknowledges that dry holes are an inevitable part of the exploration effort. With FC, the entire company can be a cost center, and all costs of exploring for oil and gas are capitalized. Companies with international operations typically treat each country as a separate cost center.

In 1977, the *FASB Statement No. 19* struck down FC with seven of the Big Eight accounting firms ruling against FC. While the FASB did not consider FC accounting an acceptable accounting method under GAAP, the SEC in 1978 declared the FC method acceptable. The SEC ruled that FC could coexist with SE and that companies could choose whichever method they desired. The FASB refused to develop the rules for FC accounting, so the SEC developed the FC guidelines. In 1979, the FASB rescinded their requirement that all companies use SE accounting. By 1986, 60% of the publicly traded oil companies had adopted FC accounting.

FC proponents say that it would not be logical to expense all dry holes and capitalize, in effect, only a portion of the effort that resulted in the discovery of oil and gas reserves. They point out that to expense the dry holes would have the effect of understating current period profits by the amount of dry holes written off. The amount to be capitalized and matched with future revenues is also understated. FC accounting attempts to allocate the dry-hole costs as though they were an integral part of the discovery process. This honors the matching principle, but violates the principle of conservatism.

CEILING TEST LIMITATION

FC accounting requires a write-down on the book value of oil and gas assets if it exceeds the SEC value of reserves. For this reason, FC companies use large cost centers. This is the *ceiling test* required by the SEC for the cost of oil and gas properties on the balance sheet. The recorded capitalized costs for producing oil and gas properties are limited to the net present value of the reserves discounted at 10%. This is the SEC value of reserves or standard measure. If the SEC value of reserves falls below the capitalized costs on the balance sheet, a ceiling write-down occurs. For example, if a company had a book value for proved oil and gas properties of $100 million, and the SEC value of these reserves was $130 million, there would be no write-down. The company would have a *cost ceiling cushion* of $30 million. In 1986, when oil prices dropped so dramatically, cushions disappeared, and many FC companies experienced substantial write-downs. The most important problem that this caused was that many companies suddenly found themselves in violation of covenants in their loan agreements.

Impairments and write-downs occur under SE accounting, too. It is usually not considered as great an issue because such a large part of exploration costs are expensed and not capitalized. But, consistent with the conservatism principle, the carrying value of SE oil and gas properties are subject to write-downs if the economic value of a property is less than the recorded value. Periodic assessments are made to ensure that the value of leases have not been *impaired* due to negative results of drilling or approaching expiration dates.

COMPARISON

With each system, lease bonus payments, related legal costs, and development drilling costs are capitalized. Capitalized costs within a cost center are usually amortized on the unit-of-production method (explained later in this chapter). Basic elements of the two systems are compared in Table 3–1.

Table 3-1 Comparison of Accounting Systems

	Successful Efforts Methods	Full Cost method
G&G Costs	Exp	Cap
Exploratory Dry Hole	Exp	Cap
Lease Acquisition Costs	Cap	Cap
Successful Exploratory Well	Cap	Cap
Development Dry Hole	Cap	Cap
Successful Development Well	Cap	Cap
Operating Costs	Exp	Exp
Which Companies Typically Use Each Method	Major Oil Companies	Smaller Independent Companies
Size of Cost Center Used	Small	Large
	Single Well, Lease or Field	Company, Country, or Hemisphere
Comment	Favored by FASB Approved by SEC	Approved by SEC

G&G = Geological and Geophysical
Exp = Expensed (Written off in accounting period)
Cap = Capitalized (Written off over a number of accounting periods)

BOOK VALUE, SEC VALUE, AND FAIR MARKET VALUE OF RESERVES

The book value of oil and gas reserves that appears on the balance sheet bears no direct relationship to reserve values under either FC or SE accounting methods. Because the SE company will expense G&G costs and exploratory dry holes, the book value of reserves will be lower than under FC accounting.

The SEC value of reserves is usually less than the market value for reserves. Analysts must look beyond the reported figures on the balance sheet and the SEC values of reserves.

COMPARISON OF ACCOUNTING IMPACT FOR A STARTUP COMPANY

Table 3-2 shows an example of a company with $10 million startup capital. In its first year, the company drills 15 wells and has two discoveries. The following table outlines the general features of how the two accounting methods would report the financial results of the first year of operations.

Under the SE method, all exploratory dry holes are expensed. For the startup company, reporting a $5.5 million loss in the first year can be devastating. This is one of the reasons why so many small startup companies prefer FC accounting. The company managed to find 1.6 million barrels of oil. The company might believe the reserves would be unfairly represented by a book value of only $2.5 million under SE.

Events affecting net income will also be represented differently under the two accounting systems. This is particularly true of a startup company. With moderate reinvestment of cash flow, the earnings of an established company would be nearly the same under either accounting system.

Figure 3–1 depicts how the income statement under the two accounting systems would reflect changes in drilling activity. It is assumed that drilling efforts result in the same degree of success as in the past. With increased exploratory drilling, net income drops under SE accounting compared to FC accounting methods. This is because SE will expense exploration dry-hole costs. Decreased exploratory drilling under both methods will increase net income initially, but the change will be greater under SE.

Table 3–2 Company Startup Results Under FC & SE Accounting

Exploration Wells Drilled	Drilling Costs ($000)	Results
6	3,000	Plugged and Abandoned
1	1,500	700,000 Barrel Discovery
7	2,500	Plugged and Abandoned
1	1,000	900,000 Barrel Discovery
15	$8,000	1,600,000 Barrels

Generalized Financial Reporting

	SE Accounting ($000)	FC Accounting ($000)
Revenue	0	0
Expense	– 5,500	0
Income*	(5,500)	0
Assets		
Cash	2,000	2,000
Property	2,500	8,000
Equity	4,500	10,000

*No income taxes or G&A costs considered.

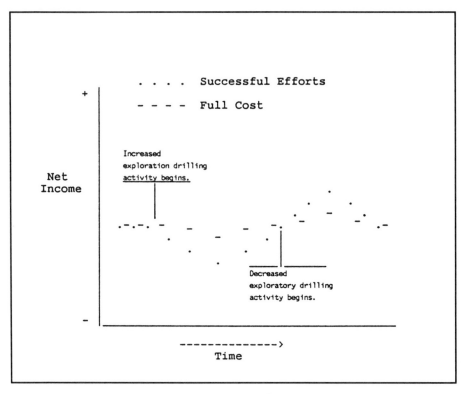

Fig. 3–1. Accounting Technique Comparison—Results of Changes in Drilling Activity

The comparison in Figure 3–2 shows the effect on earnings of an increased *rate* of discovery, that is, a greater percentage of successful wells rather than dry holes. Under FC accounting, the impact on net income is shown in later years when the additional discovered oil begins to come on stream. The difference with this scenario is that fewer dry holes are written off for the SE company. The FC company would capitalize exploration wells whether successful or dry.

For the SE company, if greater success is the result of more reserves per well as opposed to a larger ratio of successful wells, then the result may be more like that of an FC company.

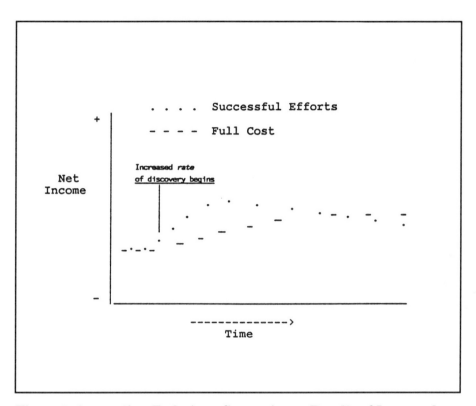

Fig. 3-2. Accounting Technique Comparison—Results of Increased Rate of Discovery

The difficulty with both SE and FC accounting methods is that increased success in exploration is not shown until subsequent years. It is helpful that the company's net reserves are reported each year so that analysts can know at least whether reserves are being increased or depleted. The SEC value of reserves helps quantify the company's success in not only replacing reserves but replacing *value*. It would not be a winning situation for a company to produce and sell high-quality reserves and replace them with low-quality, low-value reserves.

DEPRECIATION, DEPLETION, AND AMORTIZATION

Depreciation is a means of accounting for the recovery of the costs of a fixed asset by allocating the costs over the estimated useful life of the asset. When this concept is applied to mineral resources such as oil and gas reserves, it is called *depletion*. The concept is called *amortization* when the allocation of costs is applied to intangible assets. The terms depreciation, depletion, and amortization (DD&A) are sometimes used interchangeably, or more often collectively as DD&A. The importance of DD&A is that these expenses are deducted from income for federal and state income tax purposes. The depreciable life of an asset is usually determined by legislation to emulate the useful life of that asset. Table 3–3 gives some examples of basic oil industry assets.

Table 3–3 Typical Asset Lifes for Depreciation & Amortization

Intangible Drilling Costs that must be Amortized (30% of IDCs)	5 Years
Vehicles and Drilling Equipment	5 Years
Production Equipment and most Field Equipment Office Equipment Processing Plants	7 Years
Refining Equipment	10 Years
Transmission Pipelines	15 Years
Buildings	30 Years

COST DEPLETION AND PERCENTAGE DEPLETION

Depletion for tax purposes is based on the concept of the removal and sale of a wasting or depleting asset—in this case, oil and gas. Depletion is analogous to ordinary depreciation. The Internal Revenue Code authorizes a deduction from income for depletion of oil and gas properties. It is a relatively simple concept, but it is complicated by many limitations and exemptions.

Two types of calculating depletion must be considered when estimating taxable income. The two methods are *cost depletion* and *percentage depletion*. The taxpayer is entitled to the higher of either the cost or percentage depletion. Cost depletion of producing oil and gas properties is allowed under the unit-of-production method on a property-by-property basis. This method requires a reasonably accurate estimate of the remaining recoverable reserves. The basic formula is outlined as follows:

Formula for Unit-of-Production Method

$$\text{Annual Depreciation} = (C - AD - S)\,\frac{P}{R}$$

Where:

C = capital costs of equipment
AD = accumulated depreciation
S = salvage value
P = barrels of oil produced during the year*
R = recoverable reserves remaining at the
      beginning of the tax year

*If there is both oil and gas production associated with the capital costs being depreciated, then the gas can be converted to oil on a thermal basis (6 MCF of gas equals one barrel of oil).

The tax advantages of percentage depletion were eliminated for all integrated oil companies in 1975. Cost depletion is available to both independent producers and integrated oil companies.

Usually the percentage depletion allowance is higher than cost depletion. Percentage depletion allows a producer to deduct from gross income a stated percentage of gross income as an expense. Originally, in 1926, the Internal Revenue Code for oil and gas wells allowed a deduction of 27.5% of gross income from production. This method of depletion was very controversial and is no longer granted to the major oil companies, but independent companies are still allowed a percentage depletion allowance. The percentage depletion allowance since 1984 has been set at 15% of gross income. The depletion allowance is not to exceed 65% of net taxable income (computed without including depletion allowance). Prior to 1975, the limit was 50%.

The combined DD&A for many companies can be quite significant. The per-unit values that are deducted for income tax purposes can range from $3 to over $10 per barrel. While the majority of oil and gas property valuations are done on a before-tax basis, examples of before and after-tax analysis are provided in Chapter 7.

Summary and Key Concepts

Analysts understand that accounting methods can have a significant impact on reported earnings. Earnings for FC companies are usually considered to be inflated by comparison to SE companies. Full Cost companies pay a price for the opportunity to report relatively higher earnings. They must also pay relatively more in taxes. Yet, ignoring this aspect, the intrinsic value of an oil company is the same regardless of the accounting technique used.

Analysts who look at breakup value of a company ignore the book values that different accounting systems may yield. Analysis of asset values neutralizes the differences between FC and SE accounting methods. The same is true of cash flow analysis. When an analyst looks beyond reported earnings and starts analyzing cash flow, the differences between FC and SE begin to disappear.

FINANCIAL STATEMENT ANALYSIS

Nearly everyone is familiar with a company annual report. Unfortunately, many people feel the same way about company financial reports as Harriet feels about snakes (Illustration 4–1). However, things are not that bad. Financial reports can be interesting reading, with some surprises—expect the unexpected! The annual report is only one of many documents that a public company provides. The primary sources of public company information are:

Annual Report to Shareholders. Report of operating results, president's letter and outlook, and financials.

10-K. Official annual business and financial report filed with SEC (see Appendix 13).

20-F. Official annual report (similar to 10-K) filed by non-U.S. registrants.

10-Q. Official quarterly report filed with SEC.

Quarterly Report to Shareholders. Report of quarterly results—not an official filing with the SEC.

8-K. Report of unscheduled material events of importance to shareholders or the SEC.

EXPECT THE UNEXPECTED!

Harriet's last Groundhog Day outing.

Illus. 4–1

Proxy Statement. Shareholder meeting statement describing voting matters and company directors.

Registrant Statement. Official report containing a history of business and management and important financial information—must be filed before security may be publicly offered.

Articles of Incorporation and Bylaws. Charter governing management of the company, number of directors, authorized shares, voting rights, etc.

Bond Indenture. Restrictions on leverage distributions restrictive financial covenants and call provisions.

Annual Report and 10-K Report

Proper analysis of a company requires both the annual report and the 10-K report.

Actually the 10-K is all that is required as far as annual reporting to shareholders and the SEC. The annual report to shareholders is not a required filing for the SEC. The 10-K usually provides more detailed technical information than the typical annual report, but sometimes the 10-K report will make reference to items covered in the annual report.

With the industry downturn in the mid-1980s, many companies began to provide shareholders with a modified 10-K instead of a separate document for the annual report. Management would include a letter to shareholders and introductory material and then simply defer to the 10-K statement which was attached.

Sometimes the 10-K will not directly present all the standard information, but will have it *included by reference* to the annual report. This is a result of rule changes that began in 1980 by the SEC encouraging a comprehensive reporting and disclosure system known as *integrated disclosure*. The incorporation by reference procedure is used in the 10-K reports and annual reports. For example, a 10-K report may not directly include financial statements but will have them included by reference to the annual report. Because of this, both the 10-K and the annual report often are needed. A detailed summary of the information normally included in the 10-K is found in Appendix 13.

The 8-K reports unscheduled material events of importance to shareholders or the SEC. This document is not commonly seen by the average shareholder. But companies must list in the 10-K the information contained in the 8-K. This can be interesting reading and is an important place to look to see if a company has serious environmental/legal problems.

A wealth of information can be gleaned from these reports. Management is obligated to provide most of the information, but will also include nonrequired information which can be useful.

The annual report broken into its component parts is summarized as follows:

- financial highlights
- letter to shareholders
- discussion of business segments and operations
- financial statements and footnotes
- auditor's report

FINANCIAL HIGHLIGHTS

The practice of including a table of financial highlights has evolved over the years. The highlights answer very basic questions of size and value. Usually three to five years of vital statistics are summarized that provide a quick look and points of reference.

LETTER TO SHAREHOLDERS

The *letter to shareholders* and the sections devoted to presenting the accomplishments of the business segments and operations are recommended reading. Usually, these sections fall short of providing all the information an analyst might want, but additional insight can be gained by reading managements views in these sections from previous reports.

Management goes through considerable anxiety at times wording these sections properly. This is where reading between the lines can be important as well as interesting. Good news comes in paragraphs—bad news often comes in short, oblique sentences. If it appears that a certain amount of squirming is taking place in the letter to shareholders, then the rest of the report should explain why. This is where the analyst looks for smoke, knowing that if there is any, the fire will lie deeper in the report. Management is under fairly rigorous disclosure requirements and must attempt to make the letter as accurate and truthful as possible. Any attempt to deceive shareholders can have serious consequences.

DISCUSSION OF BUSINESS SEGMENTS AND OPERATIONS

The discussion of different business segments or geographic divisions of a company can be some of the more enjoyable reading in an annual report. There never seems to be complete information about the business segments, although additional segment information can be gleaned from other places in the annual report or 10-K. A picture of the different segments begins to form. Typically there should be enough information to determine operating income, earnings, DD&A, and identifiable assets associated with each segment.

FINANCIAL STATEMENTS AND FOOTNOTES

Financial statements and the accompanying footnotes are the heart and soul of the annual report or the 10-K. While financial statements do not provide answers, they do provide information. If the statements provided answers, the balance sheet would show how much a company was worth at a point in time, and the income statement would show how much money the company made during an accounting period. This is not the case.

The rest of this chapter and Chapter 5 explain how to analyze the information found in the financial statements. The financial statements are each designed to provide a concise summary of the business and financial results for a particular accounting period, or in the case of the balance sheet, a point in time. The footnotes expand on individual entries and specific events or items that require explanation.

The footnotes contain a wealth of information. When questions arise during inspection of the financial statements, the answers are usually just pages away in the footnotes. Footnotes are used to explain many balance sheet and income statement items. Without footnotes there would never be enough room to concisely depict the financial status of a company as it is done now.

Some analysts feel that the market responds almost immediately to information about earnings and dividends but takes a couple of weeks to respond to information in the footnotes. There may be some truth to this.

CONSOLIDATED STATEMENTS

If a company controls more than 50% of the voting stock of another company (subsidiary), the financial statements are usually consolidated. Where entities are *wholly owned*, the consolidation is simple. However, where less than 100% is owned by the *parent* company, minority interest accounts often are used in the balance sheet and income statements to represent these interests. This is explained further in Chapter 5.

AUDITOR'S REPORT

The auditor's report is closely associated with the financial statements. It is the auditor's responsibility to ensure that financial statements conform to generally accepted accounting principles applied on a basis consistent with that of prior years. Most texts recommend that the analysis of an annual report begin with the auditor's report. This will quickly disclose whether irregularities or unusual circumstances impinge on the company's financial status. Whether or not the analysis begins here, this section must be read. It is one thing if the company has a *clean bill of health*. If the auditor renders a *qualified opinion*, then that is quite another matter.

In a qualified opinion, the auditor calls attention to exceptions taken to items in the financial statements, or to unusual accounting practices used by the company. For instance, a qualified opinion may point out uncertainty associated with the results of pending litigation or a potential tax liability.

Usually the qualification is a simple paragraph outlining a particular concern. But the qualification paragraph often speaks volumes. A qualified opinion usually represents considerable hand wringing and worry. The market is very sensitive to this sort of thing. Whenever there is a qualified opinion, there will be further mention in the footnotes and management discussions of the issues that brought it about.

THE BALANCE SHEET

The balance sheet depicts the status of a business at a given point in time. The appropriate analogy is that it is a financial snapshot of the company. The assets, liabilities, and stockholders' equity of the company are listed with their associated accounting values. By comparison, the income statement is a moving picture.

Because of the cost principle, the balance sheet for a typical oil company will not represent the true nature of the assets.

All approaches to balance sheet analysis focus on the same basic issues:

- What is the book value of the company?
- How much working capital does the company have?
- How much debt does the company have?
- Is the company highly leveraged?
- Is the company growing?
- Is the company taking on or reducing debt?
- What is the company really worth?

A worksheet is provided at the end of this chapter as a checklist for analysis. The detailed approach to Adjusted Balance Sheet Analysis is covered extensively in Chapter 5.

THE INCOME STATEMENT

Net income is the proverbial *bottom line* for any company. But, there is more to the income statement than that. The real bottom line is cash flow, discussed in Chapter 5. Making adjustments to the income statement to arrive at cash flow for an accounting period is the primary objective of income statement analysis.

The income statement provides a dynamic vision of the business entity. It shows whether the business is profitable and how capable it is of servicing debt and honoring its other obligations.

The Statement of Cash Flows

Beginning in 1988, a *Statement of Cash Flows* (SCF) was required by the FASB instead of its predecessor, the Statement of Changes in Financial Position (SCFP). *FASB No. 95, Statement of Cash Flows*, became effective for financial statements for fiscal years ending after July 1988.

The SCF dissects and summarizes the business dealings of a company. This statement is a *derivative* statement because it can be constructed from the income statement and balance sheet.

The term "flows" is used because the statement records changes in accounts rather than absolute dollar amounts. The SCF segregates information about cash provided or used by a company into three categories:

- operating activities (Cash Flow From Operations—CFFO)
- investing activities
- financing activities

The information included in the SCF for a company helps determine:

- ability to generate future cash flows
- capacity to meet financial obligations
- success in investing strategies
- effectiveness in financing strategy

Ratio Analysis

A large part of financial analysis deals with the interrelationships between various pieces of information. Financial ratios are used to express many of these relationships. Some are not as appropriate as others when viewing companies in different industries. When estimating liquidation value, ratios have very little meaning. But comparison with industry standards gives an insight into corporate financial structure and vitality.

Financial ratios fall into five general categories. Table 4–1 lists the more commonly used ratios.

Table 4–1 Financial Ratios

Liquidity Ratios

(a) Current Ratio $= \dfrac{\text{Current assets}}{\text{Current liabilities}}$

(b) Quick Ratio or Acid Test $= \dfrac{\text{Current assets} - \text{inventories}}{\text{Current liabilities}}$

Working Capital $= \text{Current assets} - \text{Current liabilities}$

Profitability Ratios

(a) Net Profit Margin $= \dfrac{\text{Net income}}{\text{Net sales}}$

(b) Return on Assets $= \dfrac{\text{Net income}}{\text{Total assets}}$

(c) Return on Equity $= \dfrac{\text{Net income}}{\text{Stockholders' equity}}$

Activity Ratios

(a) Inventory Turnover $= \dfrac{\text{Cost of goods sold}}{\text{Value of inventory}}$

(b) Average Collection Period $= \dfrac{\text{Total accounts receivable}}{\text{Sales per day}}$

(c) Sales to Fixed Assets $= \dfrac{\text{Total sales}}{\text{Fixed assets}}$

(d) Total Asset Turnover $= \dfrac{\text{Total sales}}{\text{Total assets}}$

Leverage Ratios

(a) Interest Coverage $= \dfrac{\text{Pretax earnings + interest expense}}{\text{Interest expense}}$

(b) Fixed Charge Coverage $= \dfrac{\text{Pretax earnings + interest expense + fixed charges}}{\text{Interest expense + fixed charges}}$

(c) Cash flow to Long-term debt $= \dfrac{\text{Net Income + DD\&A + deferred taxes + exploration expenses}}{\text{Long-term debt}}$

(d) Debt to Equity $= \dfrac{\text{Long-term debt}}{\text{Stockholders' equity}}$

Valuation Ratios

(a) Dividend Yield $= \dfrac{\text{Annual dividend rate}}{\text{Stock price per share}}$

(b) Dividend Payout $= \dfrac{\text{Annual dividend rate}}{\text{Earnings per share}}$

(c) P/E Ratio $= \dfrac{\text{Stock price per share}}{\text{Earnings per share}}$

(d) Price to Cash flow $= \dfrac{\text{Stock price per share}}{\text{Cash flow per share}}$

(e) Price to Book value $= \dfrac{\text{Stock price per share}}{\text{Book value per share}}$

(f) Market Capitalization and Debt to Appraised Value of Assets $= \dfrac{\text{Market capitalization + debt}}{\text{Appraised value of total assets}}$

Further value from ratio analysis can be gained by comparing trends within a company of key ratios. This procedure gives an indication of whether conditions are improving or deteriorating.

RATIO ROULETTE

Ratio analysis has some important limitations that must be considered. Due to the differences in accounting practices, ratios can be misleading. Two otherwise similar companies using different accounting methods can look quite different. Furthermore, management can take certain short-term actions to influence their ratios. This is called *window dressing*. For instance, a company with positive working capital can improve its current ratio by paying off as many current liabilities as possible just before the balance sheet date. If Company A has $150 of current assets and $100 of current liabilities, the current ratio is 1.5. If the company pays $50 of current liabilities out of current assets, then the new current ratio is $100/50 or 2. A current ratio of 2 sounds better than 1.5, yet working capital is still just $50. A company with negative working capital would not likely payoff current liabilities out of current assets just prior to a reporting date. This would reduce the current ratio.

Care must also be taken to ensure that the definition of a ratio is consistent. Some very common ratios and terms have different definitions. For example, the ratio of debt to equity has three common definitions (see Glossary).

EXAMPLE—ATLANTIC RICHFIELD COMPANY

Financial statements (Figs. 4–1, 4–2, and 4–3) from the Atlantic Richfield Company's (ARCO) 1989 10-K provide examples for ratio analysis and other analytical techniques.

Millions of dollars except per share amounts	For the year ended December 31		
	1989	1988	1987
Revenues			
Sales and other operating revenues — including excise taxes	$16,021	$18,324	$16,977
Income from equity investments	240	48	65
Interest	355	290	288
Other revenues	199	206	249
	16,815	18,868	17,579
Expenses			
Costs and other operating expenses	8,975	10,731	10,724
Selling, general and administrative expenses	1,476	1,408	1,108
Taxes other than excise and income taxes	943	665	702
Excise taxes	670	698	547
Depreciation, depletion and amortization	1,748	1,704	1,661
Interest	799	842	991
	14,611	16,048	15,733
Income before gain on subsidiary stock transactions	2,204	2,820	1,846
Gain on subsidiary stock transactions	957	—	322
Income before income taxes and minority interest	3,161	2,820	2,168
Provision for taxes on income	1,142	1,144	932
Minority interest in earnings of subsidiary	66	93	12
Net Income	$ 1,953	$ 1,583	$ 1,224
Earned per Share	$ 11.26	$ 8.78	$ 6.68
Retained Earnings			
Balance, January 1	$ 7,562	$ 6,683	$ 6,173
Net income	1,953	1,583	1,224
Cash dividends:			
Preference stocks	(4)	(4)	(4)
Common stock	(756)	(700)	(710)
Cancellation of treasury stock	(3,119)	—	—
Balance, December 31	$ 5,636	$ 7,562	$ 6,683

Fig. 4–1. ARCO Consolidated Statement of Income and Retained Earnings

78

Millions of dollars	December 31 1989	December 31 1988
Assets		
Current assets:		
Cash and cash equivalents	$ 1,173	$ 876
Short-term investments	1,836	1,029
Accounts receivable	1,483	1,689
Inventories	710	962
Prepaid expenses and other current assets	212	201
Total current assets	5,414	4,757
Investments and long-term receivables:		
Investments accounted for on the equity method	194	168
Other investments and long-term receivables	80	130
	274	298
Fixed assets:		
Property, plant and equipment, including capitalized leases	28,431	29,279
Less accumulated depreciation, depletion and amortization	12,774	13,348
	15,657	15,931
Deferred charges and other assets	916	528
Total Assets	$22,261	$21,514
Liabilities and Stockholders' Equity		
Current liabilities:		
Notes payable	$ 577	$ 521
Accounts payable	1,078	1,156
Taxes payable, including excise taxes	409	261
Long-term debt and other obligations due within one year	704	577
Accrued interest	200	219
Other	469	530
Total current liabilities	3,437	3,264
Long-term debt	5,287	5,400
Capital lease obligations	26	265
Deferred income taxes	3,407	3,770
Other deferred liabilities and credits	3,273	2,333
Minority interest	269	235
Stockholders' equity:		
Preference stocks	1	1
Common stock, $2.50 par value;		
shares issued 167,584,194 (1989), 217,512,186 (1988);		
shares outstanding 164,186,803 (1989), 171,966,015 (1988)	419	544
Capital in excess of par value of stock	764	1,016
Retained earnings	5,636	7,562
Treasury stock, at cost	(236)	(2,909)
Foreign currency translation	(22)	33
Total stockholders' equity	6,562	6,247
Total Liabilities and Stockholders' Equity	$22,261	$21,514

Fig. 4–2. ARCO Consolidated Balance Sheet

	For the year ended December 31		
Millions of dollars	1989	1988	1987
Cash flows from operating activities:			
Net income	$1,953	$1,583	$1,224
Adjustments to reconcile net income to net cash provided by operating activities:			
Depreciation, depletion and amortization	1,748	1,704	1,661
Tax refunds	—	—	779
Gain on subsidiary stock transactions	(634)	—	(185)
Income from equity investments	(240)	(48)	(65)
Dividends from equity investments	84	31	46
Non-cash provisions in excess of cash payments	570	146	239
Net change in deferred taxes	(363)	129	79
Dry-hole expense	163	149	76
Net change in accounts receivable, inventories and accounts payable	380	(263)	173
Net change in other working capital accounts	57	114	(156)
Other	11	6	(155)
Net cash provided by operating activities	3,729	3,551	3,716
Cash flows from investing activities:			
Additions to fixed assets (including dry-hole costs)	(2,105)	(3,038)	(1,463)
Net cash provided (used) by short-term investments	(814)	1,597	(1,369)
Proceeds from asset sales	149	145	265
Payments received on notes for sales of property	—	60	234
Net proceeds from subsidiary stock transactions	1,241	—	—
Net sale (acquisition) of Britoil stock	—	242	(132)
Other	(334)	(100)	26
Net cash used in investing activities	(1,863)	(1,094)	(2,439)
Cash flows from financing activities:			
Repayments of long-term debt	(486)	(868)	(1,470)
Proceeds from issuance of long-term debt	459	219	181
Net cash provided (used) by notes payable	85	(1,026)	392
Proceeds from issuance of common stock by subsidiary	—	—	591
Dividends paid	(760)	(704)	(714)
Treasury stock purchases, including subsidiaries	(810)	(601)	(94)
Other	(29)	(13)	(3)
Net cash used in financing activities	(1,541)	(2,993)	(1,117)
Effect of exchange rate changes on cash	(28)	(23)	15
Net increase (decrease) in cash and cash equivalents	297	(559)	175
Cash and cash equivalents at beginning of year	876	1,435	1,260
Cash and cash equivalents at end of year	$1,173	$ 876	$1,435

Fig. 4–3. ARCO Consolidated Statement of Cash Flows

LIQUIDITY RATIOS

(a) Current Ratio $= \dfrac{\text{Current assets}}{\text{Current liabilities}}$

The current ratio is one of the first things to check on the balance sheet. When viewed with the amount and quality of *working capital*, the ratio becomes more useful.

The current ratio should be greater than 1, which indicates positive working capital. Working capital is current assets minus current liabilities. It represents the short-term liquidity of a firm.

The ratio for ARCO is:

(Millions of dollars except per-share amounts)

	1989
ARCO Current Ratio $=$	$\dfrac{\$5,414}{3,437}$
	$= 1.58$

	1989
ARCO Working Capital	$= \$1,977$

(b) Quick ratio $= \dfrac{\text{Current assets } - \text{ inventories}}{\text{Current liabilities}}$

The quick ratio, often called the *acid test*, shows how truly liquid and flexible the available working capital is.

An old rule of thumb suggested the current ratio should be at least 2 and the quick ratio at least 1. Many oil companies, though, are getting on fairly well with a current ratio of around 1.2 and a quick ratio of only slightly less. The trend over time is often more important than the static ratios. When a company's working capital is diminishing, that is often a bad sign.

Judgment must be exercised to adjust current assets to *quick assets* other than by simply subtracting inventories. The balance sheet item *prepaid expenses* represents expenses that normally fall due beyond the current accounting period that have been prepaid. Therefore, if the company needed these funds, they are not available. All of these items, including current liabilities, are deducted from current assets to arrive at *quick assets*.

$$\text{ARCO (1989)} \atop \text{Quick Ratio} \quad = \quad \frac{\$5,414 - 710 - 212}{\$3,437}$$

$$= \quad 1.3 \quad \text{or} \quad 130\%$$

ARCO (1989)
Quick Assets = $1,055

PROFITABILITY RATIOS

$$\textbf{(a) Profit Margin} \quad = \quad \frac{\text{Net income}}{\text{Net sales}}$$

The oil industry profit margin for 1989 was around 4.4%, compared to a ratio of around 4.9% for all public companies. The profit margin tells only part of the story.

$$\text{ARCO (1989)} \atop \text{Profit margin} \quad = \quad \frac{\$1,953}{16,815}$$

$$= \quad 11.6\%$$

$$\textbf{(b) Return on Equity } = \frac{\text{Net income}}{\text{Stockholders' equity}}$$

The return on equity (ROE) is a measure of the profitability of the capital provided by the shareholders. It receives lots of attention from shareholders and security analysts. ROE for the oil industry in 1989 was approximately 12.5%, compared to 12.6% for all public companies.

$$\begin{array}{l}\text{ARCO (1989)} \\ \text{Return on Equity}\end{array} = \frac{\$1,953}{6,562}$$

$$= 29.8\%$$

Return on equity should always be viewed within the context of the degree of financial leverage. One way of improving ROE is to use leverage with debt in the corporate capital structure. Imagine a company that earns $1 million on $10 million in equity capital. If the company can earn another $1 million on $10 million borrowed capital, then it can double its ROE. Financial leverage can increase risk. Therefore, another measure of profitability, *return on assets* (ROA), can be helpful. It puts companies, leveraged or not, on an even footing.

$$\textbf{(c) Return on Assets } = \frac{\text{Net income}}{\text{Total assets}}$$

Return on assets (ROA) for public companies in the oil industry in 1989 was 4.3%, compared to a ROA of all public companies of around 2.6%.

$$\begin{array}{l}\text{ARCO (1989)} \\ \text{Return on Assets}\end{array} = \frac{\$1,953}{\$22,261}$$

$$= 8.8\%$$

LEVERAGE RATIOS

(a) Interest Coverage $= \dfrac{\text{Pretax earnings} + \text{Interest expense}}{\text{Interest expense}}$

This ratio assesses *debt service capability*, the ability of a company to meet interest and principal payments on debt. It is sometimes called the *times interest earned* ratio. If a company has a major long-term capital lease obligation, or other contractual long-term obligations (called fixed charges), the interest coverage ratio should be amended to include them. An amended or expanded interest coverage ratio is called *fixed charge coverage*.

Many analysts would like to see at least a 3 to 1 (3:1) ratio to cover interest expense or fixed charges. Anything less than 3 begins to indicate a higher degree of risk.

ARCO (1989)
Interest Coverage $= \dfrac{\$2,204 + 799}{799}$

$\qquad\qquad\qquad = $ 3.76 or 376%

(b) Cash Flow to Long-term Debt $= \dfrac{\text{Net income} + \text{DD\&A} + \text{deferred taxes} + \text{exploration expenses}}{\text{Long-term debt}}$

The concept of cash flow is often confusing and frequently misused. There are many definitions and closely related terms such as *cash earnings*, *cash flow from operations*, *free cash flow*, and *discretionary cash flow*. This issue deserves proper attention and clarification. In the section on discounted cash flow analysis in Chapter 5, the subject gets aired properly. For now, the following example uses one common definition: cash flow is equal to net income plus depreciation, depletion, and amortization (DD&A) plus exploration expenses plus deferred taxes.

ARCO Cash flow:	1989	1988
Net Income	$ 1,953	$ 1,583
DD&A	1,748	1,704
Exploration Expenses	400	469
Deferred Taxes	(363)	129
	$ 3,738	$3,885
Cash flow per share		
(164,186,803 shares)	$22.76	$23.66

	1989	1988
ARCO	$ 3,738	$3,885
Cash flow to =		
Long term debt	5,287	5,400
=	70.7%	71.9%

Here ARCO appears to have the ability to make interest payments by a wide margin. If the ratio were around 30% or less, bankers, bond rating agencies, and management might begin to get nervous.

(c) Debt to Equity $= \dfrac{\text{Long-term debt}}{\text{Stockholders' equity}}$

ARCO (1989)
Debt to Equity $= \dfrac{\$5,287}{\$6,562}$

$= 80.6\%$

Many people refer to the debt to equity ratio as it is treated above. Others will refer to a perhaps more meaningful ratio, which is debt as a percentage of the total capitalization of a company. This seems more helpful and is called the *percentage of debt* or *percent debt*.

(d) Debt to Total Capitalization $=$ $\dfrac{\text{Long-term debt}}{\text{Stockholders' equity + long-term debt}}$

ARCO (1989)
Debt to Total
Capitalization $=$ $\dfrac{\$5,287}{\$6,562 + 5,287}$
(Percent Debt)

$$= 44.6\%$$

These are common ways to calculate debt ratios. Misleading statements are often made about a company's level of debt. For example, if someone says, "Company A has 40% debt," they may be referring to a ratio of debt to equity of 40%, or they may be referring to debt as compared to total capitalization. Sometimes the reference is clear, sometimes it is not.

VALUATION RATIOS

(a) Dividend Yield $=$ $\dfrac{\text{Annual dividend rate}}{\text{Stock price per share}}$

The average yield for oil and gas stocks historically has been around 5 to 6%.

ARCO paid $760 million in dividends in 1989 with a dividend of $4.50 per share. With a stock price of around $114 per share at January 1, 1990, the dividend yield was:

ARCO (31 Dec. 1989)
Dividend Yield $=$ $\dfrac{\$4.50}{\$114.00}$

$$= .0395 \text{ or } 3.95\%$$

(b) Dividend Payout $=$ $\dfrac{\text{Annual dividend rate}}{\text{Earnings per share}}$

ARCO (31 Dec. 1989) $ 4.50
Dividend Payout   = $\dfrac{\$\ 4.50}{11.26}$

$$= .41 \text{ or } 41\%$$

This ratio is close to the percentage of earnings that many major oil companies distribute to shareholders. The average is around 45% for the major oil companies.

(c) P/E Ratio   = $\dfrac{\text{Stock price per share}}{\text{Earnings per share}}$

The price/earnings ratio is one of the most familiar ratios in the financial industry. It is discussed further in Chapter 5.

ARCO (1989)
P/E Ratio   = $\dfrac{\$114}{11.26}$

$$= 10.1$$

(d) Price to Cash Flow = $\dfrac{\text{Stock price per share}}{\text{Cash flow per share}}$

The price to cash flow ratio is a more reliable trading ratio than P/E. This is especially true when earnings are very low or negative. At times like this, analysts will say the stock is *trading on cash flow*. To a certain extent, stocks always trade on cash flow.

$$\text{ARCO Price to Cash Flow} = \frac{\$114}{\$22.76}$$

$$= 5$$

The stock would be said to be trading at five times cash flow. This is a typical trading level for many oil stocks. Under unusual circumstances, stocks will trade at higher multiples, but the explanations can often be found in the footnotes and other information found in company reports.

(e) Stock Price Plus Debt to Cash Flow
$$= \frac{\text{Stock price} + \text{Long-term debt}}{\text{Cash flow}}$$

This ratio will often explain unusual price to cash flow ratios.

ARCO (1989)
$$\text{Stock Price Plus Debt to Cash Flow} = \frac{\$114 + 32.20}{\$22.76}$$

$$= 6.4$$

When all the claims on the cash flow are considered, it appears to be trading at more than six times cash flow. By using this type of ratio, which supposedly includes all the capital employed by the company, a common denominator is used that allows a comparison of companies with different levels of debt.

(f) Market Capitalization and Debt to Appraised Asset Value
$$= \frac{\text{Market capitalization} + \text{debt}}{\text{Appraised value of total assets}}$$

This ratio is one of the important analytical ratios for valuation and is quoted often. The market capitalization is the market price per share times the number of shares of stock. Usually analysts will treat all long-term obligations as debt. There are other more sophisticated ratios that follow this approach. One is called the McDep ratio. It is explained further in Appendix 10.

Typically oil and gas companies will have a ratio of less than 1, which indicates that the stock is *undervalued* to some degree. Ratios as low as .5 and .6 were not uncommon in the early and mid-1980s, and the difference between a ratio of .5 and a ratio of 1 could be hundreds of millions or billions of dollars. This is primarily because the market is *income driven*, and this ratio is *asset driven*. If there are assets that do not generate income or that perform less efficiently from a financial point of view, then the market will respond accordingly. The market focuses primarily on earnings ratios, return on equity, yields, and perceptions of the quality of earnings and cash flow.

An example is not yet given because the equation requires some techniques in estimating value and calculations that have not yet been discussed. The methods of appraising assets and liabilities are covered in detail in Chapter 5.

ADJUSTMENTS TO STANDARD RATIO ANALYSIS

Much of the procedure described so far is like going through the motions of analysis. It is important to understand the ratios that were calculated above. They are the same ratios that are quoted in the press and in company reports.

One of the most important things to look for and consider are the *extraordinary items*. Extraordinary items are usually nonrecurring, one-time material events that require a separate income statement entry as well as explanation in management discussion or the footnotes. These can include write-off of a segment, gain or loss on sale of a subsidiary, or negative impact of a legal decision.

Extraordinary items can have a huge impact on reported earnings. For instance, a company might report a large write-down on the value of certain investments. This write-down would reduce earnings, but the company would not have actually paid out that money in the accounting period the write-down was reported. This is called a *noncash* expense. The analyst must look for these things. Extraordinary items have many names, but one thing to look for is entries on the income statement that change significantly from one year to the next.

The ARCO income statement shows a gain on subsidiary stock transactions of $957 million in 1989. Notice that the previous year there was no entry for this item. This is the hallmark of most extraordinary events. As in the case of ARCO, net income is usually stated before and after taking into account the effects of items like this.

The job for the analyst is to try to decipher what the financial results would have been without the extraordinary events. Notice that ARCO revenues were off by more than $2 billion from 1988 to 1989. Expenses were also down, but only by $1.4 billion. This resulted in a drop in pretax income before the extraordinary item of more than $600 million.

The extraordinary item was primarily the result of the sale of controlling interest in Lyondell, a 100% owned subsidiary of ARCO. It resulted in an after-tax gain of $634 million. Notice in the Statement of Cash Flows (SCF) that this figure is deducted from the calculation of cash flows from operating activities. Net cash provided by operating activities increased from $3,551 million in 1988 to $3,729 million in 1989.

Cash flows from operating activities are often subtotaled *before* changes in inventories, accounts receivable, and other working capital accounts. It neutralizes the effect of "inventory profits." This is usually a good approximation for cash flow. This figure dropped from $3,694 million in 1988 to $3,281 million in 1989.

It does not take a rocket scientist to see that earnings were enhanced by the sale of the assets. But it is not fair to simply subtract the extraordinary item in this case. What would net income have been without the sale of Lyondell? The after-tax gain would be deducted, but the contribution to earnings and cash flow from Lyondell must be assessed as though the sale had not been made. There were $160 million in Lyondell earnings attributable to the interests sold. Adding this sum back helps to show what the earnings would have been without the sale. Determining the cash flow attributable to the interests sold can be difficult. However, the procedure for estimating cash flow for a subsidiary is the same as for the parent company.

ARCO
Adjusted Net Income and Cash Flow

	Adjusted 1989	1988
Reported Net Income	1,953	1,583
Adjustments		
Gain on sale of stock	(634)	—
Earnings attributable to		
subsidiary stock sold	160	—
Net Income Adjusted		
for Extraordinary Item	1,479	1,583
Adjusted Cash Flow		
DD&A	1,748	1,704
Exploration expenses	400	469
Deferred taxes	(363)	129
	3,264	3,885
Adjusted Cash Flow per Share	$19.88	$23. 66

This exercise shows the importance of trying to evaluate business financial results without the effects of extraordinary items. These are some of the most important adjustments that are made in the analysis of income statements.

The next adjustment that should be made is to long-term debt. ARCO has $5,287 million in long-term debt. However, there are also $3,273 million in "other deferred liabilities and credits" on the balance sheet. For all practical purposes, these two figures can be added together and treated as total long-term debt. This combined figure of $8,560 million is consistent with the 1989 interest expense of $799 million and corporate interest rates. This yields an effective interest rate of 9.3%. With these adjustments, ratio analysis begins to get interesting.

SUMMARY AND KEY CONCEPTS

One of the primary uses of ratio analysis is for screening companies or stocks. This is because analysts are often looking for prospective investments for one reason or another, and a detailed analysis is not practical. Ratios help to narrow the field.

The most important use of ratio analysis is to evaluate leverage, or the amount of debt the company uses, and the ability of the company to meet interest and principal payments (*debt service capability*). Usually financial analysis begins with the financial ratios. This is because they are readily accessible and easy to calculate. But reading the footnotes is just as important, and ratio analysis is not complete without it. Illustration 4–2 stresses the importance of the footnotes—don't be the last one to read the footnotes.

"Ya gotta start reading them footnotes, Pa!"

Illus. 4–2

HOW MUCH IS TOO MUCH DEBT?

The greater the percentage of debt, the greater the financial leverage. For example, assume that:

1. Company X can earn 15% rate of return (ROR) after-tax on invested capital.
2. The company can borrow at 10% interest.
3. The company borrows 50% of its capital.
4. Total investment is $1,000.
5. Tax rate is 34%.

With a rate of return of 15%, the company earns $150 on its investment. The company pays $50 interest (10% on $500). The after-tax cost of the interest is $33 because interest is deductible.

$ 500	Invested capital (Equity)
500	Borrowed capital
$1,000	Total capital
150	After-tax rate of return before interest expense
33	After-tax interest expense
$ 122	After-tax return with after-tax interest expense deducted

$$\frac{\$ \ 122 \quad \text{After-tax leveraged return}}{\$ \ 500 \ \text{Invested equity capital}} = 24.4\%$$

Return on Equity = 24.4%
Return on Assets = 12.2%

With borrowed funds, the return is lower at $122 instead of $150, but the rate of return goes from 15% to 24.4%. This is what is meant by financial leverage. Leverage can enhance profitability of invested capital, but it can also enhance risk. Just as leverage can magnifiy profitability, it can also magnify losses.

From a practical point of view, the optimum capital structure for a company is determined perhaps more from observation than theory. The business world is the laboratory for determining how much debt is too much. To a certain extent, survival of the fittest will demonstrate the upper limits of debt for a particular industry. The oil industry seems to have one threshold of around 40% debt as a percentage of total capitalization. Above that level, debt costs increase substantially. This relatively static measure of leverage must be complemented with a close look at the debt service capability of a company. The percentage debt alone is not sufficient. The interest coverage ratio is essential. A company should be able to cover interest and fixed charges by at least a factor of two and a more comfortable coverage would be 3:1. The interest coverage or times interest earned ratio for all companies is close to 2.2:1.

When analysis of breakup value is performed, most ratios have little meaning. Some of the valuation ratios are worthwhile under this view of a company, but most others are not. Table 4–2 summarizes key business ratios for the industry in 1990.

Table 4–2 Summary of Key Business Ratios—1990

	Majors	Independents	Pipeline and Utility
Current Ratio	1.25	1.20	1.00*
Quick Ratio	.80	.75	.90*
Debt/Equity Ratio	25–40%	40–80%	80–110+%
Debt as Percent of Total Capitalization	20–30%	30–45%	45–55%
Return on Assets	5.2%	3.5%	4.4%
Return on Equity	13.5%	7.8%	11.5%

*The current ratio has a wide range, .7–8.0.
The quick ratio can also have a wide range.

Worksheet 4-1 *Financial Statement Analysis*

Company:_____   Date:_____

Shares:_____   Source:_____

Current Trading Price of Stock:_____

	Total ( )	Per Share	Remarks
Total Revenues	_____	_____	_____
Total Assets	_____	_____	_____
Book Value	_____	_____	_____
Current Ratio			_____
Working Capital	_____	_____	_____
Long-term Debt	_____	_____	_____
Interest Expense	_____		Effective Rate _____
Other	_____		_____
Total Debt	_____	_____	_____
Debt/Total Assets			_____
Market Cap.	_____		_____
Net Income	_____	_____	_____
DD&A	_____		_____
Exploration Expenses	_____		_____
Deferred Taxes	_____		_____
Extraordinary Items	_____		_____
Other _____	_____		_____
Cash Flow	_____	_____	_____
Interest Coverage	_____		_____
P/E Ratio	_____		_____
P/CF Ratio	_____		_____

Fig. 4–4 Sample Financial Statement Analysis

Company: __ARCO__   Date: __JANUARY 1990__

Shares: __164.18 MILLION__   Source: __1989 10-K__

Current Trading Price of Stock: __$114/SHARE__

	Total ($MM)	Per Share	Remarks
Total Revenues	$16,815	$102	Down $2 Billion from '88
Total Assets	22,261		
Book Value	6,561	$40	
Current Ratio		1.6	
Working Capital	1,977	$12	
Long-term Debt	5,287	$32	
Interest Expense	799		Effective Rate 15%
Other	3,273		"Deferred Obligations"
Total Debt	8,560		Effective RATE = 9.3%
Debt/Total Assets	38% (NET DEBT = 8,560 − 1,977) 6,583		
Market Cap.	18,716		
Net Income	1,953	$11.90	
DD&A	+ 1,748		
Exploration Expenses	+ 400		
Deferred Taxes	+ (363)		
Extraordinary Items	− 634		
Other			
Cash Flow	$3,104	$18.90	
Interest Coverage	3.76:1		Using income before extraordinary gain
P/E Ratio	9.6		P/E Adjusted = 12.6
P/CF Ratio	6		

96

VALUATION OF COMMON STOCK

Numerous analytical techniques exist, and there are many ways to look at value. While a specific technique is usually most appropriate for a particular purpose, it is often prudent to use a combination of procedures. Different methods will yield a range of results. Reconciliation of the inconsistencies will provide more analytical insight than any one valuation method. The Internal Revenue Service (IRS) and the Securities and Exchange Commission (SEC) recommend a number of guidelines for estimating value.

Guidelines for Estimating Value

IRS GUIDELINES

The IRS in *Revenue Ruling 59–60* outlines several factors that must be considered when valuing a closely held business or its common stock. In later rulings, the IRS expanded the application of the 59-60 guidelines to include valuations of corporate stocks or business interests of any type for tax purposes or determination of fair market value.

IRS Revenue Ruling 59-60 factors are:

1. The nature of the business and the business history
2. The general economic outlook, and the condition and outlook of the specific industry of that business

3. The book value of the stock and the financial condition of the business
4. The earnings capacity of the business
5. The dividend-paying capacity
6. Goodwill or other intangible value
7. Sales of the stock and the size of the block to be valued
8. Comparable sales
9. Premium for control or discount for illiquidity

Obviously, these factors would not all carry the same weight. The IRS emphasizes that the estimate of value should be based on judgment after consideration of all factors. Financial analysts are given considerable latitude. The independent analyst is allowed to impose his own business judgment in emphasizing particular factors or techniques.

SEC GUIDELINES

Instructions from Rule 13(e) of the Securities and Exchange Act of 1934 outline the factors to consider when determining the fairness of a stock transaction. The SEC outlines eight factors:

1. Current market prices (of the stock in question)
2. Historical market prices
3. Net book value
4. Going concern value
5. Liquidation value
6. Price paid (for the stock) in previous transactions
7. Any reports, opinions, or appraisals
8. Any firm offers from outside parties within last 18 months

The following sections discuss each valuation technique in detail. Sometimes a valuation approach will have less meaning in one particular setting than it might in another. The analyst who becomes familiar with the many different ways of looking at value will gain expanded analytical scope. Every company is different, and the more experience the analyst has in looking at value from different angles, the more insight he will have.

Book Value

Book value of a company or shareholder equity is the sum of the common stock, paid in surplus, and retained income accounts from the balance sheet. An asset or a class of assets will be *booked* according to the cost to acquire or obtain them. The accrued depreciation, depletion, and amortization, if they apply, are subtracted. The net amount is the *book value* for that asset or group of assets. A balance sheet entry for inventories may be $10 million regardless of what the inventories are actually worth. This is the book value.

Book value often defines the most conservative value of an oil company. This is primarily because of the cost principle in accounting and GAAP as discussed in Chapter 3.

In a merger where companies are evaluated on a comparative basis, book value is seldom ignored, even though it may not carry much weight.

The appraised value of oil companies is often 1.5–3 times book value. Typically companies using Full Cost accounting will have a higher book value relative to appraised value than a company using Successful Efforts.

Book Value Multiple

In some industries, the trading value of a stock and transaction values are constantly compared to book value. The upstream oil industry is not one of them. Book value multiples are more useful in valuing businesses in the downstream sector. The large refineries are often appraised at .75–1.25 times book value. The utility industry also has established trends. Utility stocks trade at approximately 1.5 times book value. Utility acquisitions, on the other hand, range 2.2–2.8 times book value. This gives a point of reference and a means of comparison.

The most common use of the ratio compares the purchase price to the book value of the stock. For example, a company stock that sells for $30 per share with $15 per share book value sells for 2 *times book*. However, the ratio has more meaning if debt is considered. This puts leveraged and unleveraged companies on an equal footing. Suppose that the company that sold for $30 per share had $10 per share of debt. The *debt-adjusted* ratio would be:

Debt-adjusted Book Value Multiple

$$\text{Debt-Adjusted Book Value Multiple} = \frac{\text{Stock price/Share} + \text{Debt/Share}}{\text{Book value/Share} + \text{Debt/Share}}$$

$$= \frac{\$30 + \$10}{\$15 + \$10}$$

$$= 1.6$$

Considering the debt in the capital structure, the book value multiple is 1.6.

Adjusted Book Value

The adjusted book value approach has many names: *appraised value, adjusted balance sheet value, ad hoc asset value, liquidation value,* or *appraised equity.* It centers on balance sheet adjustments that convert book values to fair market values. Each balance sheet item is valued at its stand-alone market value. Sometimes specific assets, groups of assets, or business entities are segregated and valued together.

In most situations it is easy to estimate a realistic value for the individual balance sheet items. The following guidelines provide methods for assigning values to the numerous assets and liabilities commonly found on the balance sheet of an oil company.

When estimating liquidation value for the SEC, market value of a particular asset is based on timing, discount for present value, and selling costs associated with the sale of the asset. For example, consider a company that holds a 500-acre tract of undeveloped real estate with a book value of $2 million. A typical analysis is outlined in Table 5-1.

Table 5–1 Example Balance Sheet Item "Adjustment"

Real Estate (500 acres)
($ 2,000,000 book value)

Fair market value*	$3,000,000
Less commission and selling expense (7%)	210,000
	2,790,000
Discount for time to sell (assume one year = 12%)	.89
Adjusted balance sheet value	2,483,100

*Based upon comparable recent sales

This approach is a normal part of due diligence for SEC and IRS valuations. However, the quoted asset value or appraised equity of companies often does not incorporate this kind of treatment for each balance sheet entry. Quoted liquidation values for a company usually do not include the kind of detailed adjustments shown above.

Usually each balance sheet item is entered at its estimated fair market value (FMV) without adjustments for commissions and selling expenses or discounting for time to sell. The resulting appraised equity is then discounted or adjusted by a factor based on experience, the complexity of the balance sheet, and capital gains taxes, if they apply. While book value of a company represents accounting value, appraised equity represents economic value. The term appraised equity is the same as adjusted book value. Accounting book value is simply adjusted to reflect economic reality. Worksheet 5–1 can be used for the adjusted book value approach to evaluating a nonintegrated oil company.

Worksheet 5–1 Adjusted Book Value — Nonintegrated Oil Company

Company:_____   Date:_____

Shares:_____   Source:_____

Current Trading Price of Stock:_____

Appraised Values

Assets		Equities	
Current Assets	_____	Current Liabilities	_____
Other	_____	Long-term Debt	_____
Oil	_____	Deferred Taxes	_____
Gas	_____	Other Obligations	_____
Acreage Value	_____	Shareholder Appraised Equity	_____
Other Assets	_____		
Total Assets	_____	Total Liabilities and Appraised Equity	_____

Adjusted Book Value Methodology

Total current assets
- Total current liabilities
= Working capital
+ Increased value of inventories or other current assets
+ Appraised value of oil properties
+ Appraised value of gas properties
+ Acreage value of nonproducing properties
+ Other assets such as overfunded pension plan
- Long-term debt
- 50% of deferred taxes (typically)
- Other liabilities such as capitalized lease obligations
= Adjusted book value = Shareholder appraised equity

RECEIVABLES

Appraisal of receivables is based on their present value. Theoretically receivables should account for the possibility of nonpayment of some portion. It cannot be taken for granted. Sometimes a company will use latitude in calculation for doubtful accounts. If the percentage of receivables that make up the doubtful portion has changed from one accounting period to the next, it can suggest a problem. For instance, if the provision for doubtful accounts changes from 9% of receivables to 4% from one accounting period to the next, there should be a good reason. Another thing to look for is a situation where receivables are increasing significantly with flat sales. This can indicate problems with the quality of receivables.

FIXED ASSETS

Fixed assets, called property, plant, and equipment (PP&E), include buildings, equipment, vehicles, and machinery. They are represented on the balance sheet at their net depreciated value, but should be appraised at current market value. Sometimes an asset will be fully depreciated for accounting purposes, yet it may have a significant market value.

REAL ESTATE

Land owned by a company can have considerable value beyond what is shown on the balance sheet. The appraised value should reflect property values based on recent transactions of similar properties. These kind of assets are often the *hidden treasures* that are the focus of corporate raiders.

LONG-TERM DEBT

Long-term debt, and notes payable should be appraised at the present value of the amounts to be paid. Interest rates should be checked on long-term debt to ensure they are not significantly different from prevailing interest rates. Circumstances can exist where the present value of long-term debt is significantly different from the value reported on the balance sheet. If interest rates appear to be unusually high, the likely explanation is that debt is effectively understated. The footnotes disclose the rates for all bond issues. It is a good practice to quickly compare annual interest expense with average long-term debt for the year to see if the interest rates are close to prevailing corporate rates.

In 1982 Exxon had $515 million of old, low-interest rate (5.8–6.7%), long-term debt due in 2009 on their balance sheet. The company purchased $312 million of U.S. government securities with an interest rate of 14% and placed them into an irrevocable trust to provide for the repayment of the principal and interest on the old debt. Exxon was then able to remove the debt from the balance sheet. This is known as *defeasance*. It was then possible for Exxon to add $132 million to earnings in that quarter. The $132 million was the after-tax difference between the old defeased $512 million (book value) debt and the $312 million for the government securities.

The book value of debt is usually taken at face value. It is unusual to make balance sheet adjustments to long-term debt. The Exxon example was provided to point out that exceptions exist for nearly every rule. With the increased use of *call provisions* on bond and debenture issues, the problems associated with fluctuating interest rates have been softened for companies.

LIFO INVENTORIES

Refining and marketing entities that use the *last-in, first-out* (LIFO) method of inventory valuation for reporting income will normally understate the value of inventories on the balance sheet during times of rising prices. Therefore, the market value of inventories in excess of LIFO book value must be considered. The difference between book value of inventories and market value is usually outlined in the financial footnotes.

In the ARCO 1989 annual report, Footnote No. 4 explained that approximately 60% of inventories were accounted for under the LIFO method. The footnote further explained that "The excess of the current cost of inventories over book value was approximately $167 million at December 31, 1989." This kind of value in excess of book value with LIFO inventories is sometimes referred to as LIFO *reserve*.

This footnote entry, explaining the difference between book value of inventories under LIFO and market value, is fairly typical. In some instances, where large differences exist between LIFO value and market value of inventories, companies can liquidate inventory with dramatic results.

During 1982 and 1983, Texaco partially liquidated inventories which resulted in after-tax increases in net income of $206 million and $503 million, respectively. This information was explained in the financial footnotes of the Texaco 1984 annual report. Sometimes these kinds of profits are referred to as *inventory profits*.

FIFO INVENTORIES

The *first-in, first-out* (FIFO) method of inventory accounting can cause large distortions in earnings. FIFO accounting does not lend itself to manipulation like LIFO does. The FIFO method uses the earlier costs of inventories for calculation of cost of goods sold (COGS). This has the effect of yielding relatively higher earnings in times of rising prices, and lower earnings in times of lower prices for goods sold. FIFO accounting for inventories will effectively magnify the results of business cycles in reported earnings.

Theoretically, LIFO accounting will generate more realistic earnings since the current costs for inventories are used in the calculation, but FIFO will have a more realistic value of inventories. In times of stable prices, both systems would ultimately yield the same earnings and inventory values.

DEFERRED TAXES

There is considerable controversy as to the nature of the deferred tax item. Accountants treat it as a liability, but deferred taxes do not strictly satisfy the conventional definition of a liability.

Deferred taxes are created from the difference between tax accounting and financial accounting for depreciation. It is perfectly legal for a company to report lower earnings to the IRS than the earnings reported to the stockholders. This is because tax laws allow *accelerated depreciation*. For example, an asset may be depreciated by accountants using straight-line depreciation, but for tax purposes the company might use an accelerated method of depreciation as shown in Table 5–2. The deferred tax liability on the balance sheet is the result of that difference.

It is usually not appropriate, from an analytical point of view, to treat the book value of deferred taxes as debt. For valuation purposes, treating a portion of the deferred tax item as though it were debt is best. This approach acknowledges the present value of the potential stream of additional income tax payments resulting from a reversal in the timing differences.

Table 5–2 shows how a deferred tax item is created. A $1,000 piece of equipment is used as an example.

Table 5–2 Example of the Deferred Tax Item

Equipment cost = $1000

Year	Revenue	DD&A SL	DD&A SYD	Difference	— Earnings — Financial	— Earnings — Tax	Annual Deferred Tax	Balance Sheet Entry
1	800	250	400	150	550	400	75	75
2	800	250	300	50	550	500	25	100
3	800	250	200	(50)	550	600	(25)	75
4	800	250	100	(150)	550	700	(75)	0
		$1,000	$1,000	0				

SL = Straight-line depreciation for accounting purposes
SYD = Sum-of-years' digits accelerated depreciation for tax purposes

Assumed tax rate is 50%

In this example, with revenues of $800 per year, the deferred tax account reaches $100 in Year 2. Thereafter, the change in the deferred tax account is negative, and the account is zero at the end of Year 4.

DEFERRED TAXES AND THE GOING CONCERN

At some point, the deferred taxes may have to be paid off. This means that (1) corporate capital expenditure will fall off enough to allow a reversal in the timing difference that created the account and (2) the entity will remain profitable. While these two assumptions are not mutually exclusive, they do tend to contradict each other. It is unlikely that a profitable going concern would cease to reinvest capital for growth.

The timing of deferred tax payments may be so far into the future that the present value would be negligible. A common practice is to reduce the deferred tax entry to half its book value for quick-look analysis and going concern analysis. In the adjusted balance-sheet analysis, reducing the value of deferred taxes, or any balance sheet liability, will increase the appraised *equity*.

Deferred taxes can be a huge balance sheet item. The 1989 ARCO balance sheet had $3,407 million in deferred taxes. Shareholder equity was only twice that amount at $6,562 million. Treating half of the ARCO deferred taxes as a liability effectively increases appraised shareholder equity by 25%.

Occasionally tax laws reduce corporate income taxes. When this happens, companies with deferred income tax liabilities will pay less tax in future years than indicated by the deferred tax account on the balance sheet. As a result, the deferred income tax item on the balance sheet is adjusted accordingly to reflect the effective reduction in the liability. Income statements reflect a gain that increases reported income. Typically, the increases are noncash increases because the company does not actually receive cash. If taxes are increased, the deferred income tax liability will be increased, and a loss would be recorded against earnings.

DEFERRED TAXES IN LIQUIDATION

When evaluating a company's liquidation value, the book value of deferred taxes usually are treated as though they are payable at the time of liquidation.

OIL AND GAS PROPERTIES

The balance sheet adjustment for oil and gas reserves and exploration acreage is usually the most important balance-sheet adjustment. The estimate of the true value of oil and gas reserves is a key objective in the analysis of an oil company. Therefore, the focus of Chapter 7 is on considerations of value for oil and gas properties.

LONG-TERM INVESTMENTS IN STOCK

Corporations often have substantial investments in the common stock of other companies. These investments usually will come under investigation by the inquiring analyst. The analyst is mainly interested in the value of the shareholdings. Long-term stock investments are categorized according to the level of ownership in the stock of a particular company. Table 5–3 outlines the categories and the accounting treatment of each kind of ownership.

Table 5–3 Treatment of Long-term Stock Investments

Level of Ownership	Percentage of Ownership	Accounting Treatment
Noninfluential and Noncontrolling	Less than 20%	Cost method: Investments are valued on the balance sheet at lower of cost or market value
Influential but Noncontrolling	20% and 50%	Equity method: Investments are valued on the balance sheet at cost plus investors' share of income less dividends
Controlling Interest	More than 50%	Consolidated financial statements are prepared

The actual market value of shareholdings under these methods can be different from the value represented on the balance sheets. The footnotes are often helpful in providing additional information about such investments.

MARKETABLE SECURITIES UNDER THE COST METHOD

This item on the balance sheet is entered at market value or cost, whichever is less. It should be valued at its appraised value. If the balance sheet entry was based on market value, the value of the securities may have increased or decreased since the balance sheet date, and an adjustment may be necessary. Usually the footnotes will disclose the actual market value of securities as of the reporting date.

NONCONTROLLING INTERESTS UNDER THE EQUITY METHOD

The footnotes will often describe the nature of a stock investment accounted for under the equity method. As with many exercises in estimating value, the accounting entry for such an investment may not represent the actual value of the interests held.

CONSOLIDATION AND MINORITY INTERESTS

When a company owns a controlling interest of more than 50% in another company or subsidiary, the financial statements of both companies are consolidated. Imagine a parent company owning 80% of a subsidiary that has a book value of $200 million. The total assets and liabilities of the subsidiary are consolidated with the parent. But the parent company must account for the 20% that it does not own. This is called a *minority interest*. The balance sheet entry for minority interests treats 20% of the book value of the majority-owned subsidiary as a liability (usually).

The minority interest item is found most often in the liability section of the balance sheet, but sometimes is treated as equity. It does not represent an immediate claim on the company assets. It represents the proportionate interests of minority shareholders in a majority-owned subsidiary that was consolidated with the financial statements of the parent.

If the subsidiary had a negative book value, the entry may look more like an asset. The important thing is that the minority interests are based on book value. If the analyst wants to get into detail, the analysis of this balance sheet item would require evaluation of the subsidiary in terms of market value rather than book value.

Suppose the subsidiary earned $10 million. Revenues and expenses are also consolidated with the parent company, but the 20% of earnings that do not belong to the parent are deducted by the use of the minority interest item on the income statement. Sometimes the entry for minority interests can be confusing. If the subsidiary has negative earnings, the income statement for the parent company will show a positive adjustment. This is because in consolidation, the parent had incorporated 100% of the loss.

INTANGIBLE FACTORS

Intangible assets might include licenses, patents, and franchises. In theory, the value of such assets should be reflected in corporate earnings. But in situations where a license or patent require additional capital to realize their full potential, an acquiring company with available capital may perceive a higher value than the value implied by established earnings performance.

OFF-BALANCE SHEET ASSETS AND LIABILITIES

With the adjusted balance-sheet approach, the assets and liabilities that do not show up on the balance sheet must be considered. A good example would be a long-term lease obligation.

LONG-TERM LEASES

Long-term leases can represent specific liabilities that under certain conditions may not be clearly disclosed in financial statements. In 1973, the SEC issued a ruling requiring companies to disclose lease or rental commitments and the financial impact on both present and future earnings. Material lease commitments are required to be disclosed in the footnotes, but the full extent of the liability a lease may represent may not be instantly clear. It is something to keep in mind.

Analysis of a company's liquidation value treats the lease obligation as a liability that must be paid, if that assumption is consistent with the terms of the lease. Income-based analysis of the company as a going concern treats lease payments as ongoing costs of doing business. The projected lease payments would be built into the earnings or cash flow analysis.

TAX LOSS CARRY FORWARD/BACK

Under most circumstances, a company with an operating loss can carry the loss back and apply it to income in the preceding three years. If it cannot be fully used by carrying it back three years, the remaining portion can be carried forward 15 years.

The value of a tax loss carried back is straightforward since the earnings for the past three years are known. The value for the carry forward of a tax loss is less certain since it requires an estimate of future earnings against which the loss would be applied.

Occasionally, a company will have a tax loss carry-forward (TLCF) position that could conceivably be used to offset the taxable income of an acquiring company. However, the criteria established by the Internal Revenue Code is highly restrictive. Whenever a carry-forward position is an important consideration to an acquiring company, an advanced ruling from the IRS by the acquiring company is usually obtained.

The criteria governing eligibility of transferring a TLCF is primarily founded on a *continuity of interest* concept. While a corporation that incurs a loss is entitled to the TLCF, this benefit cannot be assigned to another company. If a company is merged into another company, it is possible to maintain the integrity of a TLCF. Two general requirements for continuity of interest are:

1. The acquired company should be acquired as a going concern with no major change in its nature of business.

2. If the company is acquired in a nontaxable transaction, which essentially requires the legal discontinuation of one of the acquired companies, the stockholders of the target company must hold at least 20% of the stock of the surviving company. The amount of the TLCF that can be transferred may be reduced if this condition is not met.

If it can be determined that a TLCF will survive an acquisition, then the present value of the position can be estimated. The rate at which the surviving corporate entity is capable of applying the TLCF to its before-tax earnings and the discount factor used will govern the present value of the TLCF.

PENSION PROGRAMS

Sometimes there is value in excess pension funds. The status of the fund is usually discussed in the footnotes of the annual report. There are two types of pension programs: defined benefit programs, and defined contribution programs. Under the defined benefit programs there was often the possibility of *hidden assets*. An example of this kind of plan is explained in the 1989 AMOCO annual report. Footnote No. 18, Retirement Plans, provided an estimate of the "fair value of plan assets . . ." of $2,804 million. The "projected benefit obligation" was $2,400 million. The result was an *overfunding* of $404 million "excess of plan assets over projected benefit obligation." This is the kind of hidden value that the *sharks* are searching for. However, just as pension funds can be overfunded, they can be *underfunded* as well. This can represent a liability and must be represented on the balance sheet. Another problem that is becoming a looming problem for companies is the *postretirement health-benefits* coverage liabilities. Defined benefit programs for many companies provided for a percentage of an employee's salary to be paid during retirement. In addition to that, health coverage was guaranteed. For many companies, these guarantees for postretirement health coverage are not quantified (as they should be on the balance sheet) as the liability that they represent.

Analysts inspecting an overfunded pension program had to determine if the program could be terminated or restructured in order to free up the excess funds. The restructuring process could be quite complex and expensive, requiring numerous government approvals and scrutiny. Now the overfunding of many programs is being   overshadowed with the reality of the obligations to retirees' health coverage.

OTHER POSTEMPLOYMENT BENEFITS

Unfortunately, if the chief executive officer of a company has a $5 million *golden parachute,* it will not show up as a balance sheet item. But evaluating the liquidation value of a company requires knowledge of such obligations. These types of provisions for management can be substantial. Disclosure of these types of obligations may be part of shareholder meeting/proxy material or shareholder rights plans.

LITIGATION

Potential liabilities or benefits from litigation can have a substantial impact on corporate value. Any significant litigation should be mentioned in the auditor's report, the chairman's letter to the shareholders, and the footnotes. The financial results of a lawsuit may be difficult to assess, but clues sometimes can be found that indicate the seriousness of the litigation.

ENVIRONMENTAL LIABILITIES

The greatest potential liabilities facing the industry are those concerning the environment. Spills, explosions, leaks, and contamination are becoming increasingly costly and are strictly monitored by regulatory agencies and the public. In recent years, there has been a large increase in the number of companies disclosing contingencies and commitments for environmental matters. By 1990, half of all annual reports in the petroleum industry mentioned environmental issues and contingencies.

The challenges facing the industry in the area of environmental focus include:

- oil spill legislation
- cleaner fuels
- stricter emissions controls
- offshore drilling
- air quality
- contamination and cleanup

Many companies face significant financial exposure from possible claims and lawsuits regarding environmental matters. The Environmental Protection Agency (EPA), under Superfund legislation, is designating companies as potentially responsible parties (PRPs) for contaminated sites and cleanup requirements. Estimating the potential financial impact can be difficult. The place to look for clues is examination of the legal matters item in the 10-K and the list of exhibits and 8-K filings (Item 14) at the end of the 10-K report.

There are more than 110,000 gas stations in the United States with underground storage tanks for gasoline and diesel fuel. As these facilities get older, the potential liability due to leaks increases. This is just one example. The issue of environmental exposure and potential litigation is like a field of land mines. It is expected only to get worse. Almost all companies are exposed to some degree. Analysts will look more and more into the precautions and financial contingencies that have been established.

On March 24, 1989, the Exxon Valdez, a tanker owned by Exxon Shipping Company, ran aground, spilling approximately 260,000 barrels of crude oil into Prince William Sound, Alaska. By the end of the year, Exxon had spent more than $1.6 billion cleaning up the oil spill. More than 170 lawsuits, including class action proceedings, were brought against the company as a result of the spill. In its 1990 annual report, Exxon indicated that in February 1990 an indictment had been returned in U.S. District Court in Anchorage, Alaska, charging Exxon with violation of the Refuse Act, the Migratory Bird Treaty Act, the Clean

Water Act, the Ports and Waterways Safety Act, and the Dangerous Cargos Act.

In March 1991, Exxon agreed to a $1 billion out-of-court settlement with the federal government and Alaska Gov. Walter Hickel. By that time, cleanup costs had passed $2 billion. Other civil suits and spill-related litigation from environmental groups were still pending. One month later the Alaska House of Representatives rejected the $1 billion settlement as inadequate. Subsequently, Exxon withdrew guilty pleas that had been part of the original agreement. The battle continues.

ABANDONMENT COSTS AND CLEANUP

There are situations, especially offshore with platforms, where abandonment costs are quite large. Theoretically, accounting practices should acknowledge these liabilities, but that is often not the case. Companies must make provisions to satisfy eventual dismantlement and abandonment costs.

If the analyst suspects that a situation exists where abandonment is drawing near, then this possibility should be investigated. Some companies own properties where the abandonment and cleanup costs exceed by far any tangible value of the properties. Have the funds been set aside for the abandonment costs or cleanup costs? Are they adequate?

OFF-BALANCE-SHEET COMMITMENTS

In addition to leases, there are other types of off-balance-sheet commitments. This area can be complex, and the analyst must be aware of the variations on this theme.

The *take-or-pay* agreement was one method that became very visible in the gas industry in the 1980s. Take-or-pay agreements in the petroleum industry usually involved gas purchasers that had an obligation to pay a certain minimum amount for gas even if the gas was not taken. Some of these agreements became substantial liabilities and were not disclosed in the balance sheets or other financial statements as other liabilities were.

Another example is where a company uses project financing through a joint venture or a limited partnership that may not be consolidated with the company's financial statements.

The Financial Accounting Standards Board is tightening the disclosure requirements for these types of financing.

DRILLING COMMITMENTS

In the upstream end of the oil industry, the most prominent capital expenditures are for drilling. Often commitments are made well in advance of the actual expenditure of capital. These drilling commitments can represent substantial short- and long-term obligations that do not find representation on the balance sheet.

When evaluating a company as a going concern, the matter is less important than when evaluating the liquidation value of a company.

SUMMARY

The analysis of a company balance sheet is seldom as demanding as this chapter may make it appear. The detailed discussion of each type of balance sheet item was provided as a source of reference. One never knows what will turn up.

With independent oil companies, the adjustments to the balance sheet are often straightforward and much less complicated than analysis of an integrated oil company. This is because the mix of assets is less complex and there are fewer major categories of assets. Nevertheless, the arithmetic is just the same. Worksheet 5–2 is the kind of worksheet that can be used to perform an adjusted book value analysis of an integrated oil company.

Worksheet 5-2 Adjusted Book Value—Integrated Oil Company

Company:_____   Date:_____

Shares:_____   Source:_____

Current Trading Price of Stock:_____

Appraised Values

Assets		Equities	
Current Assets	_____	Current Liabilities	_____
Other	_____	Long-term Debt	_____
Domestic U.S. Oil and Gas	_____	Deferred Taxes	_____
International Oil and Gas	_____	Preferred Stock	_____
		Minority Interests	_____
Acreage Value	_____		
		Other Obligations	_____
Refinery Operations	_____		
		Other Obligations	_____
Marketing Outlets	_____		
Other Assets	_____	Shareholder Appraised Equity	_____
Other Assets	_____		
		Total Liabilities and	
Total Assets	_____	Appraised Equity	_____

Adjusted Book Value Methodology

Total current assets – Total current liabilities
= Working capital
+ Increased value of inventories (if any)
+ Appraised value of oil and gas properties
+ Acreage value of nonproducing properties
+ Appraised value of refining operations
+ Appraised value of gas stations and marketing outlets
+ Surplus assets if pension plan is overfunded
+ Other assets
– Long-term debt
– 50% of deferred taxes (typically)
– Preferred stock (market value or liquidation value)
– Minority interests
– Capitalized lease obligations or other obligations
= Adjusted book value = Shareholder Appraised Equity

Dividend Discount Valuation

One of the most heartwarming aspects of stock ownership is the quarterly dividend payment. This is part of the reason that dividends are an emotional issue and so much attention is paid by management to the signals that are sent by an increase or reduction in dividend payments.

The dividend discount valuation technique is based on the present value of a projected stream of dividends. It is sometimes referred to as an "investment value" approach, because this technique was once considered as the basis of investment in the stock of a company. From the viewpoint of the investor, returns consist of dividends plus the capital gain on resale of the stock at some point in the future. Theoretically, the resale value is based on the price another investor would be willing to pay for the anticipated dividend stream at that time.

The dividend models usually assume a perpetual stream of dividend

payments. This technique requires an estimate of future stock performance, not only in terms of dividend distributions, but potential growth
as well. A simplified approach for estimating the value of a stock is based
on dividend rate and estimated growth. It is called the Gordon Dividend
Model.

Gordon Dividend Model

$$P = \frac{D}{i - g}$$

Where:

P = present value of dividend stream
D = dividend
i = the rate of interest
g = growth rate

This model assumes that dividends are paid annually at the end of the
year, even though dividends are typically paid quarterly.

For example, with a dividend rate of $4 per share, a discount rate of
12% and a growth rate of 7%, the present value of the dividend stream
would be:

$$P = \frac{\$4.00}{.12 - .07}$$

$$= \frac{\$4.00}{.05}$$

$$= \$80$$

The dividend rate is thus capitalized at 5%, and, under these assumptions, the stock would be worth $80 per share.

The dividend discount approach traditionally assumes the firm will continue as a going concern.

Dividends in the petroleum industry seldom provide the driving force behind stock price. The typical yield for an oil and gas company has been 5–6%. There are exceptions. The Master Limited Partnerships (MLPs), where dividend distribution is of prime importance, yield around 15%.

Capitalized Earnings

The price earnings ratio (P/E) is one of the most widely quoted statistics associated with any stock. Investors will often look first for stocks that are trading at a low P/E multiple. It is commonly used by stock analysts for estimating a reasonable trading value for a stock, although it no longer holds the exalted position it once held.

Because many companies pay no dividends, evaluating stocks on the basis of earnings rather than dividend yield makes better sense.

An earnings multiple of 20 implies a net discount rate of 5%. The assumption of growth is built into the earnings capitalization model in the same manner as in the dividend discount model.

Suppose that earnings for a stock were $5 per share and similar stocks typically traded at eight times earnings. This multiple implies a net discount rate of 12.5%. The stock should trade at $40 per share if it is truly similar to its peer stocks in the industry group. If, however, the stock is expected to grow at an annual rate of 2% per year more than other similar stocks, then the appropriate multiple would be:

$$P/E = \frac{1}{(.125 - .02)} = 9.5$$

With a multiple of 9.5, the stock with earnings of $5.00 per share would be worth $47.50 per share.

THEORETICAL P/E MULTIPLE

A derivation of the Gordon Dividend Model provides a means of calculating a theoretical P/E multiple for a company.

$$P/E = \frac{D/E}{i - g}$$

Where:

P = stock price
P/E = price earnings ratio
D = dividend
D/E = dividends as a percentage of earnings
i = the rate of interest or discount rate
g = growth rate

In the petroleum industry, dividends are approximately 35% of earnings. Assuming a 12% discount factor and a growth rate projection of 8%, the calculated P/E multiple would be:

$$P/E = \frac{.35}{12 - .08} = \frac{.35}{.04} = 8.8$$

Just as in the dividend model, when the growth rate approaches the interest rate, the equation *blows up*—approaches infinity. This model does not have lots of practical value, but it helps to show the relationship between the various factors that influence the P/E of a stock.

Dividends as a percentage of earnings are different for each company and industry group. When earnings swing with volatile oil prices, the ratios change while managements try to maintain stable dividend policy. In less volatile times, there is a general trend in dividend payout policy, which is summarized in Table 5–4.

Table 5–4 Dividends as a Percentage of Earnings

Industry Group	Dividends as a Percentage of Earnings*
Integrated International	45%
Integrated Domestic	35%
Independent Producers	20%
Natural Gas Transmission and Distribution	70%

*Dividend payout ratio

GRAHAM & DODD P/E FORMULA

The Graham & Dodd P/E formula was developed in the early 1970s to estimate a reasonable P/E ratio. This formula was empirically derived in an effort to assess the value of *growth stocks*. Growth stocks are stocks of companies that exhibit faster-than-average earnings growth. The Graham & Dodd Formula is based on the prevailing interest rate of a Aaa bond (Chapter 9) and the expected 7–10 year growth rate for a stock.

Graham & Dodd Formula for Estimating Appropriate P/E Ratio

$$P/E = \frac{37.5 + [8.8 \times g]}{i}$$

Where:

P/E = price earnings ratio

g = growth rate

i = rate of interest on Aaa bond

note in this formula that interest and growth rates are not decimal percent, i.e., a growth rate of 15% is input as 15, not 0.15.

123

For example, assuming the rate on a Aaa (pronounced "triple A") bond is 10%, the appropriate P/E for a stock with an expected growth rate of 15% would be 17.

$$P/E = \frac{37.5 + [8.8 \times g]}{i}$$

$$P/E = \frac{169.5}{10}$$

$$P/E = 17$$

THE FUNDAMENTALS HAVE CHANGED

The essential *fundamentals* are interest rates and growth. All other factors are important, but they boil down to projections of growth for a particular stock. When these fundamentals change, the overall market will respond accordingly. All of the valuation formulas indicate that as interest rates go up, stock prices and P/E ratios, in general, should go down. These formulas also show the kind of growth rate assumptions that are needed to justify certain earnings multiples.

Interest rates have changed considerably over the years. As a result of that and other factors, trends in P/E ratios have changed as well. A typical stock in the late 1940s and early 1950s traded at 8–12 times earnings. During the 1960s, multiples increased and stocks traded at 15 to 20 times earnings. The P/E ratio of the Dow Jones Industrials during the 40 years since 1940 was 14.4. In 1961, before the crash in 1962, the Dow Industrials, on the average, were trading at 23 times earnings. In 1974, the Dow P/E ratio hit a low of 6 but was more than 10 the following year. Prior to the crash in October 1987 the P/E of the Dow was more than 20. Table 5–5 summarizes some of the annual trends in interest rates and other market indicators.

Table 5-5 Historical Market Trends

Year	Dow Jones Average P/E	Dividend Yield	Moody's Aaa Corporate Bond Yield	Bank Prime	Consumer Price Index Growth "Inflation"	Long-term U.S. Government Bonds*
1973	10.7	3.8%	7.4%	8.03%	6.2%	7.12%
1974	7.7	5.0	8.6	10.81	11.1	8.05
1975	10.6	4.7	8.8	7.87	9.1	8.19
1976	10.1	4.2	8.4	6.84	5.7	7.86
1977	10.0	5.1	8.0	6.83	6.5	7.75
1978	7.3	5.9	8.7	9.06	7.6	8.49
1979	6.8	6.0	9.6	12.67	11.3	9.29
1980	7.3	6.1	11.9	15.27	13.5	11.30
1981	8.2	6.0	14.2	18.87	10.3	13.44
1982	14.3	6.1	13.8	14.86	6.1	12.76
1983	14.0	4.7	12.0	10.79	3.2	11.18
1984	9.8	5.1	12.7	12.04	4.3	12.39
1985	12.5	4.7	11.4	9.93	3.5	10.79
1986	15.8	3.7	9.0	8.33	1.9	7.78
1987	14.1	3.1	9.4	8.20	3.7	8.59
1988	9.0	3.9	9.7	9.32	4.1	8.96
1989	10.7	4.1	9.3	10.87	4.8	8.45
1990	14.6	3.6	9.0	10.01	4.5	8.61

*Data for 20-year bonds prior to 1977, 30-year bonds thereafter.
Source: Value Line, Inc., Federal Reserve Board

The capitalization of earnings is pure present value theory. But formulas based on earnings give no consideration for dividends. Therefore, no distinction is made between companies with the same earnings but different dividend rates. A company stock that pays no dividends would not likely trade at the same price as one that paid out 50% of earnings in dividends.

Establishing a value for a company or business entity using an earnings approach requires estimation of earnings growth and application of an appropriate capitalization rate. Many security analysts select an earnings multiple based on a typical P/E ratio for the appropriate industry group, or peer group of companies.

Analysts will apply a multiple to the three-year average of forecast earnings, or to current earnings. In the energy industry, the key elements in forecasting earnings are based on expectations of:

- product prices
- production rates
- costs and expenses

When an analyst goes so far as to address each of these issues in detail, it is probably best to go ahead and do cash flow analysis. The analysis of earnings falls just short of cash flow analysis.

The other factors that influence the P/E ratio are worth mentioning.

Stability. Companies exhibiting a lower degree of volatility than otherwise similar stocks may trade at a multiple of one or two points higher. The volatility, or beta, is considered by some a measure of risk.

Cash Flow Strength. The market gives more credence to strong cashflow performance than to earnings. In situations where earnings are negative, stock will trade purely on cash flow and/or asset value. This may be particularly true during periods where earnings have suffered short-term setbacks due to write-downs or unusual industry conditions. The real bottom line for a company is cash flow.

Leverage. The market appears to give some credit to low-debt companies. This is especially true in a bear market. The premium is usually one or two P/E points above the average.

Yield. Assuming all other factors are equal, especially growth expectations, the market should theoretically allow some sort of premium for companies that pay a higher dividend. Dividend paying stocks with higher yields generally do have higher P/E ratios. Some analysts believe that stock prices may be more closely related to dividend growth than to earnings growth. However, those who contest this theory point out that nondividend-paying stocks trade at higher P/E ratios than stocks that do pay dividends.

It all sounds confusing, and it is, especially for directors and management trying to decide corporate dividend policy. These relationships are general and have many exceptions.

The most important argument against paying dividends was that dividends were effectively taxed twice, as far as the shareholder was concerned. If a company paid no dividends, theoretically the shareholder would profit purely by capital gains. However, with the tax reform act of 1986, this tax differential has been virtually eliminated. With the highest personal tax rate at 31%, and capital gains tax rate at 28%, this argument for not paying dividends was no longer valid.

The earnings capitalization technique is at best a proxy for a true present value approach to estimating value. The capitalized earnings approach is closer to a rule of thumb. Fortunately, like many rules of thumb, it can sometimes provide a quick approximation of value, or at least point out an interesting trend.

The best measure of value should be based on discounted cash flow analysis.

Discounted Cash Flow Analysis

Cash flow analysis is a complex and controversial subject in the financial industry. The concept of cash flow is often misunderstood and misused due to numerous related definitions and the many variations involved. Some industries have different definitions.

CASH FLOW

The simplest, most frequently quoted formula for oil company cash flow is:

Cash Flow = Net Income
+ DD&A
+ Exploration Expenses
+ Deferred Taxes

The treatment of cash flow for most industries is referred to as net income before depreciation, or sometimes *cash earnings*. These definitions can be very helpful for quick-look analysis. Cash flow is one of the first things to evaluate on the income statement and the statement of cash flows. For segment information, such as refining and marketing operations or a pipeline segment, net income and DD&A may be all the information available for making an estimate of cash flow.

Generally, these are the formulas that are used and quoted most frequently. These simple definitions have weaknesses, but most analysts are aware of that, and they use these formulas regularly.

Full Cost companies will capitalize exploratory dry-hole costs. By adding exploration expenses and DD&A to net income, the differences between Successful Efforts and Full Cost accounting begin to disappear.

A comparison of two companies' simplified income statements in Table 5–6 illustrates the importance of cash flow.

128

Table 5-6 Earnings vs Cash Flow Comparison

	Company A Successful Efforts	Company B Full Cost
Revenues	$10,000	$10,000
Less Expenses	7,000	7,000
Less Dry-hole costs	1,000	0
Less DD&A	1,500	2,000
Net Income before tax	500	1,000
Income Tax (34%)	170	340
Net Income after tax	330	660
Conventional Cash Flow	2,830	2,660
Before Tax Cash Flow	$3,000	$3,000

The earnings for Company B are twice that of Company A, but Company A has more cash flow. The differences in accounting for depreciation will impact the taxes paid. Using before-tax net income is one way to place the two companies on a more equal footing for comparison.

EARNINGS VS CASH FLOW

The investment community does not overlook the importance and superiority of cash flow compared to earnings. Earnings and earnings multiples are quoted frequently because of the accessibility of these figures. But many analysts ignore earnings and focus on cash flow.

The accounting methodology used in the oil industry can yield very different results on reported earnings depending on the method used. By making adjustments to earnings to arrive at cash flow, the differences in FC and SE accounting are nullified. Cash flow analysis then begins to place companies on an equal footing for comparative purposes.

Still, cash flow, as most definitions structure it, does not represent the true profitability of a firm much more than earnings do.

The treatment of depreciation is an important matter, and simply adding DD&A to net income should be considered in the proper light. The usual treatment of cash flow will add all noncash expenses to net income, incorrectly ignoring the need for replenishment of assets. Analysts know there is sound reasoning behind depreciation and amortization of assets.

The best definitions of cash flow are those that acknowledge the need for capital to maintain a company as a going concern. In a situation where a company decides to self-liquidate, a pure cash flow analysis that purposely ignores the need for capital infusion is appropriate. An MLP that distributes virtually all cash flow would be viewed this way.

ADJUSTMENTS

Sometimes the cash flow calculation may have adjustments and changes that are specific to an industry or to a particular situation. A detailed cash flow analysis may include assumptions about changes in corporate strategy. Certain expenditures might be unnecessary, especially in a short-term financial crunch.

Most analysts start with net income and make the necessary adjustments to arrive at the appropriate cash flow calculation. The difference between cash flow and net income is in the adjustments made for noncash expenses and nonrecurring items. The thought of a noncash expense can be an obstacle because it is slightly abstract. However, once the concept is grasped, the door is open to an understanding of the true nature of financial analysis. Examples of the adjustments that are made to arrive at cash flow are:

- depreciation, depletion and amortization (DD&A)
- deferred taxes
- extraordinary items
    loss on sale of assets
    write-downs on book value of assets
    gain on sale of assets
- exploration expenses
- research and development costs
- changes in working capital

Net Income

Net income is the first component of cash flow analysis. Adjustments may need to be made for extraordinary one-time events that impact net income. The most obvious adjustment is for the gain or loss on the sale of capital assets. The analyst looks for these in the income statement or the statement of cash flows. Further adjustments would be necessary to predict future earnings and cash flow if income generating assets had been sold.

Depreciation, Depletion and Amortization

DD&A is usually the most significant cash flow variable. The misuse and misunderstanding of the concept of cash flow comes from focusing too much on the noncash aspect of DD&A. DD&A is a valid cost.

Depreciation expense for a computer purchased three years ago would be a noncash expense, but soon it will be time to replace the equipment. This highlights the most important aspect of cash flow theory. Many people focus on the noncash aspect and forget that, theoretically, it should match capital requirements to keep a company going.

There are three different aspects to depreciation:

1. Depreciation for tax purposes—usually some form of accelerated depreciation

2. Accounting depreciation—usually some form of straight line, though sometimes accelerated, explained in the footnotes

3. Economic depreciation—comes from physical depletion, deterioration, and technological obsolescence

Economic depreciation is a fact of life that cannot be ignored. To evaluate a company as a going concern, this aspect must be considered. To perform cash flow analysis by simply adding back depreciation ignores economic depreciation.

The difference between depreciation for tax purposes and accounting depreciation is the birthplace of deferred taxes.

Deferred Taxes

The deferred tax account on the income statement is not an actual payment of taxes to the government. In reality, the company actually still has the money and may not have to pay down the deferred tax account for some time. Because of this, deferred taxes are treated like other noncash expenses. Most analysts will add deferred taxes during the accounting period to earnings and other noncash expenses to calculate cash flow.

Extraordinary Items

The extraordinary items such as a loss or a gain on the sale of assets or write-downs on book value of assets are excluded from most cash flow calculations. This is because these one-time, nonrecurring events are not considered to be part of the normal course of business. The objective in cash flow analysis is to try to eliminate the effects of such events to get a picture of the actual cash generating capability of a company. Some extraordinary items are noncash in nature; some actually either provide cash or deplete the company's cash resources. The key element is whether or not the event is an isolated incident.

Other Adjustments

The minority interest account is one of the less common but more complicated adjustments that is made. The minority interest in consolidated subsidiaries has been discussed in Chapter 4.

Adjustments for minority interest income will overstate cash flow because the attributable earnings are actually not received in cash. Equity interests in unconsolidated subsidiaries record only the dividends received.

Exploration Expenses

By adding in the exploration expenses, virtually all the differences between Full Cost and Successful Efforts accounting are offset. Companies can be compared for their cash flow generating capability. Companies that spend more on exploration pay relatively lower taxes. Therefore a common adjustment to the exploration expense is to multiply it by one minus the tax rate $(1 - t)$. Either statutory rates or an "effective" rate can be used.

Research and Development

Another item that may be added in is research and development (R&D) costs. Corporate raiders often consider part or all of a company's R&D expenditures as available sources of cash flow to pay off acquisition debt. This instinctively bothers many people because the implications clearly are not pleasant for corporate America and global competition.

Interest Expense

Another common adjustment to cash flow is to add in the interest expense and evaluate the company's cash flow capability before debt service. This helps in comparing companies without the influence of leverage. Because interest rates are deductible, an adjustment for tax effect is usually made by multiplying interest expense by one minus the tax rate $(1 - t)$. Either the statutory rate or an effective rate can be used.

When estimating a company's value, interest expenses often are included in the cash flow forecast, and debt is subtracted from the resulting discounted cash flow value.

Free Cash Flow

Free cash flow represents cash flow available after the necessary capital expenditures have been made to sustain or maintain productive capacity. This treatment of *maintenance* capital is the fundamental difference between free cash flow and definitions of cash flow that simply add net income, DD&A, and other noncash expenses. For an oil company, maintenance capital would include funds necessary to drill wells and maintain facilities such as refineries and pipelines.

Free Cash Flow = Net income
+ DD&A
+ Exploration expenses
+ Deferred taxes
+ Other noncash expenses
− Capital expenditures required to maintain productive capacity
− Preferred stock dividends

The treatment of maintenance capital makes the difference between doing it right or wrong. Many analysts ignore this element when doing a quick analysis, but they still know the importance of this item.

One technique for estimating maintenance capital is to assess a reasonable cost to find and develop reserves. Reserve replacement costs, though not totally reliable, are widely published. Estimates of the reserve replacement costs for a particular company can be made.

DISTRIBUTABLE CASH FLOW

Distributable cash flow is cash flow before common stock dividends but after preferred stock dividends. These are the funds available for reinvestment and payment of common stock dividends. Most definitions of distributable cash flow are some variation of the cash flow theme before common dividends are distributed—hence the name.

DISCRETIONARY CASH FLOW

Discretionary cash flow is a term that is used fairly frequently. As defined here, it represents virtually all available cash flow. Out of these funds, dividends can be paid and exploration ventures undertaken. Similar definitions do not consider dividends on common and preferred stocks a discretionary item, so they are deducted. The rationale behind this is that management really does not have much latitude to consider dividend obligations a truly discretionary matter.

The following definition of discretionary income is from the ENRON 1989 annual report. This definition is consistent with most treatments of the concept of discretionary cash flow.

Discretionary Income. Net income (loss) adjusted to eliminate the effects of DD&A, lease impairments, deferred taxes, property sales, other miscellaneous noncash amounts, and exploration and dry-hole expenses.

Compare the definitions of discretionary cash flow found in the 1990 Maxus and ORYX annual reports.

Maxus 1990 Annual Report

Discretionary cash flow is net income (loss) plus noncash items and exploration expense, reduced by preferred dividends.

ORYX 1990 Annual Report

Discretionary cash flow is the cash from operating activities, before changes in working capital, plus the cash portion of exploration expenses.

The definitions almost sound as if they refer to different things—they are virtually identical.

CASH FLOW FROM OPERATIONS

Cash flow from operations (CFFO) is the amount of cash taken in during a given accounting period. It is provided in the very first section of the statement of cash flows (SCF).

The CFFO figure is sometimes treated as cash flow. Occasionally this is acceptable, although it is not the same as the cash flow figures normally quoted and used for estimating value of a company or forecasting long-term profitability. The main difference between the CFFO and cash flow is the treatment of increases or decreases in the components of working capital. Most analysts do not explicitly address the changes in working capital for basic quick-look cash flow analysis. This is one reason why the SCF will often summarize net cash flows provided by operating activities *before* changes in components of working capital.

An important thing to consider here is that not all successful efforts companies treat dry-hole costs in the same manner on the statement of cash flows. Probably about half of the SE companies will add dry-hole costs as an adjustment to earnings in calculating CFFO. The other half do not.

VALUATION ANALYSIS OF CASH FLOW ESTIMATES

Cash flow is used two different ways for appraising value. The best approach is the discounted (corporate) cash flow method based on pro forma projections of revenues, expenses, DD&A, and capital requirements. The other method simply capitalizes cash flow or uses a cash flow multiple, which is a proxy for a true discounted cash flow analysis.

PRO FORMA CASH FLOW ANALYSIS

When analysts decide to perform detailed analysis of a company, a pro forma cash flow model is a standard tool. An example cash flow model with standard components is constructed in Table 5–7.

This example indicates the need for a company to increase working capital (W/C) as it grows. The need for additional working capital is a valid expense. The cash flow stream grows from $83 million in Year 1 to $104 million in Year 8. The present value for the eight-year projection is $428 million, discounted at 15%. Interest expense is included in the cash flow projection, and corporate debt is simply subtracted from the present value estimate.

Table 5–7 Cash Flow Pro Forma

Company X
($ Millions)

Projected Free Cash Flow	Year 1	Year 2	Year 3	Year 4	Year 5	Year 6	Year 7	Year 8
Net Income	31	35	37	41	44	48	52	56
+ Extraordinary items	5	4						
+ DD&A	43	43	42	42	42	42	42	42
+ (1 – t) Interest Exp.	2	2	2	2	2	2	2	2
+ Deferred Taxes	4	4	4	5	5	5	5	6
+ Exploration Costs	12	12	12	12	12	12	12	12
– Required Capital*	(10)	(10)	(10)	(10)	(10)	(10)	(10)	(10)
– Increase in W/C	(1)	(1)	(1)	(1)	(1)	(1)	(1)	(1)
– Dividends	(3)	(3)	(3)	(3)	(3)	(3)	(3)	(3)
Total Free Cash Flow	83	86	83	88	91	95	99	104
Discount Factor (15% DCF)	.93	.81	.71	.61	.53	.46	.40	.35
Discounted Cash Flow	$77	70	59	54	48	44	40	36

Total (8 Years)	$428 million
Less Debt	30 million
Present Value less Debt	$398 million

* Treatment of this item includes assumptions about estimated reserve replacement. If the company produced 1.0 million barrels of oil in 1990 with $10 per barrel replacement costs, the required capital would be at least $10 million in order to replace production.

$(1 – t)$ is the tax adjustment for the deductibility of interest expenses. Exploration expenses also are adjusted in this way. Either the statutory tax rate or an "effective" tax rate may be used.

Capitalized Cash Flow

Capitalization of cash flow and the use of a cash flow multiple are simplified approaches to estimating value. Pro forma cash flow analysis is not a quick-look method. The use of a multiple with cash flow is similar to the earnings multiple approach, but is nearly always more appropriate.

A cash flow multiple of 5 implies a capitalization rate of 20%, but it capitalizes an implied infinite stream of cash flow.

There are many estimates of the value of an entity or company that are based on a multiple of either:

- current period cash flow
- average of past three years cash flow
- average of three years projected cash flow

Choice of an appropriate multiple is usually based on experience and trends from past transactions.

The most common usage of the cash flow multiple is based on the less complicated definitions of cash flow. A multiple of five times year 1 cash flow from Company X in Table 5–7 (simply net income + DD&A + exploration expenses + deferred taxes) yields a value of $450 million (5 times $90 million).

An example of the capitalization of cash flow is shown below. Capitalizing cash flow in this manner assumes an infinite life for the cash flow stream, and in this example a continuous growth rate of 3%. With a discount rate of 20%, the present value less debt is $458 million.

$$PV = \frac{CF}{i - g}$$

Where:

PV = present value
CF = cash flow
i = interest rate or discount rate
g = growth rate

$$PV = \frac{\$83 \text{ Million}}{.20 - .03}$$

$$= \$488 \text{ Million}$$

less debt of $30 million

$$= \$458 \text{ Million}$$

This technique is sometimes used to make an estimate of *residual value*. Residual value is the present value of potential future revenue beyond what is forecast in a pro forma cash flow analysis. In the example in Table 5–7, the residual value would be the value of cash flow beyond year 8. Residual value does not receive a lot of attention. Often a corporate acquisition will be based on an 8–12-year cash flow projection.

CASH FLOW LIFE

The term *cash flow life* is sometimes used. With the use of algebra, the dimensions associated with the price/cash flow ratio will reduce to *years*. Thus reference to "five year's cash flow" is the same as a cash flow multiple of five.

Cash Flow Multiples

In the early 1980s, leveraged buyouts were taking place at multiples of three to four times free cash flow. The ratio increased to four to five times free cash flow by 1985. After that, transactions were taking place at multiples of up to 6 and 7. These higher multiples were the result of increasing competition and availability of debt financing through *junk bonds*. Unfortunately, the higher prices proved to be too much in many cases. The higher multiples of 6–7 required cash flow growth in order to pay down acquisition debt. Otherwise, buyers were in trouble. The lower multiples of 3–4 allowed buyers to service debt even under moderate conditions of stagnant or negative cash flow growth in the early stages after the acquisition.

Some analysts go one step further. They put companies on an equal footing for comparison by adjusting for debt in the capital structure. A cash flow multiple will make high-debt companies look cheap compared to low-debt companies. This approach is similar to the debt-adjusted book value multiple approach. In the following example, a stock trading at $30 per share has $7 per share cash flow. The price/cash flow multiple not accounting for debt is 4.3. Incorporating debt of $10 per share into the equation gives a better view.

Debt-adjusted Cash Flow Multiple

$$\text{Debt-adjusted Cash Flow Multiple} = \frac{\text{Stock Price/Share} + \text{Debt/Share}}{\text{Cash Flow/Share}}$$

$$= \frac{\$30 + \$10}{\$7}$$

$$= 5.7$$

OPERATING INCOME MULTIPLE

An operating income multiple is sometimes used as a method of valuation. It is similar to the cash flow multiple method.

Operating income is defined as the difference between business revenues and the associated costs and expenses, exclusive of financing expenses, extraordinary items, or ancillary activities. Even though the interest is a legitimate expense, it is usually excluded from the calculation of operating income.

Operating income is also called *net operating income* (or loss) and *net operating profit* (or loss).

This information is commonly a part of the reported segment information in an annual report or 10-K report. The operating income multiple is usually applied to a particular segment, such as refining and marketing operations. Theoretically, the multiple chosen for appraising a segment (or company) should be based on experience and the nature of the segment being evaluated. Multiples of operating income used for appraisals range 4–8 for refining and downstream segments of the industry. The operating income multiple is used for quick-look appraisals and depends on many factors. The technique is almost always more meaningful when used in conjunction with other valuation methods.

Comparable Sales

A *comparable sale*, as the name implies, is a comparative means of estimating value. In many ways, it is one of the most important analytical methods. Evaluating the prices paid for other companies or assets is the acid test for valuation theory. Theory must conform to the realities of the market.

The comparable sale approach to estimating value of a company is based on the hope of finding similar companies that have recently changed hands. Comparable sales of nearly identical companies can be hard to find, and it can be difficult to make a comparison fit a particular situation. Fortunately, the many ways of making comparisons can lend insight into an analysis. Companies can be compared to each other or to general industry trends and statistics. Typical standards of comparison used are:

• cash flow analysis or cash flow multiples
• earnings trends and multiples
• estimated breakup value
• book value and book value multiples
• total assets
• basic unit of value or unit of production

One of the common unit-of-value comparisons made in the oil industry is the comparison of the dollars paid per barrel for a company's oil and gas reserves.

The market for production acquisitions in the United States is quite active. The information from these transactions provides the means of comparison.

There are a number of ways to look at comparable sales figures. Some analysts distinguish between the price paid for reserves in the ground for production acquisitions versus the prices paid for reserves in the large corporate mergers. The average price paid per barrel in production acquisitions is generally higher than for company acquisitions. Table 5–8 summarizes acquisition prices for oil and gas production acquisitions as compared to average U.S. wellhead prices.

Production from the Gulf of Mexico will often receive a premium of from $1.50 to $2.00 per barrel over average onshore production acquisition prices. This is partly due to the fact that the average Gulf of Mexico oil well produces around 180 to 200 BOPD (see Appendix 3). The royalty rates are also generally lower offshore, and there are no state severance taxes in federal waters.

In the refining industry, unit-of-production comparisons are often made on the basis of distillation capacity. A transaction will be measured in terms of the dollars per daily barrel. This is the basic unit of production for a refinery. If a 100,000 barrel-per-day refinery sold for $400 million, the comparative price paid is $4,000 per daily barrel. This gives an analyst a means of comparison with another perhaps similar refinery. This is discussed further in the section on refineries later in this chapter.

Table 5–8 Summary of Acquisition Prices per Barrel

Year	Average U.S. Wellhead Price		Gas Price Parity	Weighted Average Acquisition Price/bbl (Crude Oil Equivalent)	
	Oil $/bbl	Gas $/MCF		BTU $/bbl	Price $/bbl
1979	12.64	1.18	56%	4.75	5.45
1980	21.59	1.59	44%	11.20	14.70
1981	31.77	1.98	37%	6.20	6.37
1982	28.52	2.46	52%	8.03	10.26
1983	26.19	2.59	59%	6.68	7.88
1984	25.88	2.66	62%	7.64	8.71
1985	23.88	2.63	66%	6.72	8.55
1986	12.66	1.38	65%	5.71	6.78
1987	15.60	1.65	63%	4.98	6.85
1988	12.58	1.69	80%	5.77	6.67
1989	15.89	1.71	65%	4.55	6.26
1990	19.75	1.69	51%	4.39	5.65

Source: Wellhead Prices from Energy Information Administration 1990. Estimated prices from *Oil & Gas Journal*. Acquisition Values from Daniel Johnston & Co., Inc.

Replacement Value

Replacement value is an important financial tool used in evaluating many businesses and types of assets. As a valuation technique for a nonintegrated oil company, though, it has limited value. The issue is discussed when corporations consider entering the oil industry. The cost to start from scratch to build an oil company can be measured in terms of estimated dollars, time, and risk.

One way of viewing replacement value of reserves is to examine reserve replacement costs in the industry or for a company. These costs include both finding costs and development costs for reserves. Quite often, companies decide that a more efficient way to replace reserves is to simply purchase them on Wall Street. For instance, this might happen when a company finds that reserve replacement costs are around $9 per barrel, but reserves can be purchased for $6 per barrel. This example is uncomfortably realistic.

The value of a refinery in terms of replacement cost is also meaningful. The replacement value of a refinery would be the costs associated with construction of a new facility. With environmental considerations, inflation, and industry structure, the cost to build a new refinery in the United States substantially exceeds the cost to buy a similar facility. Estimating the replacement value is considered a normal part of the evaluation process of a refinery or similar businesses. It will usually identify the upper range of value.

Combined Appraisal Techniques

In most situations, using a combination of valuation techniques is better than any single method. Wherever practical, as many techniques as possible should be applied. This will provide insight beyond the perspective given by a single valuation technique. Too often, one technique will generate a value that logic would not support. That is when the perspective of another approach is invaluable.

Once a number of estimates of value are made, the analyst must judge which one to use, or how to weigh the values in arriving at an answer.

THE FACTORED APPROACH

In the *factored approach*, a weight factor is applied to different estimates of value to arrive at a *weighted value*. This approach is used in many different ways and for different reasons. Regulatory bodies favor this approach for due diligence and fairness opinion work where third-party estimates of value are required to protect independent shareholders. It is assumed that the analyst will use common sense, experience, and sound business judgment in deciding how to assign weight factors.

In Table 5-9, the value of Company A is based on three separate valuations. Each technique gave a different value. In this approach, the different techniques were used to estimate value of Company A, with a weight factor applied to each.

Table 5–9 Example Valuation Using the Factored Approach

Valuation Technique	Company A Value $MM	Weight Factor	Weighted Value $MM
Discounted Cash Flow	230	60%	138
Capitalized Earnings	180	10%	18
Adjusted Book Value	300	30%	90
Total		100%	$246

EXPECTED VALUE THEORY

A single valuation method would not be appropriate when takeover speculation influences the value of a stock. Suppose that Company X has been trading at $8 per share, which is considered an appropriate trading value for the company as a going concern. Suppose, too, that there is speculation that Company X is a takeover target. If the estimated acquisition price is $12 per share, based on the expected tender offer and liquidation value, it would appear the stock is a bargain at $8 per share.

Expected Value Theory is the best way to evaluate circumstances such as this. The analyst must estimate the probability that the takeover may succeed. In this case, assume there is a 30% chance that Company X will be taken over with a successful cash tender offer of $12 per share. The expected value of the stock can be calculated by weighting the values according to the estimated probabilities. This approach is shown in Table 5–10.

Table 5–10 Expected Value—Technique

	Stock Value	Estimated Probability	Expected Value
Unsuccessful Takeover	$8.00	70%	$5.60
Successful Takeover	$12.00	30%	$3.60
TOTAL		100%	$9.20

The *expected value* of the stock under these circumstances is $9.20 per share. If the market agrees with the acquisition price assumptions and a 30% chance of the acquisition happening, then takeover speculation will drive the price up to $9.20 per share. The investor will buy the stock under these assumptions as long as it is sufficiently below $9.20 per share to cover brokerage and transaction fees.

MERGER—RELATIVE COMBINATION

Mergers are other instances where the expected value approach is used. Suppose Company X and Company Y intend to merge. Both companies are evaluated to arrive at their respective comparative values. Assume that Company X has a stronger balance sheet, while the strength of Company Y is in earnings quality. Table 5–11 shows how the distribution of relative values might look.

Table 5–11 Example Valuation for Merger—Relative Combination

Valuation Technique	Percentage of Combined Value		Weight Factor
	Company X	Company Y	
Discounted Cash Flow	40%	60%	50%
Capitalized Earnings	45%	55%	30%
Net Assets	54%	46%	20%
Weighted Averaged	44.3%	55.7%	100%

In this example, the Company X share would be 44.3%. Thus the Company X shareholders would own 44.3% of the merged entity. The weighting leans heavily toward discounted cash flow results. There are many ways to do this, and there is no certain formula for deciding how to weigh the different factors. Another example may have weighted net assets by a factor of 80%. Every situation is different. Regulatory agencies allow a wide latitude for management and financial advisors to exercise their business judgment in these matters.

Worksheet 5–3 is the kind of form that might be used in evaluating a company using a number of different estimates. When this is done with a weight factor applied to all or some of the methods, it is called the *factored approach*. This kind of approach is strongly recommended. An example of this kind of analysis is provided in Figure 7–12 at the end of Chapter 7.

Worksheet 5–3 Corporate Valuation Summary

Company:_____ Date:_____

Shares:_____ Source:_____

Current Trading Price of Stock:_____

	Observed or Appraised Value ( )	Weight Factor	Weighted Value
Market Capitalization + Debt	= _____		
Book Value _____ X _____	= _____	____%	_____
Adjusted Balance Sheet Value	= _____	____%	_____
Adjusted Earnings _____ X _____	= _____	____%	_____
Cash Flow _____ X _____	= _____	____%	_____
Discounted Cash Flow Analysis	= _____	____%	_____
TOTAL WEIGHTED VALUE		100%	_____

$$\frac{\text{Market Capitalization + Debt}}{\text{Appraised Value of Assets}} = \underline{\quad\quad} = \underline{\quad\quad\quad} \%$$

PERFORMANCE ANALYSIS

Corporate performance is viewed in many different ways. In addition to accounting and financial measures, there are other tools used by analysts and corporate management that are helpful. It is important to understand the industry within which a company resides, and one way is to compare a company with its peers. There are many yardsticks—some are better than others—but it helps to know some of the standards and boundary conditions. This is a useful exercise for company management as well as outside analysts.

Peer Group Analysis

Peer group analysis provides insight into the value and vitality of a company. The techniques can be enlightening and may signal a warning or confirm other information. Peer group analysis is a common part of corporate planning and analysis that allows management a way of monitoring corporate progress.

Individually, comparative statistics have limited value, and, depending on the circumstances, may be of no value. Taken together as part of the analytical process, peer group analysis adds perspective and insight.

There are a multitude of ways to compare a company with its peers. The comparisons can include every conceivable financial ratio, as well as statistics such as those found in this chapter. Tables 6–1 and 6–2 summarize general statistics that provide a framework for comparison of oil companies. These statistics come from a number of sources, many of which are summarized in Appendix 12.

Table 6-1 Peer Group Analysis—Independent Producing Company (1989)

Annual Revenues per Employee	$300,000–$600,000*
Total Assets per Employee	$250,000–$600,000
Reserves per Employee Barrels of Oil Equivalent (MBOE)	150–350 MBBLS
Production Per Employee (BOE per Day)	50–70
Number of Net Wells Per Employee	4–6
Reserve-life Index Oil	7–9 Years
Gas	8–10 Years
Average Reserves Per Well	
Oil Well	30–60 Mbbls
Gas Well	400–800 MMCF
Average Production Rate Per Well	
Oil Well	8–30 BOPD
Gas Well	100–300 MCFD
Reserve Replacement Ratio Oil	85%–115%
Finding Costs	$5–$6 per barrel
Price/Cash Flow	5.5–7.5
Long-term Debt as Percentage of Total Capitalization	30%–45%
Return on Assets	3.5%
Return on Equity	7.8%

*With $16 to $18 per barrel oil
Source: Various—See Appendix 12

Table 6-2 Peer Group Analysis—Integrated Major Oil Company (1989)

Annual Revenues per Employee		$600,000–$1,100,000*
Total Assets per Employee		$800,000–$1,000,000
Reserve-life Index	Oil	9–11 Years
	Gas	10–13 Years
Average Reserves Per Well		
	Oil Well	100–250 Mbbls
	Gas Well	600–3000 MMCF
Average Production Rate Per Well		
	Oil Well	25–70 BOPD
	Gas Well	1000–3000 MCFD
Reserve Replacement Ratio		90%–110%
Finding Costs		$4–$5 per barrel
Price/Cash Flow		4.0–5.5
Long-term Debt as Percentage of Total Capitalization		20%–30%
Return on Assets		5.2%
Return on Equity		13.5%

*With $16 to $18 per barrel oil
Source: Various—See Appendix 12

REVENUES PER EMPLOYEE

With volatile oil and gas prices, revenues per employee can have limited value. It is an easy statistic to obtain, though, and helps to show quickly if a company is unusual in comparison to its peers. These statistics are indexed to oil prices of $16 to $18 per barrel. The uncertainty created by price volatility can be eliminated by another comparison—production per employee.

The main difference between the majors and independent producers is that revenues per employee for refining and marketing operations are over twice as much as for the upstream end of the business. A general summary of revenues per employee statistics is provided in Table 6–3. It shows some interesting differences.

Table 6–3 Annual Revenues per Employee Statistics

	Revenues per Employee Reference Year 1989 ($ thousands)
Exploration and Production	$300–600
Refining and Marketing	700–1,200
Oil Service Industry	85–120
Gas Transmission/Utility	225–350

TOTAL ASSETS PER EMPLOYEE

The total assets per employee is usually less enlightening than other statistics. But it is often included as a part of detailed comparative analysis.

PRODUCTION PER EMPLOYEE

Production per employee is less subject to change due to volatile prices. Production statistics are also more reliable than reserve estimates, so this statistic is a more meaningful statistic than reserves per employee.

RESERVES PER EMPLOYEE

Reserves per employee is of limited value by itself. But taken with the other statistics, it provides an indication of the maturity and development status of a company's reserve base.

This is the type of statistic that is more useful with practice and experience. Other statistics can provide better indications of potential for profitability.

NUMBER OF NET WELLS PER EMPLOYEE

The number of net wells per employee is based on the total net interest a company has in its wells. For example, a company that owns a 10% interest in a total of 12 wells has 1.2 *net wells*. It is expected that the higher the net wells per employee, the greater the efficiency. Be careful: there are many exceptions. A company with an average interest of 1% in 120 wells would also have 1.2 net wells. All wells require some attention and administrative expense. Therefore, the company with 1.2 net wells out of 12 would very likely be more efficient than the company with a 1% interest in 120 wells.

This statistic begins to have additional meaning when used in conjunction with the net-to-gross ratio.

NET-TO-GROSS RATIO

In the 10-K report, the total number of wells and the net interest in those wells is listed. In the previous example, where the company owned 1.2 net wells out of 12, the net-to-gross ratio was 10%. This is often worth a look. For example, the liquidity of a production portfolio with a net-to-gross ratio of 2% may be substantially different than identical daily production from a portfolio with a net-to-gross ratio of 45%.

The same is true of the company acreage portfolio. Gross and net acreage is inventoried in the 10-K report. Furthermore, whether the company is operator, or to what degree the company operates, can have a bearing on value.

A typical operating company may have an average net interest of 25–50% in wells it operates. On the other hand, the average interest in nonoperated wells will often range 5–15%.

RESERVE LIFE INDEX (RLI)

The reserve life index (RLI) is slightly abstract, but it is used extensively. It represents the total reserves of a company divided by the annual production. Ideally, the RLI should depict the ratio of year-end developed reserves to annual production. If a company has 12 MMbbls on the books and is producing at a rate of 2 MMbbls per year, the RLI is six years. Twelve MMbbls of reserves divided by 2 MMbbls annual production equals six years.

Many people are uncomfortable with this statistic. This is because it represents the number of years of production a company would have if there were no production decline and no reserve additions. These are unrealistic assumptions. A property with a RLI of six years will likely produce for more than 12 years. Furthermore, each year during the past 10 years 15,000 to more than 30,000 oil wells were abandoned or shut in in the United States. The average producing life for those wells was 28 years.

Nevertheless, this is a useful method for checking the quality of a company's reserves and comparing reserve estimates with hard production data.

Most mature production portfolios have a RLI of around 8 years. A RLI of 12 or more would almost certainly indicate either overstated reserves, curtailed production, or undeveloped reserves. An RLI of 4 would most likely suggest either understated reserves or steeply declining reserves. These possibilities have strong implications on the value of the booked reserves. Calculation of the index gets a bit complicated when reserve acquisitions change the picture.

While there is much discussion about subjective and inherently inaccurate reserve reports, production information provides hard data.

From 1986 to 1988, Sonat Inc. (SONAT) had a RLI for total developed and undeveloped oil reserves of around 3.3 years. The RLI for SONAT's proved reserves was closer to 2.2 years. Obviously, the reserves were significantly understated. This is what an analyst looks for.

Many factors influence the rate at which reserves will produce in a given development. These include engineering limitations, economic factors, geologic setting, fluid quality, etc. Nevertheless, whatever the reason, the implications are clear to the analyst, and a low RLI sends a strong signal.

By looking at the reserves per well and production rates, the analyst begins to see a clearer picture.

AVERAGE RESERVES PER WELL

The average reserves per well statistic is based on the number of net wells and the proved developed reserves on the books. The possibility that production is curtailed may be indicated by high per-well reserve figures. Significant curtailment of oil production is rare. Gas production is more likely to be limited by market demand.

If it appears that a large reserve base is not matched by appropriate production rates, it is usually because additional drilling is required, even though reserves are classified as developed. This might be confirmed by a high RLI and further reading in the annual report and 10-K. On the average, a U.S. oil well has 40,000 to 50,000 barrels of remaining recoverable reserves. Gas wells have around 500 million cubic feet of gas (MMCF) remaining. By contrast, a Gulf of Mexico oil well may have 600,000 barrels of oil.

AVERAGE PRODUCTION RATE PER WELL

Calculating the average production rate per well is a convenient way to get a feel for the pulse of a company. The implications of value can be significant. The difference between a company with 25 barrel-per-day (BOPD) wells and a company with 5 BOPD wells could be the difference between profitability and bankruptcy. The average producing rate per well for a company is one of the first things to inspect. For reference, Appendix 3 shows production statistics for key energy states.

PARETO'S LAW—THE 80/20 RULE

Pareto's Law, the law of the trivial many and the critical few, or commonly known as *the 80/20* rule, has many applications. It is an important analytical concept. It allows the evaluation engineer or the securities analyst to maximize efficiency by concentrating their efforts on key elements to get the greatest effect. Assume, for example, a company with 100 wells that produce at a combined rate of 1,200 BOPD. The production rates of the wells owned by any company have a diverse range. It would not be unusual for 20 of the 100 wells to produce 80% of the total production. Therefore, the 20 best wells could be producing at a rate of 960 BOPD (48 BOPD each) with the other 80 wells producing at an average rate of 3 BOPD each. This kind of distribution is commonplace in the industry. This is the 80/20 rule for the oil industry—"80% of the production comes from 20% of the wells." In a foreign country, 80% of the production may come from 20% of the fields.

With this in mind, the concept of an average production rate per well as a comparative tool loses some of its appeal. However, the analysts evaluating companies from public information accept this and understand the limits of these analytical tools. Examples of per-well production statistics are found in Appendix 2 and Appendix 3.

RESERVE REPLACEMENT RATIO

The reserve replacement ratio helps to indicate whether a company is at least managing to find oil and gas to replace produced reserves. The reserve replacement ratio for a company is determined by inspecting the reserve disclosure information commonly found in the 10-K report. This information shows how much oil and gas a company has produced during the fiscal year. It also shows how much of the produced oil and gas has been replaced either through exploration efforts, revisions to reserve estimates, or with production acquisitions. The reserve replacement ratio commonly is based on the reserves added through exploration and development efforts (additions) and revisions to previous estimates. Reserve replacement ratios based on additions and revisions are typically 100–115%. This includes foreign operations. However, reserve replacement in the United States has not kept pace with production for the past few years. Reserve replacement in the United States typically ranges 80–90%, but this figure would drop to around 50% if only additions (and not revisions) were considered.

It is best to view trends in company performance in reserve replacement rather than on a given year. A three to five-year average may be a more reasonable measure of whether a company has the ability to stay in the exploration business. Some analysts make an honest effort to look beyond the reserve replacement ratio and determine if reserve value is being replaced. If less valuable reserves are being found to replace high-quality production, this is not good. Unfortunately, it is difficult to place a value on recently discovered reserves. The analyst working with public information is limited in his ability to estimate required capital costs, operating costs, production rates, and the various factors that determine reserve value.

PRODUCT PRICES

Average product prices received during the previous year are standard information in a 10-K report. Checking the price information can signal if a company has any unusual characteristics such as lower or higher than normal oil prices.

Lower-than-normal Oil Prices

Low prices may indicate heavy oil production—not always a bad sign, but one must consider the implications. Heavier oils normally carry higher operating costs, and heavy oil properties may be more difficult to sell. It may also indicate sour crude production that also sells for less.

Crude oil value depends primarily on density (American Petroleum Institute [API] Gravity) and sulfur content (sweet or sour). There is no formula for determining the discount for heavy or sour crude. During 1988, West Texas sour crude generally sold for $.80 to $1.40 per barrel less than West Texas Intermediate (WTI). A comparison is provided in Table 6–4 to show the differences that exist between inferior crudes and sweet light crudes.

Table 6–4 Wellhead Oil Price Comparison
(1988 Average Prices)

Product—Crude Source	API Gravity	Prices $/BBL
West Texas Intermediate	33°	15.10
West Texas Sour	30 – 33°	13.80
East Texas	38°	15.29
Alaska Cook Inlet	30°	12.53
Mid-Continent Oklahoma	36°	15.25
California Long Beach	27°	12.80
U.S. Heavy Crudes	15 – 20°	12.00

As a point of reference, crude oil with an API gravity of 35° can look and feel much like common motor oil. The *heavy* crudes (12–15°API), by comparison, can be pretty ugly. Even on a hot day, these kinds of crude are typically thick and sticky. They are also more costly to refine. This is why heavier crude oils sell for less. According to one rule of thumb, heavy crude should sell at a discount of around $0.20 to $0.30 per API degree difference. Thus, if WTI (33° API) sells for $15.00 per barrel, a 20° API crude should sell for $2.60 to $3.90 per barrel less ($0.20 to $0.30 times the 13° API difference). In the 1960s, when oil prices were around $3 per barrel, the discount for each degree decline in API gravity was around $0.02 per barrel. For high-sulfur content crude, the discount was $0.03 per barrel, or about 1% change in price per degree of API gravity. The relationship is much the same now. The discount for sour crude is shown by the $1.30 per barrel difference between WTI and West Texas Sour. Prior to 1988, the price differential between the two on the *spot market* had been $0.80 to $0.85 per barrel.

Higher-than-normal Oil Prices

Higher-than-average oil prices may indicate good quality, light oil production—not necessarily a good sign, but not bad news.

Higher-than-normal Gas Prices

High gas prices can be a concern if they are significantly higher than normal market prices. There is always the risk that there may be undue downward pressure on prices. Market forces in the short term may not have effect due to contract terms, but in the long term, the market will exert its influence.

Lower-than-normal Gas Prices

Low gas prices may indicate a potential for improvement in pricing. Certainly there is less risk with low prices than with precariously high gas prices.

SUCCESS RATIO

Companies' 10-K reports outline the results of exploration and development drilling. The success ratios in these reports represent only the *technical success* of drilling. This information is less meaningful than one might hope. In some areas, drilling success is practically guaranteed in terms of technical success, while *commercial success* may be no better than general industry standards.

Most analysts pay little attention to these figures. Certainly if a company indicates that it has participated in 30 wells during the year and none of the wells is successful, then the analyst may be on to a significant piece of information about the company.

Risk Factors

The most familiar element of risk associated with drilling is the dry-hole risk. Drilling under the best conditions is risky, and it would not be unusual for even a development well program to have 25% of the wells dry. Wildcat wells worldwide are dry 87% of the time. Furthermore, there are worse things than a dry hole. Some areas require that a well be completed and *fractured,* or *acidized,* before it can be determined whether or not commercial quantities of hydrocarbons are present. Some wells can be worse than the normal dry hole because both dry hole and completion costs can be lost if insufficient oil or gas is found.

FINDING COSTS

As a means of providing a meaningful comparison between companies, finding costs can sometimes be interesting. There have been situations where a company has had finding costs that far exceed the posted price of the product. These figures are not often published but can be estimated from income statement figures footnotes and reserve disclosure. Published finding costs for the early 1990s ranged from $4 to $6 per barrel. Major oil companies' finding costs were generally about $1 lower than finding costs of the independent oil companies.

EVALUATION OF ASSETS AND RELATED SEGMENTS

A knowledge of the characteristics and values of oil industry assets is the key to scrutinizing an oil company balance sheet. Analysts familiar with the industry use numerous standards of comparison, known industry multiples, and rules of thumb. Outlined in the following pages are common valuation tools used in the industry for estimating value of certain related assets or business segments. The major segments of the petroleum industry are:

- oil and gas properties
- master limited partnerships (MLPs)
- refineries
- gas stations and marketing outlets
- pipelines and natural gas
- foreign operations

Oil and Gas Properties

The most appropriate method for evaluating oil and gas properties is discounted cash flow analysis. Discounted cash flow analysis is the workhorse of acquisition teams, bank engineers, and independent consultants. For those who read through an annual report and try to make mental adjustments to balance sheet values, a detailed cash flow analysis is impractical. Typically, public documents do not provide sufficient information to perform detailed cash flow analysis. There are ways, however, of examining reported information to get a better understanding of oil and gas asset values.

The key factors influencing the value of producing oil and gas reserves are: product prices, capital and operating costs, production taxes, and the timing of production. Analysts have a number things they look for to determine quality and value of reserves:

- book value of reserves
- SEC value of reserves
- average production rate per well
- reserves per well
- average prices
- production rates and reserve life index (RLI)

Analysts will sometimes talk about *high-quality reserves.* Usually, the reference is made to fast-producing, short-life reserves with a low RLI. The value of these reserves is slightly higher on a per-barrel basis because present value discounting does not have as great an effect. Many analysts will attribute up to a $1 premium for high-quality oil reserves. For example, if reserves are selling at an average price of around $5 per barrel, high-quality, fast-producing reserves might be appraised at $6 per barrel. Gas prices are expected to increase at a disproportionately higher rate than oil prices. Because of this, where long-life oil is usually discounted on a per-barrel basis, long-life gas reserves may actually have a premium.

The unit of value in the petroleum industry is a barrel of oil (bbl) or a thousand cubic feet of gas (MCF). When referring to acquisitions, transactions are often calibrated in terms of barrels of oil (bbls) or millions of cubic feet (MMCF) of gas purchased at some value per unit, such as $6 per barrel in the ground or $0.75 per MCF.

Reference is often made to a *barrel of oil equivalent* (BOE) or *crude oil equivalent* (COE) used to equate gas to oil when referring to reserves in the ground. This is usually based on the heating value equivalency, in British Thermal Units (Btu) of natural gas and oil. A barrel of oil has about the same heating value as 6 MCF of gas.

Almost all $/BOE quotations are based on the Btu relationship of oil and gas. A better comparison in many situations is the relationship of price equivalency. It compares the financial value equivalent of gas to oil.

Table 7-1 Summary of U.S. Oil Well Production Statistics

		OIL WELL		
		Average		Units
Daily Production Rate	4	13	40	BOPD
Decline Rate	10	12	15	%
Royalty	18.75	20	25	%
Severance & Ad Valorem Taxes	4	7	10	%
Monthly Operating Costs	800	1,200	2,500	$
Well Depth		4,500		ft
Reserve-life Index	6	8	10	years
Remaining Recoverable Reserves	15	44	65	Mbbls
Total Cumulative Reserves	35	60	100	Mbbls

If oil is selling for $20.00 per barrel and gas is selling at $1.50 per MCF, the price relationship is 13:1. The reason the 6:1 thermal relationship is used so frequently is that it is a standard that does not change. In contrast, when oil and gas prices change, the price equivalency also changes.

The basic unit of production in the oil industry is a producing oil or gas well. An understanding of standards and statistics associated with oil and gas wells strengthens the analytical process. Tables 7–1 and 7–2 summarize production statistics and other information for U.S. oil and gas wells. Some of these statistics have already been discussed in Chapter 6.

Table 7–2 Summary of U.S. Gas Well Production Statistics

	GAS WELL Average			Units
Daily Production Rate	100	200	400	MCFD
Decline Rate	8	10	14	%
Royalty	18.75	20	25	%
Severance & Ad Valorem Taxes	3	5	8	%
Monthly Operating Costs	700	1,000	2,000	$
Well Depth		5,500		ft
Reserve-life Index	8	10	12	Years
Remaining Recoverable Reserves	.3	.5	2	BCF
Total Cumulative Reserves	.6	.9	5	BCF

DAILY PRODUCTION RATE

The United States has over 610,000 oil wells. The average production rate for these wells is 13 BOPD. Three fourths of these wells are stripper wells. A stripper well produces at an average rate of less than 10 BOPD. The stripper wells in the United States produce at an average rate of less than 3 BOPD. The nonstripper wells average over 40 BOPD (see Appendix 2). The average U.S. gas well produces at a rate of 220 MCFD. Americans have to try harder. A typical North Sea oil well produces initially at a rate of 10,000 BOPD. North Sea oil wells now produce around 4,000 BOPD each. Middle Eastern wells can often produce more oil during an extended test than a typical U.S. oil well will produce in 28 years. Appendix 5 summarizes production statistics for various countries.

The value of oil and gas reserves is quite sensitive to the average production rate of the wells. This is an important variable in assessing quality of reserves.

DECLINE RATE

A decline rate of 10–15% is representative of most production portfolios in the United States. This would be equivalent to a reserve life index of around 7. It is unusual to see normal production declining at a rate of less than 10% per year.

One exception to normal production decline is tight, low-permeability reservoirs that have characteristically low decline rates. Some reservoirs decline at significant rates. One example is production from fractured rocks. The Austin Chalk oil production has a distinctively steep decline rate that approaches 75% in the early stages of production and will *settle in* after 6–12 months at decline rates of from 35–50%.

ROYALTY

The age-old landowners' *royalty* of one-eighth (12.5%) has not changed much, but during boom periods or in hot areas, landowners are sometimes able to get up to a three-sixteenths (18.75%) royalty. Many land deals include geologist and promoter royalties that are added on. It is unusual, therefore, to see royalties less than three-sixteenths. Royalties of greater than 25% would be considered to be cruel and unusual. Oil companies with inhouse landmen and geological staff usually pay only landowner royalties and federal royalties on federal acreage in the United States. Outside the United States, the concept of a landowner royalty is almost unheard of. Reported reserves in annual reports are *net* reserves; that is, the royalty has been deducted.

SEVERANCE AND AD VALOREM TAXES

Severance and ad valorem taxes are a normal part of business for the oil and gas producer. These taxes vary substantially from one area to another. Severance taxes are normally levied by states, with counties and with other elements administering ad valorem taxes. Ad valorem taxes are not a severance tax but for analytical purposes are often treated as such. These taxes combined can range from 1% of the revenues to more than 15%. Appendix 4 summarizes severance and production taxes for major oil and gas producing states.

WELL DEPTHS

The average depth for wells drilled in the United States these days is around 4,600 feet. Oil wells, on the average, are slightly shallower at 4,000 feet, with the average gas well depth at 5,500 feet. The depths for producing wells range from less than 100 feet for many low production stripper wells to more than 25,000 feet for deep gas wells.

Drilling costs begin to increase substantially beyond 10,000 feet. Many companies will specify a particular depth limit (often 10,000) as an investment criteria threshold. Operating costs are also sensitive to well depths.

OPERATING COSTS

Operating costs are generally broken down into three categories:

• normal daily expenses
• surface maintenance
• subsurface maintenance and repair (workover)

Nearly 95% of all oil wells in the U.S. are on some form of artificial *lift* to bring oil to the surface. Equipment for artificial lift requires maintenance and adds to the cost of production. The depth of a well has a large impact on operating costs because of the workover operations for downhole maintenance and repair. Wells require regular workover and maintenance. On the average, a well will require a major workover with downhole equipment and tubulars (if they exist) pulled out of the hole every three years. Table 7–3 summarizes average U.S. operating costs for oil and gas wells.

Table 7–3 (1989) Oil and Gas Well Operating Costs

	Oil Well		
Average Well Depth (ft)	Primary Recovery Operations ($/Month)	Secondary Recovery Operations ($/Month)	Gas Well ($/Month)
2,000	900	1,810	740
4,000	1,167	2,570	1,040
8,000	1,650	3,900	1,700
12,000	2,275		2,160
16,000			2,600

Source: Energy Information, Administration Costs and Indices for Domestic Oil and Gas Field Equipment and Production Operations 1987–1989

Operating costs vary substantially depending on which part of the country wells are located. Table 7–4 compares the average monthly operating costs per well for different areas around the United States.

Table 7–4 (1989) Regional Oil Well Operating Costs

Region	4,000 ft Oil Well Operating Costs ($/Month)
California	1,465
Oklahoma	868
South Louisiana	1,410
South Texas	1,347
West Texas	890
Wyoming	1,019
Average	$1,167

Source: Energy Information, Administration Costs and Indices for Domestic Oil and Gas Field Equipment and Production Operations 1987–1989

DISCOUNTED CASH FLOW ANALYSIS

Evaluation of oil and gas properties in the industry is done almost exclusively with discounted cash flow (DCF) analysis. Many rules of thumb are used for quick estimates of value by those who make production acquisitions or production loans, but the bottom line is invariably determined with DCF analysis. Table 7–5 outlines the types of costs, expenses, deductions, and taxes associated with U.S. oil production. The example starts with a wellhead price of $20 per barrel.

Table 7–5 United States Production Cost and Fiscal Structure

Terminology	$/bbl	Royalties, Costs, and Taxes
Wellhead Price	$20.00	
	– 3.75	18.75% (three-sixteenths) Royalty
Net Revenue	16.25	
	– 1.63	10% Severance, Ad Valorem and Production Taxes
	– 4.15	Operating Costs
	– 1.45	General and Administrative Costs
Before-tax Cash Flow	9.02*	
	– 5.15	Depreciation, Depletion and Amortization
Before-tax Net Income	3.87	
	– .31	8% State Income Tax
	3.56	
	– 1.21	34% Federal Income Tax
After-tax Net Income	$2.35	
	+ 5.15	Depreciation, Depletion and Amortization
After-tax Cash Flow	$7.50	

*Most discounted cash flow analyses are performed at this (before-tax) stage.

The DCF method unfortunately is not practical for most people who are trying to evaluate a company's annual report or 10-K.

ESTIMATING VALUE—THE DOLLAR-PER-BARREL METHOD

One of the most frequently quoted statistics that accompanies news of an acquisition is the amount paid per barrel for reserves.

A common rule of thumb values oil reserves in the ground at approximately one-third of the posted wellhead price. For oil, this works fairly well in obtaining a quick estimate of value. For gas reserves, the value can often approach 50% or more of the wellhead price.

Two cash flow models for oil production and gas production are shown in Tables 7–6 and 7–7. They show how the present value of reserves is a function of declining production, price forecasts, operating costs, and taxes. These are typical but somewhat simplified cash flow models used by companies that buy or sell production. Table 7–8 shows the relationship between value in dollars per barrel and dollars per daily barrel for short- and long-life reserves. The longer-life reserves are worth slightly less on a $/bbl basis because of present value discounting. Gas reserve estimates normally do not have as large a discount per MCF for long-life reserves because gas prices are expected to rise significantly compared to oil prices. On a heating value basis, gas sells for less than half the value of oil.

The value of reserves on a $/BOPD basis is strongly influenced by timing of production. While the difference in value between long-life and short-life reserves can be about $1 per barrel, the dollar-per-daily-barrel method shows a more dramatic difference between long-life and short-life reserves. Table 7–8 indicates a difference of $10,000 per daily barrel for reserves with a RLI of 6 and reserves with a RLI of 10. However, this sensitivity analysis does not account for likely undeveloped reserves often associated with a RLI of 10. Few mature producing properties actually have a RLI greater than eight (8).

Figures 7–1 and 7–2 demonstrate how sensitive oil and gas reserve values are to the average production rate of a well. It is a basic concept that a well making 20 BOPD should be more valuable than 2 wells making 10 BOPD each. The market value of producing oil and gas reserves can be estimated empirically by using these graphs.

An unfortunate aspect of the dollar-per-barrel estimate is that it does not account for production timing and implies that value is more a function of reserve volume than production rate. The dollar-per-daily-barrel method has its weaknesses too, but using the two methods in conjunction with each other can help give some meaning to an annual report or 10-K.

Table 7–6 Present Value of Producing Oil Reserves

Year	Oil Price ($/bbl)	Net Volume (bbls)	Net Revenue ($)	Operating Costs ($)	Sev. & Ad Val Taxes ($)	Capital ($)	Before Tax Net Cash Flow ($)	Discounted Present Value 18.0% ($)
1	20.00	5,100	102,000	20,550	10,200	0	71,250	65,591
2	20.80	4,488	93,350	20,244	9,335	0	63,771	49,751
3	21.63	3,949	85,434	19,975	8,543	0	56,916	37,630
4	22.50	3,476	78,189	19,738	7,819	0	50,633	28,369
5	23.40	3,058	71,559	19,529	7,156	0	44,874	21,307
6	24.33	2,691	65,491	19,346	6,549		39,596	15,933
7	25.31	2,368	59,937	19,184	5,994		34,759	11,853
8	26.32	2,084	54,854	19,042	5,485		30,327	8,764
9	27.37	1,834	50,203	18,917	5,020		26,265	6,433
10	28.47	1,614	45,946	18,807	4,595		22,544	4,679
11	29.60	1,420	42,049	18,710	4,205		19,134	3,366
12	30.79	1,250	38,484	18,625	3,848		16,010	2,386
13	32.02	1,100	35,220	18,550	3,522		13,148	1,661
14	33.30	968	32,234	18,484	3,223		10,526	1,127
15	34.63	852	29,500	18,426	2,950		8,124	737
		36,254	884,451	288,127	88,445	0	507,879	259,587

Input Parameters	
Oil Price Escalation	4.0%
Production Decline	12.0%
Severance & Ad Valorem	10.0%
Monthly Operating Costs	$1,500
Variable Costs ($/bbl)	$0.50
Discount Rate	18.0%

Valuation	Summary
$/BOPD	$18,578
$/bbl	$7.16
RLI (Yrs)	7.1
Operating Costs $/bbl	$4.03

172

Table 7–7 Present Value of Producing Gas Reserves

Year	Gas Price ($/mcf)	Net Volume (MMCF)	Net Revenue ($)	Operating Costs ($)	Sev. & Ad Val Taxes ($)	Capital ($)	Before Tax Net Cash Flow ($)	Discounted Present Value 18.0% ($)
1	2.00	73	146,000	29,000	14,600	0	102,00	94,267
2	2.10	66	137,970	27,540	13,797	0	96,633	75,388
3	2.21	59	130,382	26,226	13,038	0	91,117	60,242
4	2.32	53	123,211	25,043	12,321	0	85,846	48,099
5	2.43	48	116,434	23,979	11,643	0	80,811	38,371
6	2.55	43	110,030	23,021	11,003		76,006	30,584
7	2.68	39	103,979	22,159	10,398		71,422	24,355
8	2.81	35	98,260	21,383	9,826		67,051	19,377
9	2.95	31	92,855	20,685	9,286		62,885	15,401
10	3.10	28	87,748	20,056	8,775		58,917	12,228
11	3.26	25	82,922	19,491	8,292		55,139	9,698
12	3.42	23	78,362	18,982	7,836		51,544	7,683
13	3.59	21	74,052	18,523	7,405		48,123	6,079
14	3.77	19	69,979	18,111	6,998		44,870	4,803
15	3.96	17	66,130	17,740	6,613		41,777	3,790
		580	1,518,313	331,940	151,831	0	1,034,541	450,366

Input Parameters	
Gas Price Escalation	5.0%
Production Decline	10.0%
Severance & Ad Valorem	10.0%
Monthly Operating Costs	$1,200
Variable Costs ($/MCF)	$0.20
Discount Rate	18.0%

Valuation	Summary
$/MCFD	$2,252
$/MCF	$0.78
RLI (Yrs)	7.9
Operating Costs $/MCF	$0.40

Table 7–8 Reserve Values—Long-life vs. Short-life Reserves

	RLI	Production Decline Rate	Present Value	
			$/bbl	$/BOPD
Short-life Reserves	4	25%	$7.80	11,000
	6	15%	7.25	15,300
Normal	8	10%	7.05	20,500
	10	6%	6.85	25,200
Long -life Reserves	12	4%	6.70	28,900

Sensitivity Analysis based on: $20 per barrel wellhead price and a discount rate of 18% before tax

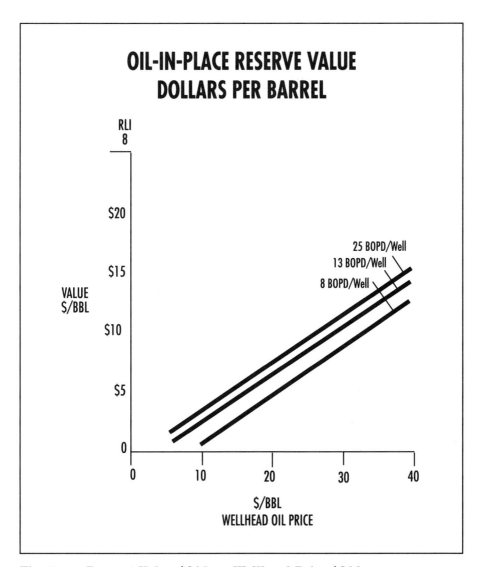

Fig. 7–1. Present Value $/bbl vs. Wellhead Price $/bbl

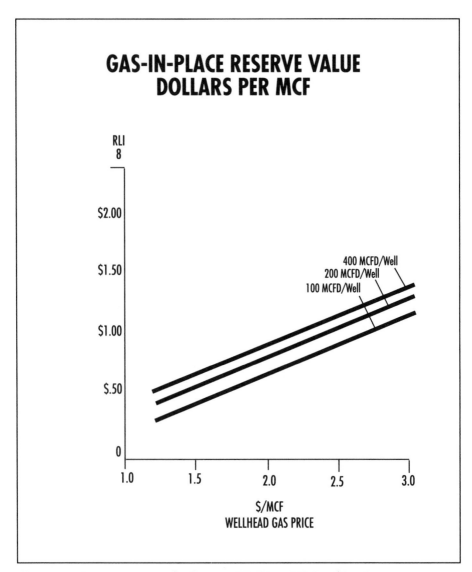

Fig. 7-2 *Present Value $/MCF vs. Wellhead Price $/mcf*

ESTIMATING VALUE—THE DOLLAR-PER-DAILY-BARREL METHOD

Estimating value using the dollar-per-daily-barrel method as it is depicted in Figures 7–3 and 7–4 is based on experience, discounted cash flow sensitivity analysis, recent transactions, and specific expectations of oil and gas prices. It is a quick-look technique that emulates the results of a detailed cash flow analysis for a property.

For example, if a property producing 100 barrels of oil per day (BOPD) sells for $1.4 million, then the value per daily barrel of production would be:

$$\$1,400,000/100 \text{ BOPD} = \$14,000/\text{BOPD}$$

This technique is much less common than many others. The main reason is that it is extremely sensitive to the production decline rate. Long-life reserves have a much higher value in terms of dollars per daily barrel. This can be seen in Table 7–8 and in Figures 7–3 and 7–4. For example, assume that a property with a reserve-life index of 10 is producing at a rate of 100 BOPD. The average well produces 25 BOPD, and oil prices are at $20 per barrel and expected to remain relatively stable. The estimate of value under these conditions would be $23,000 per daily barrel, or $2.3 million. If, however, the RLI were closer to six years, the value would be $15,000 per BOPD or $1.5 million.

Estimating value using the dollar-per-daily-barrel method (Figures 7–3 and 7–4) can complement the dollar-per-barrel method. While the values derived by the two techniques should be close, this seldom happens.

The differences between the two values provide valuable insight into the quality and nature of an oil and gas company's principal assets. In situations where reserve figures have either been exaggerated or understated, there can be substantial differences. Large differences between the two estimates of reserve values are not unusual.

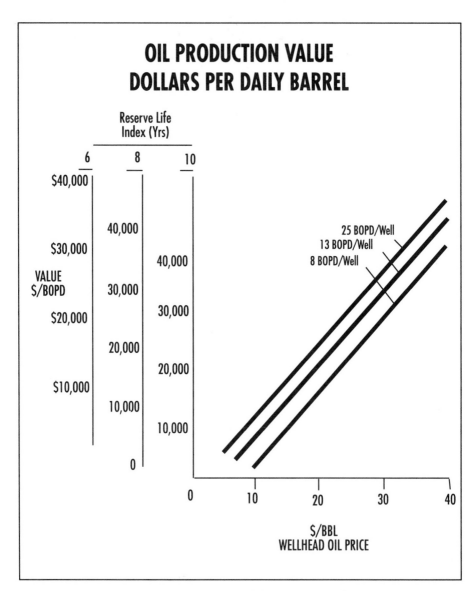

Fig. 7–3. Present Value $/BOPD vs Wellhead Price $/bbl

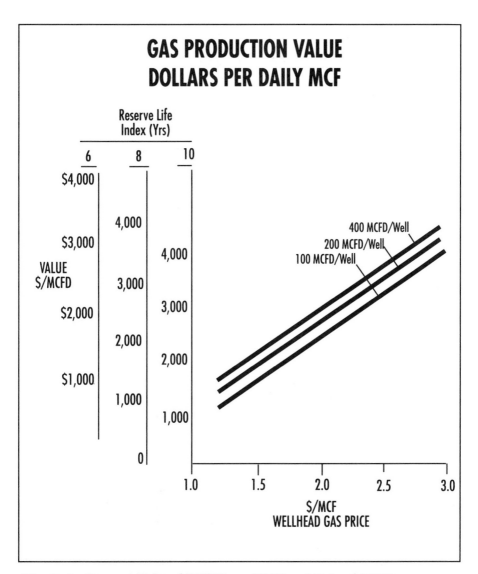

Fig. 7–4. Present Value $/MCFD vs. Wellhead Price $/MCF

THE MIDWAY-SUNSET EXAMPLE

An example is outlined to show how these graphs can be used together to see more than one dimension of reported information. On November 29, 1990, the Dallas Morning News reported that Oryx Energy Company (ORYX) had sold interests in a California field for $642 million. ORYX reportedly sold 140 million barrels of slightly heavy crude that was producing at a rate of 29,000 BOPD. The production was from the Midway-Sunset field, the second largest field in California, discovered in 1894. In 1990, the wells in this field produced an average of 14 BOPD each. The article explained that while reserves at the time were valued at $5.50 to $6.00 per barrel, ORYX sold their interests for around $4.60 per barrel. One analyst said of the transaction, "It's on the low side of a fair price, but it's not disastrous by any means."

At the time, the four-week average futures' price for West Texas Intermediate was $30.50. The value of $4.60 sounds low in comparison, but most people at the time did not expect prices to stay that high for long. Furthermore, the sales price amounted to more than $22,000 per daily barrel. From this perspective, the deal was right in the ball park for acquisitions at that time, especially considering that the field produces heavy oil that can sell at a substantial discount. The crude from the Midway-Sunset field is around 13° API, which has historically sold for around $5 per barrel less than West Texas Intermediate (WTI) crude (see Table 6–4).

Figures 7–1 and 7–3 are used to illustrate the two different views. Figure 7–1 indicates that a $4.60 per barrel acquisition price would be consistent with an expected wellhead price of around $17 per barrel. The value of $22,000 per daily barrel corresponds to a wellhead price of more than $20 per barrel. This is a big difference. The seemingly low price per barrel is explained by the reserve life index (RLI), which is around 13 years, and by the relatively low quality of the crude. The RLI of 13 years is quite high. It indicates a strong likelihood that additional drilling may be required to produce the reserves in a reasonable time.

180

ADJUSTED SEC VALUE OF RESERVES

In accordance with provisions of the *Statement of Financial Accounting Standards No. 69*, oil companies report the standardized measure of discounted net cash flows for oil and gas reserves. This is often referred to as the SEC value of reserves.

Many analysts will simply substitute the SEC value of reserves for the book value of oil and gas properties on the balance sheet to arrive at an adjusted balance sheet appraisal. This approach is a place to start, but there are a few things to consider when using SEC values. The 10-K report will disclose the average price received for oil or gas sold during the fiscal year. However, the SEC value of reserves found at the back of the 10-K uses year-end prices for oil and gas valuation. These year-end prices are held constant and not escalated unless actual contract terms have escalation factors built in. The SEC value of reserves is the closest many analysts will get to a discounted cash flow analysis of the oil and gas assets of an oil company. However, there are a number of things to look for:

- What were the average product prices during the year?
- What were the year-end product prices used in the SEC valuation? (Sometimes this is disclosed in the 10-K.)
- How do the year-end prices compare to projected prices?
- What value per barrel does the SEC estimate represent?
- What value per daily barrel does the SEC estimate represent?

After reviewing the SEC values, many analysts will venture an educated guess at an adjusted SEC value. This is usually done when prices used in the SEC calculation are considered to be substantially different than forecast prices.

CASH FLOW MULTIPLE

When the information is available, a multiple of cash flow provides a rough estimate of the value of producing properties. The market for oil and gas production in the United States typically will pay from three to six times (annual) cash flow for a mature portfolio of oil or gas production. This corresponds to payouts of from four to seven years. Payout typically will be greater than the cash flow multiple for a production acquisition because production and cash flow are characterized by a decline rate.

The cash flow multiple is not quite the same as the often-used term *payout*. Payout is the amount of time it takes for an investor to get his investment back. If a producing property did not have a decline rate, the cash flow multiple and the payout would be the same.

VALUATION OF UNDEVELOPED RESERVES

Undeveloped reserves often represent a considerable asset, yet they can be difficult to evaluate. Fortunately, undeveloped reserves are included in the SEC value of reserves in the 10-K. The most difficult aspect for analysts is that the required capital costs to develop these reserves is unknown. Usually analysts will simply attribute to undeveloped reserves one half the value per unit given to proved developed producing reserves. For example, if a company's developed reserves based on prices, quality, and timing, are appraised at $6.50 per barrel, then undeveloped reserves will be appraised at $3.25. This approach is very common. It is usually about all that can be done with the information available.

ACREAGE VALUATION

Exploration acreage is an important component of a company's asset portfolio. While information on the location and amount of net acreage is available in the 10-K, it is often difficult to estimate the market value of the acreage. There are a couple of very important reasons for this. The 10-K will summarize net developed and net undeveloped acreage. The analyst would prefer to know more about the net undeveloped acreage. Some of this undeveloped acreage has proved undeveloped reserves attributed to it, and the rest does not. When an analyst attributes value to proved undeveloped reserves, he is indirectly accounting for some portion of the net undeveloped acreage portfolio. But how much? This usually cannot be determined.

It is a common practice for analysts to estimate value of developed and undeveloped reserves and also to attribute value to acreage even though, indirectly, some value has already been given. Ordinarily, in a mature, well-balanced portfolio of oil and gas assets, the acreage component will represent 15% of the portfolio value. It can be higher. There are always exceptions, but this is the place to start. A reasonable range would be 10–20% of the overall portfolio value. An analyst should be cautious when attributing a greater share of value to this element of the corporate asset base. Acreage values are based on:

- acreage position (size) and continuity
- location
- geological conditions
- expiration date for leases
- regional drilling success ratios
- potential size of discovery (if successful)
- costs of drilling/exploration in the area

Undeveloped acreage can have substantial value. When evaluating an acreage position, it is important, if possible, to determine if expiration dates will have a large impact on the acreage value. Even more important is a company's drilling commitments or obligations associated with the acreage. These obligations may have a significant negative impact on the value of acreage.

This is one of the toughest parts of an oil company to evaluate based on published information. The analyst must get by on little information and few hints. Sometimes there is more information. If a company has a lot of value in acreage, which is not represented by production or booked reserves, there may be information to indicate this in management discussions. The SEC requires an inventory of acreage in the 10-K report. This is the place to start.

Table 7–9 outlines general acreage values for comparison and reference, but the information must come with a warning. This kind of generalization is very difficult to make. Acreage values vary from one side of a county to the other, and from one geological trend to the next. There are exceptions to every rule. With fluctuating oil prices, acreage values change, too, although not quite as wildly.

Table 7-9 Comparative Range of Acreage Values

	Low ($/Acre)	Most Likely ($/Acre)	High ($/Acre)
ONSHORE U.S.			
Boom Area	200	250	400
Active Area	75	100	125
Moderately Active Area	10	50	75
Inactive Area	2	5	10
OFFSHORE U.S.			
Active Area	150	250	500
Inactive Area	25	50	100

During the late 1980s, broad portfolios of onshore acreage in the United States were appraised by various analysts at $30 to $100 per acre.

The minimum bid requirement for offshore acreage in federal waters of the Gulf of Mexico was reduced from $150 per acre to $25 per acre in April 1987.

ANALYZING RESERVE INFORMATION IN THE 10-K

Sometimes the only means available to an analyst to compare one company with another are the methods outlined in this chapter. Detailed cash flow analysis is not practical for every situation. There are many well-documented weaknesses associated with rules of thumb, but for estimating values and getting a quick indication of value, they can be helpful. When the only source of information is an annual report or a 10-K report, these methods may be the only tools available.

The disclosure requirements for oil companies now provide quite a bit of information. Worksheets are helpful for organizing the most important information. Worksheets 7-1 and 7-2 can be useful in collecting information. Figures 7-5 and 7-6 provide examples of the kind of information that can be gleaned from a 10-K report, and analysis of that information.

184

Worksheet 7-1 10-K Oil and Gas Information and Analysis

Company:_____ Source:_____ Date:_____

INPUT	Current Oil Price:			
COUNTRY		_____	_____	_____
Proved Developed Reserves				
Oil ( )		_____	_____	_____
Gas ( )		_____	_____	_____
Proved Undeveloped Reserves				
Oil ( )		_____	_____	_____
Gas ( )		_____	_____	_____
Total Proved Reserves				
Oil ( )		_____	_____	_____
Gas ( )		_____	_____	_____
Annual Production				
Oil ( )		_____	_____	_____
Gas ( )		_____	_____	_____
Net Wells				
Oil		_____	_____	_____
Gas		_____	_____	_____
Prices				
Oil ($/BBL)		_____	_____	_____
Gas ($/MCF)		_____	_____	_____
Lifting Costs per Unit				
Oil ($/BBL)		_____	_____	_____
Gas ($/MCF)		_____	_____	_____

CALCULATIONS				
Current Oil and Gas Prices		_____	_____	_____
Average Daily Production Rate				
Oil (BOPD)		_____	_____	_____
Gas (MCFD)		_____	_____	_____
Average Production Rate				
Per Well Oil (BOPD)		_____	_____	_____
Gas (MCFD)		_____	_____	_____
Average Reserves Per Well				
Oil ( )		_____	_____	_____
Gas ( )		_____	_____	_____
Reserve Life Index (Years)				
Oil		_____	_____	_____
Gas		_____	_____	_____
Price Parity Relationship (MCF/BBL)		_____	_____	_____
Barrels Oil Equivalent				
Proved Reserves ( )				
Thermal 6:1		_____	_____	_____
Price Parity		_____	_____	_____

Worksheet 7-2 Oil and Gas Property Valuation From 10-K Information

Company:_____ Source:_____ Date:_____

Current Oil and Gas Prices   _____ _____
Year-end Oil and Gas Prices   _____ _____

Book Value of Reserves . . . . = _____

SEC Value of Reserves _____   _____

                                               = _____

"Adjusted" SEC Value of Reserves _____ X _____ = _____

Average Daily Production

_____ Oil (BOPD) _____ X _____ $/BOPD = _____
_____ Oil (BOPD) _____ X _____ $/BOPD = _____
_____ Gas (MCFD) _____ X _____ $/MCFD = _____
_____ Gas (MCFD) _____ X _____ $/MCFD = _____

Total Value of Producing Reserves . . . . = _____

Reported Reserves
_____ Oil (MBBLS) _____ X ____ $/BBL = _____
_____ Oil (MBBLS) _____ X ____ $/BBL = _____
_____ Oil (MBBLS) _____ X ____ $/BBL = _____
_____ Oil (MBBLS) _____ X ____ $/BBL = _____
_____ Gas (MMCF) _____ X ____ $/MCF = _____
_____ Gas (MMCF) _____ X ____ $/MCF = _____
_____ Gas (MMCF) _____ X ____ $/MCF = _____
_____ Gas (MMCF) _____ X ____ $/MCF = _____

Total Developed _____ + Undeveloped _____   = _____

Cash Flow from Oil and Gas _____ X ____   = _____

Proved Oil and Gas Reserves   = _____

Book Value of Unproved Properties _____

_____ _____ Acres X ____ $/Acre = _____
_____ _____ Acres X ____ $/Acre = _____
_____ _____ Acres X ____ $/Acre = _____

            Acreage Total . . . . . _____

    Oil and Gas Reserves + Acreage Total . . . . . _____

Company: FOREST OIL CORP.   Source: 1989 10-K   Date: 3/1991

Current Oil and Gas Prices $21.50 WTI
                                2.30
Year-end Oil and Gas Prices $20.77

Book Value of Reserves . . . . = $318MM

SEC Value of Reserves   U.S. $281.2 MM
                        CANADA   44.9 MM   = $326 MM

"Adjusted" SEC Value of Reserves $326MM X 1.1 = $359 MM

Average Daily Production

U.S. Oil (BOPD) 1,046 X 25,000 $/BOPD = $26 MM
CA   Oil (BOPD)   465 X 25,000 $/BOPD = 12
U.S. Gas (MCFD) 94,822 X 2,200 $/MCFD = 209
CA   Gas (MCFD) 5,260 X 1,800 $/MCFD =   9

Total Value of Producing Reserves . . . . = $256MM

Reported Reserves
U.S. DEV.   Oil (MBBLS)   5,765 X 7.00 $/BBL = $40MM
CA DEV.   Oil (MBBLS)   2,206 X 6.50 $/BBL = 14
U.S. UNDEV. Oil (MBBLS)   1,215 X 3.50 $/BBL =   4
CA UNDEV.   Oil (MBBLS)   76 X 3.25 $/BBL =   —
U.S. DEV.   Gas (MMCF) 186,324 X 1.10 $/MCF = 205
CA DEV   Gas (MMCF)   27,183 X .60 $/MCF = 16
U.S. UNDEV   Gas (MMCF)   49,539 X .55 $/MCF = 27
CA UNDEV   Gas (MMCF)   9,858 X .30 $/MCF =   3

Total Developed $275MM + Undeveloped $34MM = $309 MM

Cash Flow from Oil and Gas $86 MM X 5   = $430MM

Proved Oil and Gas Reserves   = $366MM

Book Value of Unproved Properties $79MM

U.S. ONSHORE   208,000 Acres X 75 $/Acre = $16 MM
Gulf of Mex.   55,700 Acres X 150 $/Acre =   8
CANADA   34,000 Acres X 125 $/Acre =   4

                    Acreage Total $28MM

Oil and Gas Reserves + Acreage Total $394MM

Fig. 7–5 Sample 10-K Oil and Gas Reserve Analysis

187

Company: FOREST OIL CORP. Source: 1989 10-K Date: 3/1990

INPUT	Current Oil Price: $21.50 WTI		
COUNTRY	U. S.	CANADA	
Proved Developed Reserves			
Oil (MBBLS)	5,765	2,206	
Gas (MMCF)	186,324	27,183	
Proved Undeveloped Reserves			
Oil (MBBLS)	1,215	76	
Gas (MMCF)	49,539	9,858	
Total Proved Reserves			
Oil (MBBLS)	6,980	2,282	
Gas (MMCF)	235,863	37,041	
Annual Production			
Oil (MBBLS)	382	170	
Gas (MMCF)	34,610	1,920	
Net Wells			
Oil	23.3	8.1	
Gas	104.7	12.9	
Prices			
Oil ($/BBL)	$18.07	17.67	
Gas ($/MCF)	2.31	1.18	
Lifting Costs per Unit			
Oil ($/BBL)	—	—	
Gas ($/MCF)	$0.28	$0.42	

CALCULATIONS			
Current Oil and Gas Prices	$21.50/$2.30		
Average Daily Production Rate			
Oil (BOPD)	1,046	465	
Gas (MCFD)	94,822	5,260	
Average Production Rate			
Per Well Oil (BOPD)	45	58	
Gas (MCFD)	906	408	
Average Reserves Per Well			
Oil (MBBLS)	247	272	
Gas (MMCF)	1,780	2,107	
Reserve Life Index (Years)			
Oil	15	13	
Gas	5.4	14	
Price Parity Relationship			
(MCF/BBL)	7.8	15	
Barrels Oil Equivalent			
Proved Reserves (MMBBLS)			
Thermal 6:1	46.3	8.5	
Price Parity	37.8	4.8	

Fig. 7–6 Sample Valuation of Oil and Gas Properties

Master Limited Partnerships

The forerunner of the Master Limited Partnership (MLP) was the royalty trust. Royalty trusts provided unitholders an opportunity to own a direct working interest in oil and gas production. By doing this, one layer of income tax was avoided. This was the principal advantage of the royalty trust.

The royalty trust was first used when the Tidelands Royalty Trust B was formed in 1954. This trust was established by Gulf Oil Corporation to provide for the administration and liquidation of rights to interests in 60 offshore tracts in the Gulf of Mexico.

The trusts distributed royalties to unitholders who then paid income tax after adjusting for the depletion allowance credit. The royalty trust concept did not catch on immediately. It surfaced again after 14 years when the North European Oil Royalty Trust was created in 1975. This was the result of the liquidation of the North European Oil Company. This trust held overriding royalty interests in oil and gas producing properties in the Federal Republic of Germany.

In 1979 Mesa Petroleum Company formed the Mesa Royalty Trust. Mesa transferred to the trust an overriding royalty in producing properties in Kansas, New Mexico, Colorado, and Wyoming. This was the beginning of renewed interest in the royalty trust concept.

In 1980, the Houston Oil Royalty Trust, the Permian Basin Trust, and the San Juan Basin Royalty Trust were formed by Southland Royalty Company. The royalty trusts passed cash flow and write-offs directly through to investors.

Also in 1980, the oil and gas industry developed a new financial vehicle—the MLP. The first MLP was formed in 1981 by Apache Petroleum Company. The MLP concept, like the royalty trust, evolved essentially to eliminate corporate taxes.

A company formed an MLP by placing assets into a separate entity. The entity could be formed by combining, or rolling up, existing limited partnerships into an MLP and, therefore, was called a *roll up*. An advantage of the roll up was that units could be traded. This provided unitholders with liquidity, which they previously did not have.

If the entity were created by spinning off producing properties owned by the company forming the MLP, it would be called a *drop-down* MLP. Units of the entity would be sold then to investors who become limited partners. Investors considered oil and gas properties in an MLP to be worth more than they would be ordinarily because one level of taxation (corporate taxes) was avoided. Also, a significant percentage of cash flow was usually distributed to shareholders. A large part of distributions, especially in the early stages, were treated as return of capital, and thus were not taxed as ordinary income.

MLPs differed primarily in the degree of public ownership and in the designated use of cash flow. Some distributed a small portion of cash flow and reinvested the rest, while some were designed to distribute most of the cash flow.

The measure of success of an MLP was based on its perceived ability to maintain distributions. The MLP concept provided a good example of the liquidation value of an oil and gas company. The average MLP distributed 75% of cash flow to unitholders. Some distributed virtually all cash flow, usually in quarterly dividends.

Investors were usually willing to pay a higher premium for an MLP in exchange for the higher yield. In the mid-1980s, MLPs typically traded at around six times cash flow compared to three to four times for the major oil companies. Many analysts felt that some of the MLPs traded at a premium to their underlying asset value.

The 1986 Tax Reform Act dramatically changed the picture for MLPs. The losses generated in the early stages of the drilling programs could no longer be offset against the ordinary income of an investor. These passive losses could only be offset against other investment income. In 1987, the IRS ruled that income from MLPs was to be treated as portfolio income, and losses could no longer be used to offset other income.

The MLP vehicle was no longer as attractive as it had been. Many companies began considering ways of restructuring these entities by rolling them back into the corporate structure.

VALUATION

Valuation of an MLP focuses on the reserve base and cash generating capability. The ability of the entity to maintain distributions to unitholders is the bottom line. Most MLPs are characterized by high yields, but also by the fact that they are slowly liquidating their reserve base. Reinvestment for exploration and development drilling is low by comparison to an independent oil company.

The primary objective with analysis of an MLP, therefore, is to evaluate the value of the reserves. The methods for estimating reserve values are the same for an MLP as for an oil company.

Refineries

Evaluation of the upstream end of the business is quite different from the downstream sector. While the upstream activity is described as an extractive industry, the downstream end is heavily into the manufacturing and marketing realm.

INDUSTRY STRUCTURE

The refining industry underwent significant change and retraction during the 1980s. The escalation of oil prices during the 1970s and early 1980s was followed by reduced demand from 18.5 million barrels per day in 1979 to 15.2 million barrels per day in 1987. Table 7–10 shows how the refining industry expanded in distillation capacity until 1981. The retrenchment was done at the expense of many small refineries that were shut down during the 1980s. This was followed by a declining trend in operating capacity, which finally turned around in 1986 and 1987 as demand increased slightly.

Refinery capacity is rated in terms of *barrels per calendar day* (B/CD). This is the actual rated volume in barrels per day of distillation capacity. The distillation unit is the first step in the refining process. Another measure of capacity is *barrels per stream day* (B/SD), which is the rated amount running at full capacity for short periods. When someone mentions a 120,000 barrel a day refinery, they are usually referring to the distillation capacity in B/SD. Sometimes it is difficult to tell if quoted distillation capacity is referring to B/CD or B/SD. There is not a big difference. Most people use 330 stream days when rating refinery capacity. Usually stream-day capacity is about 6% higher than the rated B/CD capacity.

An operating level of 90% or higher is a comfortable, efficient operating rate for a refinery. Break-even operating rates are around 80–85% of capacity. At less than 80% utilization, the profitability of a refinery usually drops off dramatically.

Pressures on the refining industry pushed the utilization rate below 70% in the early 1980s. The industry saw profit margins reach a five-year low in 1985, even with the relatively lower oil costs at that time.

Table 7–10 United States Refining Capacities—Yearly Averages

Year as of 1 Jan	Number of Refineries	Capacity Barrels per Calendar Day	Capacity Utilization
1975	259	15,478,000	81.9%
1976	256	15,678,000	81.9
1977	266	16,912,600	86.3
1978	285	17,619,000	85.1
1979	289	18,050,900	80.7
1980	297	18,708,000	74.1
1981	303	19,370,000	68.2
1982	273	18,601,000	69.8
1983	225	17,007,000	73.3
1984	220	16,689,000	79.6
1985	191	15,898,198	77.9
1986	189	15,258,200	82.8
1987	187	15,288,300	79.9
1988	185	15,327,746	85.1
1989	188	15,418,738	86.7
1990	190	15,558,923	87.6

Source: *Oil & Gas Journal*

The rash of refinery closings which occurred in the early 1980s were primarily due to overcapacity and the inability of the small refiners to compete without the *entitlement program*.

The Entitlement Program

In 1959, the government imposed quotas on the import of cheap foreign oil. This helped the small independent refineries because they were allowed to use up to 75% foreign crude as feedstock. Following the 1973 embargo imposed by OPEC, the federal government started the entitlement program, which required major integrated companies to share the available crude. This situation encouraged the proliferation of small refineries, often with less than 25,000 barrels per day capacity. Their existence was justified solely on the basis of the entitlement subsidies.

Prior to decontrol in 1981, there were 183 nonmajor refineries in the United States supplying 25% of the country's oil products. From 1981 to 1985, 131 of these refineries shut down. These were mostly the smaller refineries as shown in Table 7–11.

Table 7–11 Summary of Refinery Shutdowns

Year	Number of Shutdowns	Capacity Barrels Per Stream Day	Average Refinery Size Barrels Per Stream Day
1981	23	450,940	20,000
1982	57	493,930	9,000
1983	11	501,350	45,000
1984	29	668,535	23,000
1985	11	186,400	17,000
1986	3	78,000	26,000
1987	0	–	–
1988	1	300	300
1989	1	18,800	18,800
Total	136*	2,397,655	
Weighted Average			17,700

*Includes inactive refineries
Source: *Oil & Gas Journal*

As of January 1, 1985, there were 98 companies in the petroleum refining business compared to about 180 companies in 1981. The optimum size for a refinery is 100,000 B/CD or larger. The smaller refineries, especially those below 50,000 B/CD, have a tough time competing. The larger refineries have greater economy of scale and can survive longer in lean periods with narrower margins. The smaller refineries that survived the shakeout of the early 1980s survived mainly because they have a market niche and are geographically insulated.

FINANCIAL ANALYSIS AND EVALUATION OF REFINERIES

There are a number of ways to approach the evaluation of a refinery. The first step is to assess the book value of the refinery or the refining segment.

BOOK VALUE AND BOOK VALUE MULTIPLE

Book value of the refining segment of an oil company is often provided on the balance sheet or in supplemental information. While oil and gas assets bear little relationship to book value, this is not true of refining and storage facilities. The book value represents actual construction costs or purchase price less DD&A.

Refineries are sometimes appraised on the basis of a multiple of book value. An appraisal based on 1.25 times book value might not be unreasonable in an up-market. In a down-market, the refinery may sell for as low as 75% of book value. Regardless of book value, during the early 1980s small refineries were often worthless. Some even had negative value when mothballing or abandonment costs were considered.

CASH FLOW AND OPERATING PROFIT MULTIPLES

Typically, refining and marketing operations are part of an integrated company, and information is limited to whatever is disclosed in the segment data of the annual report or 10-K. Fortunately, segment information usually provides earnings and DD&A attributable to each segment. This at least gives a general indication of cash flow for each segment.

Refining and marketing segments are often appraised at from four to six times operating income, or five to seven times cash flow. While many analysts will report an appraisal based on one of these multiples, they usually are sure to check that the appraisal fits other techniques of valuation.

COMPARABLE SALES

Comparable sales of refineries can be difficult to find because there is not an active market for them. Refineries are not bought and sold every day. Perhaps 7 to 10 refineries may change hands each year, yet during the early 1980s, many more simply closed down.

Analysts and the press like to compare refinery sales on the basis of dollars paid per B/SD capacity. For example, if a 100,000 B/SD refinery sells for $400 million, the next step is to point out that it sold for $4,000 per daily barrel. This approach is convenient for a quick approximation of value. It focuses on the basic unit of production for a refinery, the distillation capacity.

Analysis can go deeper with an estimate of the complexity of the processing operations. This adds an important dimension to the evaluation of a refinery. The most common index for comparing refineries and quantifying refinery complexity is the Nelson Complexity Index. Unfortunately, the complexity index of a refinery is seldom published. Many refinery employees do not even know what the complexity of their particular refinery is.

NELSON COMPLEXITY INDICES

The Nelson Complexity Index for refinery construction costs is a relative measure of how many upgrading units the refinery has. The index was developed by Wilbur L. Nelson in the 1960s to quantify the relative cost of components that make up a refinery. The Nelson index compares the costs of various upgrading units, such as a catalytic cracker or a reformer, to the cost of a crude distillation unit. After the raw crude is processed in the distillation unit (or units), the components are then processed in the various upgrading and other processing units. The rated capacity of a refinery refers to the crude distillation unit capacity. Beyond that, there are numerous components that can be added. The computation of the Nelson Index is an attempt to quantify the relative cost of a refinery based on the cost of all the various upgrading units.

Nelson assigned a factor of 1 to the distillation unit. All other units are rated in terms of their cost relative to this unit. For example, assume a crude distillation unit costs $200 per B/SD to construct. That is, a 50,000 B/SD unit would cost $1 million ($200/B/SD X 50,000 B/SD). If another component costs $600 per B/SD to build, it would have a complexity factor of 3. Each unit has a complexity factor related to the construction cost as it compares to the cost of the distillation unit.

Calculation of the complexity rating of a refinery is done by multiplying the complexity factor for a given unit by the percentage of crude oil it processes. Consider the case of a refinery with crude distillation capacity of 50,000 B/SD and a vacuum distillation capacity of 30,000 B/SD. The complexity factor for the vacuum distillation unit is 2. The throughput of the vacuum unit relative to the overall crude distillation capacity is 60%. The contribution of the vacuum unit to the overall refinery complexity would be equal to 1.2—.6 times 2.

IMPLICATIONS ON COST AND VALUE

The average complexity rating for a refinery in the United States is around 10. A refinery with a Nelson Complexity Index of 10 would be considered a *medium conversion* facility. A refinery with a complexity of 12 should cost 20% more to build than a similar sized refinery, all other things being equal. Unfortunately, all other things are seldom equal, and, even if they were, the relationship is not perfect. However, it does help to improve an estimate of value.

DUPLICATION AND ECONOMIES OF SCALE

Nelson was careful to point out that the cost of a 50,000 B/SD refinery with a complexity of 12 would not necessarily be the same as that of a 100,000 B/SD refinery with an index of 6. Many other factors are involved. The information normally available does not indicate the number of units used to accomplish a particular process. Small units have relatively higher per-unit construction costs. Nelson estimated that a duplication of units such as two 40,000 B/SD units, instead of one 80,000 B/SD unit, would increase the construction costs by a factor of 25%. Four units instead of one would increase costs by a factor of 60%.

The amount of duplication for larger 300,000 B/SD refineries reported by Nelson averaged 2.7 units, rather than one for each process. The industry average is 1.5 units for each process instead of one unit.

A typical refinery from each of three major refining regions is summarized in Table 7–12.

Table 7–12 Refinery Comparison

	Mid-continent	Gulf Coast	West Coast
Capacity (B/SD)	45,000	200,000	120,000
Nelson Complexity Index	7.5	10.0	12.5
	Low Conversion	Medium Conversion	High Conversion

The *Oil & Gas Journal* publishes capacity ratings of refineries in and outside the United States. The information found in the *Oil & Gas Journal Annual Refining Survey* is a good place to start. This issue of the *Journal* is usually published toward the end of March each year and lists the capacity ratings of all refineries in the United States. A listing of capacity ratings of international refineries is found in the *Oil & Gas Journal Worldwide Report* at the end of each year.

Figure 7-7 is an example from the *Oil & Gas Journal Annual Refining Survey*, which reports refinery distillation capacity ratings and the capacity of each upgrading system.

	Crude capacity		Vacuum	Thermal	Charge capacity, b/sd Cat cracking		Cat	Cat hydro-	Cat hydro-	Cat hydro-	Alky.	Production capacity, b/sd Aromatics-			Hydrogen	Coke
Company and location	b/cd	b/sd	distillation	operations	Fresh feed	Recycle	reforming	cracking	refining	treating	*Poly.	isomerization	Lubes	Asphalt	(MMcfd)	(t/d)
MISSISSIPPI																
Amerada-Hess Corp. — Purvis	30.000	⁴31.579	20.000	⁸8.000	²16.000		²5.800			²5.800	³3.500					250
										⁶6.000						
Chevron U.S.A. Inc. — Pascagoula	295.000	310.000	243.000	⁵75.000	⁷64.000		²90.000	⁷68.000	¹96.000	¹48.000	¹¹6.200	⁷5.500		20.000	¹215.0	4,000
									⁶63.000							
									⁴30.000							
Ergon Refining Inc. — Vicksburg	16.800	18.300	12.000						⁵3.800				3.600	12.000	⁷2.5	
Southland Oil Co. — Lumberton	5.800	6.500												3.500		
Sandersville	11.000	12.500												5.100		
Total	358.600	378.879	275.000	83.000	80.000		95.800	68.000	192.800	59.800	19.700	5.500	3.600	40.600	217.5	4,250

Fig. 7-7 Oil & Gas Journal Annual Refining Survey, p. 96 Oil & Gas Journal, Mar. 18, 1991.

Table 7-13 provides a summary of the general indices for the various refinery processes. This format was chosen because of the readily available information from the *Oil & Gas Journal* and the fact that the Nelson Indices are the most common source of this information available.

By using this table, an estimate of refinery complexity can be made. The value of the refinery can then be estimated by using the graph in Figure 7-9. This graph is based on refinery sales and appraisals in the late 1980s. For example, a 100,000 B/SD refinery with a complexity index of 8 would have a value of around $3,000 per B/SD. This would yield a

198

refinery value of around $300 million. When this estimate is used in conjunction with other valuation methods, such as book value and cash flow multiple, a better feel for the refinery value may be obtained.

In Figure 7–8, the complexity index for the 310,000 B/SD Chevron Pascagoula refinery is estimated at around 12. The value of this refinery should be between $1.1 billion to $1.3 billion.

Table 7–13 Generalized Refinery Complexity Indices

Refining Process	Generalized Complexity Index
Distillation Capacity	1
Vacuum Distillation	2
Thermal Processes	6
Catalytic Cracking	6
Catalytic Reforming	5
Catalytic Hydrocracking	6
Catalytic Hydrorefining	3
Catalytic Hydrotreating	2
Alkylation/Polemerization	10
Aromatics/Isomerization	15
Lubes	10
Asphalt	1.5
Hydrogen (MCFD)*	1

*Units are reported in MMCFD in *Oil & Gas Journal* vs MCFD for Nelson Complexity Index calculation.

(After: W. L. Nelson, "The Concept of Refinery Complexity." *Oil & Gas Journal*, Sept. 13, 1976.)

The main weakness of this model is in the use of broad categories to which a single complexity factor is applied. For example, the processing category of Aromatics/Isomerization, assigned a complexity factor of 15, includes various processes, each with a different complexity factor. Recently published indices demonstrate the variation as shown in Table 7-14.

Table 7-14 Aromatics/Isomerization Process Complexity Indices

Aromatics/Isomerization	Nelson Complexity Index
Isomerization	3
Polymerization	9
Benzene, Toluene, and Xylene (BTX) manufacture	20

Source: Gerald L. Farrar, *Oil & Gas Journal*, Oct. 2, 1989, p. 90

Approximately 5% of refinery processing in the United States falls into the Aromatics/Isomerization category.

It is recommended that this approach be treated as an educated guess rather than scientific methodology. It is convenient, but should be considered within the context of other available data. For example, two otherwise similar refineries, one operating at 75% capacity and the other at 90%, will have significantly different value. Smaller refineries with 50,000 B/SD capacity or less generally do not sell for as much per unit as larger refineries with the same complexity rating.

Worksheet 7–3   Refinery Complexity Analysis

```
Refinery:_____        Date:_____

Location:_____        Source:_____
```

Refining Process	Capacity (B/SD)	%	Generalized Complexity Index	Index
Distillation Capacity	_____	____	1	_____
Vacuum Distillation	_____	____	2	_____
Thermal Processes	_____	____	6	_____
Catalytic Cracking	_____	____	6	_____
Catalytic Reforming	_____	____	5	_____
Catalytic Hydrocracking	_____	____	6	_____
Catalytic Hydrorefining	_____	____	3	_____
Catalytic Hydrotreating	_____	____	2	_____
Alky/Poly	_____	____	10	_____
Aromatics/Isomerization	_____	____	15	_____
Lubes	_____	____	10	_____
Asphalt	_____	____	1.5	_____
Hydrogen (MCFD)	_____	____	1	_____

```
                                               --------

             Nelson Complexity Index Total     _____
```

Refinery: CHEVRON   Date: April 1991

Location: PASCAGOULA, MISS.   Source: 18 MARCH, 91 O&GJ

Refining Process	Capacity (B/SD)	%	Generalized Complexity Index	Index
Distillation Capacity	310,000	100	1	1.00
Vacuum Distillation	243,000	78.4	2	1.57
Thermal Processes	75,000	24.2	6	1.45
Catalytic Cracking	64,000	20.6	6	1.24
Catalytic Reforming	90,000	29.0	5	1.45
Catalytic Hydrocracking	68,000	21.9	6	1.32
Catalytic Hydrorefining	189,000	61.0	3	1.83
Catalytic Hydrotreating	48,000	15.5	2	.31
Alky/Poly	16,200	5.2	10	.52
Aromatics/Isomerization	5,500	1.8	15	.27
Lubes	0	—	10	—
Asphalt	20,000	6.5	1.5	.10
Hydrogen (MCFD)	215,000	69.4	1	.69

Nelson Complexity Index Total   11.75

Fig. 7–8 Sample Refinery Complexity Analysis

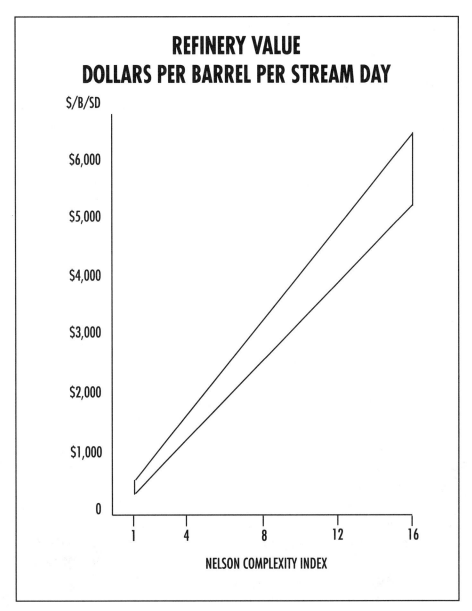

Fig. 7–9 Comparative Valuation Based On Refinery Complexity

REFINERY REPLACEMENT COST

The prices paid in transactions during the late 1980s represented only 60%–70% of the replacement cost of a refinery. The cost to build a modern, medium conversion refinery in the United States in 1991 would range from $5,500 to more than $6,500 per daily barrel. The costs, lead time, and environmental regulations make it nearly prohibitive at this time. It is easier and cheaper to buy refining capacity.

In the mid-1980s, refineries were selling for quite a bit less. This was due primarily to overcapacity. The outlook is much better for the refining industry. Refineries are operating in higher, more comfortable capacity utilization ranges. Strong growth in product demand is expected. The 1990s should be a better decade for the refining industry.

The footnotes and segment information provide data about the book value, earnings, and cash flow attributable to the downstream segment.

Other important factors include: storage facilities, water access, pipeline connections and the capability of refining operations to meet expanding environmental regulations such as low-sulfur diesel or reformulated gasoline.

Gas Stations and Marketing Outlets

The distribution and marketing segments of the industry were subjected to widespread realignment due to mergers in the 1980s. For example, the Chevron-Gulf merger resulted in situations where the new company had two stations (a Gulf and a Chevron station) at the same intersection, just across the street from each other.

Self-service was practically nonexistent in the 1960s. By 1975 self-service accounted for 22% of total gasoline sales. By 1989, self-service accounted for 80% of sales throughout the United States, although self-service is illegal in New Jersey and Oregon.

In metropolitan areas, major oil companies typically market their products through company-owned outlets. In rural areas, the major companies will often sell through brand-name stations leased or owned by *jobbers*. Jobbers are independent businesses that market gasoline and products either through brand name or non-brand name stations. The gasoline marketing industry is rapidly expanding its base to include the convenience store and special services, such as car washes and car-care centers. Modernization is taking place, particularly with the new point-of-sale credit card terminals at the gas pumps.

True service stations receive 50% or more of their business from gasoline sales. Revenues for them range from $600,000 to $1,200,000. The average annual sales was $900,000 from 1984 to 1988. In 1989, this average increased to $1 million. There were 105,561 service stations in 1987, with an average of six employees per station. In 1990, the number of stations had risen to 111,657.

Valuation of a gas station, or a marketing network consisting of a number of stations, is difficult because the profitability of this segment of a company, if it has one, is seldom reported separately. However, there are some guidelines for making an estimate of value.

There are many considerations that cannot be determined from a typical annual report or 10-K.

Value depends on the average markup on the gasoline, and this can be strongly influenced by full-service facilities. Other factors to consider, if the information is available, are whether the property is owned or leased, the primary term of the lease, type of dealership, and size and location of the facilities. The value of the real estate can be an overriding factor. Additional income generating activities would add value to a gas station business.

A small service station may pump 55,000 to 75,000 gallons per month. The average is around 100,000 gallons per month. Volume pumpers may sell 200,000 to more than 300,000 gallons per month.

Gasoline retailers make $0.03 to $0.06 net profit per gallon. Assuming a station sells 100,000 gallons per month, this yields an annual profit on gasoline sales of $36,000 to $72,000. Assuming the value of the station ranged 8–12 times earnings (profit), the value range would be $288,000 to $860,000.

CONVENIENCE STORES

The convenience store (C-stores or minimarts) industry is growing. There were 67,500 outlets in 1987. This was up 6% from the previous year. Total industry sales increased by 11% to $59.6 billion in 1987. Gasoline sales account for approximately 34% of the convenience store sales. The typical C-store pumps from 30,000 to 40,000 gallons of gasoline per month.

C-store sizes range from 800 to 3,500 square feet of floor space. The average profit margin on C-store products is 30% of gross sales. Delicatessen products can carry a 50% profit margin, while soft drinks have a profit margin of up to 70%.

A new convenience store costs $500,000 to $750,000 on the average. The main difference in costs depends on the location. Urban C-stores must spend around twice as much for land as rural locations.

A rule of thumb in the service station industry for valuation of a gas station is that it is worth $0.75 to $1.50 per gallon per month for the gas sales element alone. Therefore, a 100,000 gallon per month gas station would be worth from $75,000 to $150,000, plus other assets. Any additional assets, such as real estate or a convenience store facility, would be added to this. The cost for a new gas station, including purchasing land, can range from $300,000 to $500,000.

Some analysts also compare value of marketing operations on a dollar-per-daily-barrel basis. The range of value is appraised roughly at from $5,500 to $6,500 per daily barrel. With this yardstick, the value of a facility selling 100,000 gallons per month at 42 gallons per barrel would be from $440,000 to $515,000.

Table 7–15 gives a range of values of marketing outlets.

Analysts must contend with limited information when dealing with the refining and marketing segment of an integrated oil company. Usually the book value, identifiable assets, earnings, and cash flow information is commingled. This makes it difficult to segregate the refining from the marketing assets for detailed analysis. Moreover, the annual report and 10-K do not often mention how many marketing outlets are owned and how many are leased. Furthermore, some

Table 7–15 Marketing Outlets—Gas Station Valuation

Facility	Range of Value ($ Thousands)
Gas Station 65,000 gallons per month	$ 200 – 350
Gas Station 100,000 gallons per month	350 – 500
Gas Station 150,000 gallons per month	450 – 650
Small Station 50,000 gallons per month with 1,000 ft² C-store	300 – 500
Small C-Store 30,000 gallons per month with 1,500 ft²	375 – 550
Large C-Store 40,000 gallons per month with 3,500 ft² C-store	650 – 900
Super Station 100,000 gallons per month with 1,000 ft² C-store	650 – 800
Super Station 200,000 gallons per month with 2,000 ft² C-store	900 –1,000

times it is difficult to know just how many of each kind of marketing outlet the company has (owned or leased). There are many considerations of value that are not quantified for the analyst.

Many analysts are aware of the information and statistics outlined in this chapter. Without detailed information, analysts usually must make some general assumptions and make an educated guess at the value of this far downstream segment of a company. Analysts in the late 1980s were appraising marketing outlets at from $400,000 to $500,000 each.

TANKERS

Tankers haul crude oil or petroleum products in bulk. Their size is measured in deadweight tons (DWT). This is the total tonnage (in long tons) of cargo, fuel, water, and stores the ship can carry. Over the years, the size of tankers has grown with demand. Until the 1950s, the T-2 with 16,500 DWT capacity was standard. By the mid-1980s, Very Large Crude Carriers (VLCCs), with over 175,000 DWT, and Ultra Large Crude Carriers (ULCCs), with 300,000 tons, were used. (One long ton equals approximately 7.5 barrels.)

Transportation costs for crude oil from the Persian/Arabian Gulf to the United States (Houston) on a VLCC are approximately $1.25 per barrel.

The average tonnage for a fleet will range from 70,000 to 150,000 DWT per ship. Exxon's fleet of 66 vessels had a combined capacity of 4.8 million DWT in 1989—72,000 DWT average. Amerada Hess has 22 vessels with a combined tonnage of 3 million DWT. The average vessel size in the Amerada fleet is 140,000 DWT. More often than not, this is all the information about a company's fleet that will be available.

The value of a tanker in the early 1980s dropped as world demand for crude and products dipped. For a while, there was a glut of tanker capacity. A range of values is outlined in Table 7–16.

Table 7–16 Summary of Tanker Values

Type	Tonnage DWT	Barrels	Value Old - New ($MM)
T-2	16,500	115,500	5–10
	50,000	375,000	15–20
LCC	100,000	750,000	20–35
VLCC	175,000	1,225,000	25–50
VLCC	250,000	1,875,000	30–55
ULCC	350,000	2,652,000	40–75
ULCC	450,000	3,375,000	60–90

Pipelines and Natural Gas

The pipeline industry in the United States includes the transportation of natural gas, carbon dioxide (CO_2), crude oil, and refined products. Other commodities moved by pipeline are coal, water, and petrochemicals. The natural gas pipeline industry is divided into two categories: distribution and transmission.

A further breakdown of gas transmission companies can be made into intrastate and interstate companies. Intrastate companies, as the name implies, collect and distribute gas within one state and are regulated by less stringent controls than are interstate companies. Interstate transmission companies are heavily regulated by the Federal Energy Regulatory Commission (FERC). The FERC is a regulatory agency of the Department of Energy (DOE). Through the administration of the Natural Gas Policy Act of 1978 (NGPA) and the Natural Gas Act of 1938, the FERC has authority over financial and accounting policies as well as rates charged by these companies for gas or tariffs.

Gas transmission usually begins with the collection or *gathering* of gas at the wellhead from the original producer, but occasionally from other gas transmission companies. The transmission companies deliver the gas to someone other than the ultimate user, i.e., the utilities or local distribution companies (LDCs). The transmission operation could be equated to wholesaling rather than retailing.

Gas distribution companies include the gas utilities. These companies sell gas at the retail level to residential, commercial, and industrial users. Typically, gas distribution companies are heavily regulated by local and state bodies. Figure 7–10 depicts the general structure of the gas pipeline industry.

Gas utilities are subject to control by agencies in the states in which they operate. Like other regulated utilities, gas distribution company regulation is generally based on the price of gas or services charged to customers. Many gathering systems that transport gas from the wellhead to transmission facilities are not regulated.

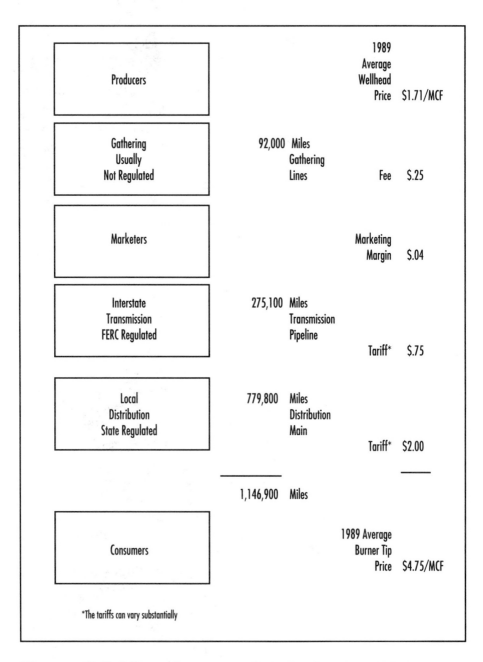

Fig. 7–10 United States Gas Pipeline Industry Structure 1989

Liquids pipelines are different from gas pipelines in that, since early 1981, the price of crude oil and refined products has been free of government control. Liquids pipelines can be divided into two types: crude oil lines and product lines. Mechanically, the operation of these two types of pipelines is similar. The differences between the two and the factor that limits switching from one to the other are the connections to source of supply and the market.

There were approximately 230 companies involved in the interstate pipeline industry in 1990. These companies commonly have more than one type of pipeline. Gas transmission companies often have sister companies that are distribution companies. Companies involved in liquids transportation by pipeline commonly have both crude oil and refined products lines.

INDUSTRY GROWTH

The natural gas industry growth has tracked GNP growth in the United States by a factor of about 75%. That is, if GNP grows by 3% per year, demand for natural gas will grow by 2.25%. Some analysts predict industry growth to outpace GNP in the late 1990s. Gas is the leading fuel for heating homes with a 57% market share in 1988. Revenue distribution for the natural gas industry is broken down in Table 7-17.

Table 7-17 Gas Industry Revenue Structure—1989

	1989 Revenues ($ Billions)	Percent of Total	Average 1989 Gas Price $/MCF
Residential	$ 26.2	55.2%	$5.46
Commercial	11.1	23.3	4.78
Industrial	9.6	20.2	2.81
Other	.6	1.3	3.55
Total	$47.5	100.0	
Weighted Average			$4.75

The average wellhead price for natural gas in 1989 was $1.71 per MCF with over 17,871 BCF of marked production. The average price for residential consumers was $5.46 per MMBtu.

THE WEATHER FACTOR

The market is gauged by calendar year degree days, defined as the average number of degrees below 65 degrees Fahrenheit (°F) times the number of days. Thus if the average temperature for the day drops to 55°F, that equals 10 degree days for that one day. The U.S. average is 4,700 calendar year degree days. It ranges from a high of 6,500 in New England to around 2,500 in the Southwest. The average monthly usage in the United States is 1.5 TCF per month. In December 1989, the weather was 26° colder than normal. This resulted in gas deliveries 22% above normal for that time of year. The country used 2.3 trillion cubic feet (TCF) of gas that month. Annual records of around 2.4 TCF usually occur in January. Sometimes reference is made to *heating season degree days*. The heating season in the United States is October through March. A comparison of calendar year and heating season degree days further illustrates the importance of the cold weather months:

1988   Calendar Year Degree Days   4,798

1988   Heating Season Degree Days   3,622

Seasonal variations in gas demand range from lows of 1.1 TCF per month to 2.2 TCF per month in the winter months. This is why so much discussion in the gas industry focuses on the winter heating season.

RATE DETERMINATION

Regulatory commissions attempt to protect consumers and utility shareholders by setting rates on tariffs or consumer prices that allow a fair rate of return for the utility. The applicable rule is usually stated as follows:

> The public utility, under efficient and economic management, is to be permitted the opportunity to recover revenues sufficient (a) to cover proper operating expenses,

depreciation expense, and taxes and (b) to provide a return on investment adequate to compensate existing investors and attract new capital.

Regulations vary significantly from one state to another, but the basic elements are the same whether or not the entity is under FERC or state control. The steps in establishing utility rates are outlined as follows:

1. Determination of revenue requirement
   • Determine cost of service
   • Determine rate base
   • Calculate the cost of capital
2. Determination of test year
   • Normalization of test year
3. Develop rate design

REVENUE REQUIREMENT

The basic equation used for regulating utilities is known as the *revenue requirement* formula:

Public Utility Revenue Requirement Formula

$$RR = E + d + T + (V - D)r$$

Where:

RR = revenue requirement

E = operating expenses and *cost* of gas

d = depreciation expense

T = taxes

V = gross value of investments used in serving the public

D = accumulated depreciation

r = allowed rate of return on net investment

$(V - D)$ = *rate base* also known as net investment

$(V - D)r$ = earning allowed on the rate base (*cost of capital*)

COST OF SERVICE

The revenue requirement, also referred to as the *cost of service*, includes raw materials, operating expenses, and the cost of transmission and distribution. The cost of gas represents nearly 80% of the operating expense for most gas distribution companies. Increases in the cost of purchased gas are usually passed directly on to consumers, although regulatory bodies monitor prices paid to ensure that consumers are not paying an unfair price for gas. The other major expense that is included in the cost of service is depreciation.

RATE BASE

The net investment, or the *capital employed* for a utility, is referred to as the *rate base*. The rate base consists of direct plant and equipment as well as working capital. Sometimes assets are excluded from the rate-base determination. Regulatory bodies may elect to omit certain investments or excess working capital from the rate base. The essential concept in the utility industry is the *used and useful* concept. Assets employed by a utility may not be included in the rate determination as a part of the rate base unless they are both used and useful.

The rate base for a company may be less than the actual net investments, but will seldom be greater. Furthermore, utilities are often unable to obtain timely rate increases. Because of this, companies will often earn less than the authorized rate of return. Regulatory bodies will typically allow a return on equity from 12.5–15.5%. The average is close to 14%.

The method used in determining how much earning to allow on the rate base is very similar to the determination of cost of capital discussed in Chapter 2. The capitalization structure (percentages of debt and equity) of the company is used to determine cost of capital. If regulatory bodies consider that the cost of capital is abnormally high because of too much equity financing, the regulators may use a theoretical capital structure for the company. For example, if a utility has only 20% debt, the cost of capital would likely be higher than a utility with industry average debt of around 50%. Therefore, the regulatory body may use the industry average debt percentage for determining the rate of return for the utility. This is why some pipeline industry executives talk about being *penalized for being underleveraged.*

DEFERRED TAXES AND THE COST OF CAPITAL

The abstract nature of the deferred tax item was briefly mentioned in Chapter 2 when the concept of cost of capital was discussed. It was discussed further in Chapter 4. The components that comprise the corporate capitalization structure, as it is normally explained, consist of debt and equity. The structure could be further subdivided to include debt, preferred stock, equity, and deferred taxes. Deferred taxes effectively represent an interest-free loan from the government. Regulatory bodies usually require utilities to treat deferred taxes as a zero-cost source of capital in determination of cost of capital, or determination of rate of return on rate base.

TEST YEAR

The *test year* is used to determine basic elements of the revenue requirement. A test year is also used for determining the number of units of sales volume over which to distribute the revenue requirement. The test period may be modified or *normalized* to adjust for unusual situations. For example, suppose that sales during the test year were 90 BCF of gas, but that the test period included a relatively mild winter. The forecast sales volumes for the rate period during which the rates would be applied would most likely be consistent with a normal winter. Therefore, the test year might be normalized to what might be expected for more typical weather.

RATE DESIGN

Once the revenue requirement is determined, it is distributed among the customer classes on the basis of a particular *rate design*. Rate design focuses on what rate to charge each class of customer. Typical rate designs charge less for each unit as usage increases. High volume industrial users will typically pay less for each thousand cubic feet (MCF) of gas purchased. A simplified example is used here with only one class of customer.

Assume that a regulatory commission and a company have agreed on a revenue requirement of $400 million per year. Assume further that, based on the normalized test year, expected sales are 95 BCF in the next rate period. A revenue requirement of $400 million divided by the 95 BCF of gas expected to be sold per year (95 million MCF) yields a rate of $4.21 per MCF.

Table 7–17 illustrates the results of the various rate designs in the United States. High volume industrial customers pay about half the rate paid by residential consumers.

BOOK VALUE MULTIPLES

Gas transmission and utility companies that have been acquired give some indication of the perception of company acquisition value in the market. While the upstream oil industry may seldom make a comparison of acquisition price to book value, it is commonplace in the gas utility industry. This is because regulatory bodies will seldom allow a change in rate base due to a change in ownership. Rates are based on original cost. Any premium over book value will be ignored by regulatory agencies, and this will dilute the rate of return an investor could expect to earn. Nevertheless, utilities are often appraised and acquired on the basis of a multiple of book value. A common trading range for gas pipeline stocks is 1.5–2.0 times book value and acquisitions of gas transmission companies have been taking place at around 2–2.2 times book value.

CASH FLOW MULTIPLES

A traditional valuation multiple for pipeline company appraisal is five times cash flow. Pipeline company acquisitions generally range from five to six times cash flow.

Foreign Operations

Foreign operations are difficult to evaluate from the vantage point of a 10-K report. Usually, there is little information to aid in the analysis of the foreign segments of a company. Segment information will most often allow only a few clues, such as cash flow (net income + DD&A only), reserves, and SEC value of reserves. Every country has different geology, costs, laws, and fiscal regimes. Generalizations are impossible to make.

COUNTRY RISK

There are many elements of risk in doing business overseas. The concept is usually termed *country risk*. The first thing that comes to mind with foreign operations is the specter of nationalization or expropriation of assets. This is a valid concern, but not quite the risk it once was. Countries pay a severe penalty for expropriating the assets of a foreign company. There are other risks associated with foreign operations that are more likely to occur. Analysis of the oil industry and the politics of a country can give some indication of stability. There are a number of things to consider, but they will not be found in the company annual report. Some basic considerations are outlined as follows:

1. How stable is the government?
2. What type of government does the country have?
3. Are the citizens rioting?
4. What kind of neighbors does the country have?
5. Is the country at war or contemplating war?
6. How much of the country is in rebel-held territory?
   There are more than a few companies that have
   secured exploration licenses in rebel territory.
7. How old is the leader?
   Quite often a dictator can be much easier
   to deal with than a democratic government.

Democratic governments have a habit of changing
the tax laws regularly.

8. Is the country a net importer of crude oil?
   Countries that must import oil are usually
   more accommodating to outside oil companies.
9. What is the oil potential of the country?
10. What does the average well produce?
    The prospects must be good enough to
    justify the added expenses and risk.
11. How good are communications and transportation facilities?
12. What is the rate of inflation?
13. What is per capita income in the country?
14. What are the fiscal (tax law) conditions in the country?
    Unfortunately, this information is seldom available.
    The terms under which companies operate in a
    foreign country can vary widely from one
    company to another.

VALUATION OF FOREIGN OIL AND GAS RESERVES

Evaluating the reserves or other assets a company has in a foreign country can be difficult. The fiscal conditions of every country and every province are different. Often each company will have an individually negotiated contract with a host government. The SEC value of reserves quoted in the 10-K is the best source of information about foreign oil and gas reserves. Foreign operations are always segregated. The 10-K SEC value of reserves on a per-unit basis in foreign operations can be compared to the SEC value of the U.S. reserves. Adjustments to the SEC values are somewhat similar.

If the SEC value of reserves in the 10-K report are based on an obsolete oil price, the analyst can make some mental adjustments. If the SEC value of reserves are based, for example, on $12 per barrel oil in the 10-K and oil prices have changed since the reporting date to $18 per barrel, an upward adjustment will often be in order.

FOREIGN EXCHANGE

Foreign exchange laws control the amount of funds that can be expatriated or repatriated, or the amount of local currency that can be converted into an outside currency. Repatriation restrictions are usually imposed to control the level of foreign currency in the host country. For this reason, liquid assets in a foreign subsidiary may be worth less than book value.

Fluctuating exchange rates also add risk to foreign operations.

FOREIGN POTENTIAL

The oil industry in the United States is very mature. This can be seen by the vast number of wells, and by the average rate of production per well, which is quite low. Many foreign countries still have potential for large discoveries with which the onshore United States cannot compete. Alaska may be the one exception. Furthermore, in many countries the chances of making a discovery are also higher than in the United States. The odds are simply better.

Summary

Evaluation of a company in the oil industry can become very complicated and exotic. The industry is certainly capital intensive, but it also has a strange blend of highly evolved technical elements and the sometimes spectacular aspects of risk and reward that make it unique.

Cash flow analysis is the key to both quick-look techniques and detailed analysis of oil companies. Analysts will usually focus on cash flow first and work from there.

It is also important when evaluating oil companies to become familiar with the various assets and methods of estimating the individual asset values. The valuation worksheets of Amerada Hess in Figures 7–11 and 7–12 provide examples. Each business segment and asset group is distinct and requires a different analytical approach.

Company: AMERADA HESS   Date: April 1990

Shares: 81.147 MILLION   Source: 1989 10-K

Current Trading Price of Stock: $45/SHARE

( )

Current Assets	1,951	Current Liabilities	1,458
Other	—	Long-term Debt	2,349
Domestic U.S. Oil and Gas	1,901	Deferred Taxes	199
International Oil and Gas	2,641	Preferred Stock	—
		Minority Interests	—
Acreage Value	282	Other Obligations	103
Refinery Operations	1,725	Other Obligations	—
Marketing Outlets	262		
Tankers	825	Shareholder Appraised Equity	5,487
Other Assets	—		
Total Assets	$9,596	Total Liabilities and Appraised Equity	$9,596

(a) Current Assets and Liabilities from the Balance Sheet
(b) Deferred Taxes = 50% of Value from Balance Sheet
(c) U.S.   Oil   203 MMBBLS @ $6.00/BBL
(d)   Gas   1,050 BCF @ $.65/MCF

(e) Foreign   Oil   367 MMBBLS @ $5.75/BBL
(f)   Gas   1,328 BCF @ $.40/MCF

(g) Acreage U.S.   1,589,000 @ $75/Acre
                  Foreign   3,249,000 @ $50/Acre

(h) Refining   575,000 BOPD @ $3,000/B/SD
                         V.I. Refinery NC Index = 7.5

(i) Marketing   380 Hess Stations @ $500,000 each
                         102 C-Stores @ $700,000 each

(j) Tankers   22 @ $37.5MM each, average 140 DWT

Fig. 7-11 Example Adjusted Balance Sheet Valuation

Company: AMERADA HESS   Date: April 1990

Shares: 81.147 MILLION   Source: 1989 10-K

Current Trading Price of Stock: $45/SHARE

	Observed or Appraised Value ($ MILLIONS)	Weight Factor	Weighted Value
Market Capitalization + Debt =	$7,761		
Book Value $2,561 X 2 =	$5,122	— %	—
Adjusted Balance Sheet Value =	$5,487	30 %	$1,646
Adjusted Earnings $325 X 14 =	4,550	10 %	455
Cash Flow $925 X 5 =	4,625	10 %	463
Discounted Cash Flow Analysis =	5,200	50 %	2,600
TOTAL WEIGHTED VALUE		100%	$5,164

$$\frac{\text{Market Capitalization + Debt}}{\text{Appraised Value of Assets}} = \frac{\$7,761}{\$9,596} = 81\ \%$$

Fig. 7-12 Example Analysis Using the Factored Approach

CORPORATE RESTRUCTURING

THE FAR SIDE By GARY LARSON

"And now Edgar's gone . . . Something's going on around here."

Illus. 8–1

Nothing like a bit of black humor to introduce a sensitive subject. The disappearance of Edgar in Gary Larson's Far Side Cartoon (Illustration 8–1) is a caricature of the oil industry in the 1980s. This was a frustrating time in the oil industry with companies and jobs disappearing at a merciless pace.

The terms *merger* and *acquisition* (M&A) are used together to depict the arena of corporate restructuring. An acquisition differs from a merger in that an acquisition is a broad term that encompasses mergers. In an acquisition, a buyer acquires a *target company*, or *target*, through the purchase of assets, purchase of stock, or a merger. In a merger, two companies are combined. A *statutory merger* is a transaction where one company survives as a legal entity and the other does not. In a *statutory consolidation*, all companies involved cease to exist as legal entities, and a new corporate entity is created.

History

Like many economic and natural phenomena, mergers come in waves. The wave of mergers and acquisitions of the 1980s was the fourth episode of hyperactivity in the M&A history of the United States. A brief summary of the preceding events sheds some light on the latest surge of activity.

THE FIRST WAVE (1889–1904) MONOPOLIES

The first wave created many of the great monopolies, including General Electric, U.S. Steel, and Standard Oil. More than 300 corporate combinations similar to Rockefeller's Standard Oil developed during this period. Around 70 combinations concentrating in heavy manufacturing were monopolies. This wave involved over 15% of the country's industrial assets.

THE SECOND WAVE (1925-1930) OLIGOPOLIES

Mergers and acquisitions during this period involved more than 12,000 companies. The mergers were on a smaller scale than the preceding wave. Only around 10% of the nation's assets were involved this time. The usual objectives were to control the market, and many vertical mergers were constructed.

THE THIRD WAVE (1967-1969) CONGLOMERATES

During the third wave of acquisitions, approximately 25,000 companies were taken over. At the peak in 1969, there were more than 6,000 acquisitions in that year alone. By 1968, more than 100 of the 1962 Fortune 500 companies had disappeared.

THE FOURTH WAVE (1980-1990)

This wave began with the large oil industry mergers of 1980 and 1981. When Dome Petroleum made a tender offer for 13% of Conoco, the industry was shocked to see more than 50% of the shareholders tender their shares, despite the opposition of the Conoco board of directors. Conoco was doomed. Dome ended up with Hudson's Bay Oil and Gas, a 53% owned subsidiary of Conoco. This was Dome's objective from the start. Du Pont acquired the rest of Conoco. Prior to the tender offer by Dome, Conoco stock had been trading at $50 per share. Du Pont paid more than $3.8 billion cash and 82 million shares of Du Pont stock. Prior to the merger, Du Pont stock had traded at $45 per share. The equivalent price paid represented a premium of more than 60% to the Conoco shareholders.

Following the Conoco takeover, the entire oil industry came under scrutiny. From 1981 to 1984, oil industry mergers accounted for 25% of all M&A activity. One difference between this fourth wave and the acquisitions of the 1960s was in the premium paid to shareholders. In the 1960s, the average premium was roughly 10–20%. In the 1980s, premiums were 40–50%, with some extreme examples of premiums of more than 100%.

Corporate management always monitors the stock price. While an oil company stock will usually trade at less than its appraised breakup value, the spread between trading value and breakup value must not be allowed to grow too large.

Merger and Acquisition Driving Forces

Typically, the market focus is on income, and the underlying asset value of a stock is ignored. Because of this, there are situations where the market value of a stock is considerably undervalued relative to asset value. These undervalued situations were the driving force behind the oil and gas industry mergers and acquisitions of the early 1980s.

The primary difference between trading values of stocks and the M&A sales price is that the market consensus of value views a company as a going concern and measures value by earnings and yield. The liquidation value or breakup value is usually greater for oil and gas companies, yet the market will seldom respond unless there is takeover speculation. Oil company stocks, in many cases, were worth more dead than alive, and the differences were often substantial. In the early 1980s, it was not unusual for an energy stock to be trading at half its appraised breakup value. The difference between market value and appraised liquidation value of the stock is called *breakup margin*.

Analysts looking for acquisition candidates would assume that a successful acquisition, hostile or friendly, would require at least a 35%–50% acquisition premium. Suppose for example, that stock for Company X trades at $10 per share with breakup value for the stock estimated at $20 per share. Assuming a 40% premium would be required, the breakup margin would be $6 per share.

	$/Share
Stock trading price	$10
Acquisition premium (40%)	4
Breakup margin	6
Stock liquidation value	$20

Assume that Company X has 20 million shares, and suddenly the exercise becomes interesting. Typically, a raider would identify a situation such as this and begin to buy stock at the market rate until it held slightly less than 5% of the target company's stock. As long as the raider kept its position in the target company at less than 5%, it would be under no obligation to disclose its intentions. When the raider was ready, it would then commence the tender offer with an initial offer of 25–35% above market price.

Ultimately, the takeover, if successful, would be consummated at a premium of 40–50%. If the raider were successful, the profit would essentially be the ultimate breakup value less the acquisition cost. However, if the raider were unsuccessful in the takeover attempt, it would often receive a premium for its stock position when the target company repurchased the shares. This simplified example is summarized in Table 8–1.

In this example, an unsuccessful raid, in terms of return on investment and internal rate of return, is actually better than a successful acquisition. Failure could be very profitable. This gave rise to what is known as *greenmail*. It appeared in many cases that the prospect of losing was actually a raider's objective. The ability of the raider to arrange acquisition funding was at times suspect, but the raiders could manage to fund acquisition of 5% of the stock.

The greenmail was particularly bitter for the target company shareholders. In addition to the premium the raider received for his stock, the target company often had to pay the legal and investment banking services incurred by the raider. There were numerous instances where the combination of these reimbursed expenses and additional profit

Table 8–1 Anatomy of a Raid

COMPANY X
20 million shares

Trading Value $10/share
Appraised Value $20/share

	Successful Raid ($MM)	Unsuccessful Raid ($MM)
Time frame	1 Year	6 Months
Purchase Price		
5% of the stock	$10	$10
95% of the stock		
(40% premium)	$266	
Legal & Financial	$7	$2
Pay off Debt	$30	0
Total	$313	$12
Value of Stock	$400	$15
Margin	$87	$3
Reimbursed Expenses	0	$2
Total Profit	$87 million	$5 million

margins paid to the raider amounted to nothing less than greenmail on the order of $50 to $150 million and more. Because of this, companies started writing *antigreenmail provisions* into their corporate charters.

Margins and profits like those shown in Table 8–1 were not unusual in the energy industry mergers of the 1980s. By 1985, when speculation of mergers or takeovers became widespread, margins began to shrink. After that, the number of viable takeover candidates began to diminish. Table 8–2 shows how the oil industry mergers picked up steam in the early 1980s to peak in 1984 and 1985.

Table 8-2 Milestones in Oil Industry Mergers and Acquisitions

YR	BUYER	COMPANY ACQUIRED	VALUE (Millions)	YR	BUYER	COMPANY ACQUIRED	VALUE (Millions)
76	RJ Reynolds	Burmah Oil & Gas	522		BHP—General Elect	Utah International	2,400
	Marathon Oil	Ecol Ltd	403		Marathon Oil	Husky Oil Co.	505
					Santa Fe Internatnl	WXY Geothermal	350
78	Dome Petroleum	Seibens O&G (60%)	400				
				85	Coastal	American Nat Res	2,452
79	Shell	Belridge	3,600		Royal Dutch/Shell	Shell (USA)	5,700
	Mobil	General Crude Oil Co	792		InterNorth	Houston Natural Gas	2,300
	Carter O & G	Hamilton Brothers O&G	522		Midcon Corp	United Energy	1,160
					Hamilton	Energy Reserve Group	500
80	Freeport Minerals	McMoRan	2,300		Meridian Oil Co	Southland Royalty Co	730
	Dome	Kaiser Pet Ltd	700		Adobe Resources	Madison Oil Co	708
	Sun	Texas Pacific	2,300		Broken Hill U.S.	Monsanto Oil Co	745
	Shareholders	Valero Energy	700				
	Getty Oil Co	Reserve Oil & Gas	628	86	U.S. Steel	TXO	3,700
					Occidental Pet.	Midcon	1,600
81	Du Pont	Conoco	7,800		Shareholders	Anadarko Pet Corp	500
	Dome	Hudson's Bay O&G	1,700		CSX Corp	Sea Land Corp	742
	Kuwait Pet Corp	Santa Fe Intl.	2,400		Atlantic Pet	Ultramar Pet	785
	Elf Acquitane	Texas Gulf	2,400		Louisiana Land & E	Inexco	405
	Sulpetro Ltd	Candel Oil Ltd	550				
				87	LaSalle—OXY	United Gas Pipe Line	620
82	U.S. Steel	Marathon	6,750		Reo Tinto Zink	BP Minerals	4,300
	Occidental	Cities Service	4,100		British Petroleum	SOHIO	7,900
					Goodyear—Exxon	Celeron O&G	650
83	Diamond Shamrock	Natomas	1,400		Introprovincial Pipeline	Home Oil Co Ltd	1,100
	Phillips Pet Co	General American	1,140				
	CSX Corp	Texas Gas Resources	1,100	88	British Petroleum	Britoil Plc	4,340
	InterNorth	Belco Petroleum	800		Total CFP	CSX O & G Corp	612
	Goodyear Tire	Celeron Corp	833		Amoco Canada	Dome Pet	5,500
	Burlington N.	El Paso Co	1,300		Elf Acquitaine	RTZ Corp O&G Div	594
	OXY—Southland	Citgo Pet Corp	800		ESSO Res Canada	Sulpetro	680
	Williams Companies	Northwest Energy Co	886		Sun Exploration	Spin-off	6,000
					Trans Can. Pipe Line	Encor Energy (97%)	1,100
84	Chevron	Gulf	13,400		Southdown Inc	Moore McCormack	530
	Texaco	Getty Oil	10,100				
	Phillips	Aminoil	1,600	89	Panhandle Eastern	TX Eastern	3,223
	Mobil	Superior	5,800				
	Texas Eastern	Petrolane Inc	1,000	90	Imperial Oil	Texaco Canada	4,900
	Southern Pacific RR	Santa Fe Industries	5,200				

In addition to the arena of M&A, there are three basic capital restructuring strategies available to management to enhance stock value and shareholder wealth:

- Spin-off of assets
- Leveraged buyout (LBO)
- Share repurchase

These strategies are demonstrated using a simplified adjusted balance sheet of Company X as shown in Figure 8–1. The appraised value of assets is used rather than book value. Other information is included to show the impact on the balance sheet and on share prices as a result of the different strategies.

COMPANY X
(adjusted balance sheet)

(\$ Millions)

Current Assets	\$50	Current Liab.	\$30
Oil and Gas	150	Long-term Debt	30
Acreage	10	Appraised	
Other	10	Equity	160
	\$220		\$220

10 Million Shares

Appraised Value \$16 per Share

Current Trading Value \$8 per Share
(50% of appraised value)

Debt/Equity Ratio 18.8%

Fig. 8–1 Company X Adjusted Balance Sheet Before Restructuring

Spin-Off (MLP)

The rationale behind most spin-offs is the assumption that, as a separate entity, the spun-off assets will gain a better market response than as part of the whole organization. This approach is simply the unraveling of the conglomerate, and the associated market penalty for integration, diversification, or conglomeration.

In the following example, Company X decides to spin-off half of its oil and gas reserves.

It is assumed that half the oil and gas reserves are spun off, with no immediate tax effect, as a Company X Master Limited Partnership. It is further assumed that the Company X MLP will achieve a market capitalization equal to the appraised present value of the reserves. Figure 8–2 illustrates the results of the restructuring.

With this restructuring strategy, shareholders now hold a share of the Company X MLP for each share of original Company X stock. The combined value of a share of the company's stock and a unit of the MLP is summarized as follows:

	Share Price	
	Before	After
Company X MLP	0	$7.50
Company X Common Stock	$8.00	4.25
	$8.00	$11.75

In this example, the shareholders have achieved a 47% increase in the market value of their holdings in Company X. The debt/appraised equity ratio of Company X has increased from 18.75 to 35%. While the stock was trading at 50% of appraised value prior to restructuring, the market value of the two securities after the spin-off is 73.4% of appraised value.

COMPANY X—Before Spin-off of MLP
($ Millions)

Current Assets	$50	Current Liab.	$30
Oil and Gas	150	Long-term Debt	30
Acreage	10	Appraised	
Other	10	Equity	160
	$220		$220

NEW COMPANY X—With MLP Spun off

Current Assets	$50	Current Liab.	$30
Oil and Gas	75	Long-term Debt	30
Acreage	10	Appraised	
Other	10	Equity	85
	$145		$145

10 Million Shares

Appraised Value $8.50 per Share

Current Trading Value $4.25 per Share
(50% of appraised value)

Debt/Equity Ratio 35%

MLP appraised value = $75 Million (10 Million units)

Fig. 8–2 Corporate Restructuring—Spin-off

THE RESTRUCTURING OF DIAMOND SHAMROCK

In 1987 Diamond Shamrock Corporation spun off its marketing and refining segment to shareholders in a separate company, Diamond Shamrock R&M, Inc. (DRM). The program included a share repurchase program for 20 million shares at $17 per share, and shareholders received a share in DRM for every four shares held in the parent company that had changed its name to Maxus Energy Corp. (Maxus).

Prior to the restructuring, Mesa Limited Partnership had attempted to acquire Diamond Shamrock. The attempt was unsuccessful. Mesa had made a stock exchange offer first in November of 1986, and then a cash tender offer for 20% of the stock that was withdrawn in early 1987. In September and early October of 1986, before Mesa made the initial offer, Diamond Shamrock stock was trading between $11.50 and $12.00 per share. The share values following the spin-off are summarized in Table 8–3.

Table 8–3 MAXUS—Diamond Shamrock R & M—Spin-off

	Share Value		
	Before 9/86	After 5–6/87	
Diamond Shamrock Corp. (100 Shares)	$1,175	$ 340	Share Repurchase Program (20 Shares) $17.00/Share
		920	MAXUS (80 Shares) $11.50/Share
		325	Diamond Shamrock R&M (20 Shares) $16.25/Share
	$ 1,175	$1,585	
		$ 410	Increase—35%

Leveraged Buyout

Typically, an investor group purchases all of the stock of a company in a leveraged buyout (LBO). It is sometimes called *going private*. Usually about 10% of the purchase price is provided up front by the investor group, while the rest is borrowed. An LBO candidate is characterized by strong cash flow. As a rule of thumb, a successful LBO should retire the acquisition debt out of cash flow within five to six years.

An LBO by management, or a management buyout (MBO), is effectively the same as an LBO, but more specifically includes management of the company being acquired in the acquisition team. The LBO does not necessarily mean that management is involved as buyers.

An LBO could be structured so that the executive officers of Company X borrow the funds and tender for 100% of the shares. Assuming a 50% premium would be required, management would need to borrow $120 million. The shareholders gain a 50% increase in value. The new company structure after the LBO is shown in Figure 8-3.

In this example, management borrowed 100% of the acquisition funds. On paper, management has made $40 million, the net appraised value. The total combined debt now equals 82% of the total assets.

Share Repurchase

In a share repurchase tender offer, a company offers to buy back a specific amount of stock at a given price. The tender offer price is usually at a premium of 10–15% above the stock's market price. The tender offer usually has an expiration date of three to four weeks. The company can set limits on the amount of stock it will repurchase, but can reserve the right to extend the offer or buy more stock than specified.

COMPANY X—Before LBO
($ Millions)

Current Assets	$50	Current Liab.	$30
Oil and Gas	150	Long-term Debt	30
Acreage	10	Appraised	
Other	10	Equity	160
	$220		$220

NEW COMPANY X—After LBO

Current Assets	$50	Current Liab.	$30
Oil and Gas	150	Long-term Debt	120
Acreage	10	Appraised	
Other	10	Equity	40
	$220		$220

Fig. 8–3. Corporate Restructuring—Leveraged Buyout

Share repurchases may be done with excess capital, if it is available. Debt may also be used to finance a repurchase program. The disadvantages are that financial strength may be reduced as net worth drops and debt is incurred. The market usually responds favorably to a stock repurchase program. It sends a strong signal of management optimism.

Company X could decide to repurchase 25% of its outstanding stock. Assume that Company X borrowed $22 million to repurchase 2.5 million shares at a 10% premium above market price. The resulting impact on shareholder wealth is demonstrated in Figure 8–4.

COMPANY X—Before Share Repurchase
($ Millions)

Current Assets	$50	Current Liab.	$30
Oil and Gas	150	Long-term Debt	30
Acreage	10	Appraised	
Other	10	Equity	160
	$220		$220

NEW COMPANY X—After Repurchase

Current Assets	$50	Current Liab.	$30
Oil and Gas	150	Long-term Debt	52
Acreage	10	Appraised	
Other	10	Equity	138
	$220		$220

7.5 Million Shares

Appraised Value $18.40 per Share

Current Trading Value $9.20 per Share
(50% of appraised value)

Debt/Equity Ratio 37.7%

Fig. 8–4 Corporate Restructuring—Share Repurchase Program

Appraised equity decreased 13.7% from $160 million to $138 million. Equity per share increased 15% from $16.00 to $18.40 per share. Assuming the stock would trade at 50% of appraised value, the new share price would be $9.20 per share. Essentially, the company will have purchased $22 million of reserves at 45% less than the present value of those reserves. The ability to obtain properties at a lower price than would be available elsewhere is the main reason for a stock repurchase program. A repurchase program can also have a beneficial effect on stock prices by enhancing shareholder value and in some cases reducing volatility in stock prices.

Most share repurchases by corporations take place when the stock is trading at a value that is perceived by management to be low. For example, if the P/E ratio is 5, the effective return would be 20%. If the dividend yield is high, the company may benefit from savings on dividend payments. From the shareholders' point of view, a share repurchase can also result in tax savings. Dividends are taxed at the corporate level and at the shareholder level. Therefore, if excess cash is distributed to shareholders in a stock repurchase, corporate income tax is avoided.

FAIR PRICE REQUIREMENT

With transactions involving independent shareholders, management has a fiduciary duty to represent them fairly. Management is obligated to make full and complete disclosure of all facts pertinent to the transaction. This is particularly important with a share repurchase or an MBO. In each of these cases, management may have knowledge that shareholders do not have.

In 1984, Royal Dutch Petroleum Company acquired the minority shares of its subsidiary, Shell Oil Company. The Royal Dutch/Shell Group indirectly controlled 69.5% of the outstanding common stock of Shell Oil and had direct representation on the board of directors. On December 3, 1990, the *Oil & Gas Journal* reported that a Delaware chancery court had awarded $30 million to former Shell Oil Company stockholders. The court ruled that the Shell Oil Company board of directors had failed in their fiduciary duty of *complete candor*. The court determined that Shell had failed to fully disclose $1 billion in oil and gas reserves.

VALUATION OF BONDS AND PREFERRED STOCK

People once thought of bonds as long-term investments. This is no longer the case. Investors do not buy bonds any more with the intention of holding them until maturity. They buy bonds in the hope that interest rates will decline and bond prices will rise. While they wait for this to happen, they can collect interest.

A frequent comparison is made between shareholders who actually have purchased a piece of the company, and bondholders who have simply loaned money to the company. However, shareholders, like their counterparts, seldom feel the warmth of ownership. They simply buy a stock with the hope that the stock price will rise, and while waiting, they can often collect dividends.

Bonds

It is important for an analyst to understand a company's financial needs and its capital structure. The basic tools of bond and credit analysis must be understood and applied.

Bonds are sold primarily by corporations, municipalities, and the federal government, and state and federal agencies. Typically, bond traders refer to bond issues as *municipals, corporates, governments,* or *agencies.*

When a corporation incurs long-term debt through a bond issue, it has certain obligations. First, it must redeem the debt certificate at face value. Second, fixed periodic payments must be paid to the debt holder. The face value of bonds is usually $1,000. This is also called *par value*, or *principal*. Municipal bonds usually carry a face value of $5,000. Unlike corporate bonds, interest on municipals is exempt from federal income tax. State and local taxes can usually be avoided as well if the bond holder is a resident.

Bonds can sometimes be backed by collateral, but are usually only backed by the *full faith and credit* of the borrower. Such uncollateralized bonds are called *debentures*.

Bonds and preferred stock are *senior securities*, which represent corporate indebtedness, while common stock signifies ownership. Common shareholders can benefit from corporate growth through increased dividends or stock price increases. Bondholders or preferred stockholders cannot benefit directly from such growth. They are only entitled to repayment of fixed interest payments and principal. If the company fails, they have preferential rights over the common shareholders and must be paid before the common stockholders receive anything.

The market for bonds is several times larger than the stock market. At times bonds have accounted for as much as 80% of all new corporate financing. Nearly the same number of individuals who own bonds own common stock. Most bonds are purchased by big institutions, pension funds, and insurance agencies. They are governed by the bond ratings and the levels of risk they will accept.

Bonds are thought to be a safer and more conservative investment than common stock. While common stock can experience erratic price changes, bond prices generally are not as volatile, although bond prices will fluctuate with changes in interest rates. This is referred to as *interest rate risk*. If interest rates go up, bond prices go down. If interest rates go down, bond prices go up. But if interest rates go down, bonds can often be redeemed by the borrower with a *call option*. If the bonds are *callable*, the borrower may redeem the bonds and then borrow elsewhere at lower rates. Interest rates must go down far enough to justify exercising the call option. A call option, or *call provision*, associated with a bond is a right of the bond issuer to repurchase the bonds at a predetermined price. Usually, call provisions require that bonds be redeemed at face value plus one additional coupon payment.

The maturity of bond certificates is usually 10–30 years. The periodic payments made to the debt holder are referred to as the *coupon*. The coupon is stated as a percentage of face value, such as a 10% coupon. The expected return on a bond involves more than just the coupon rate. While face value of a bond is usually $1,000, a bond does not always cost $1,000. It may cost more, or it may cost less.

The formula for the value of a bond is:

$$V = R \frac{1 - \left[\frac{1}{(1 + i)^n}\right]}{i} + \frac{\$1,000}{(1 + i)^n}$$

Where:
  V = bond value
  R = the payment per period (coupon)
  n = the number of periods
  i = applicable market interest rate

This formula combines the present value formulas for the payment stream (coupons) and the payment of the face value of the bond (in this case, $1,000) at maturity. For example, if the market rate of interest is 10%, an investor should be willing to pay $878 for a $1,000 bond that pays an $80 per year coupon and matures in 10 years.

$$V = \$80 \frac{1 - \left[\frac{1}{1/(1 + .10)^{10}}\right]}{.10} + \frac{\$1,000}{(1 + .10)^{10}}$$

$$= \$80(6.15) + \$1,000/2.59$$

$$= \$492 + \$386$$

$$= \$878$$

YIELD AND YIELD TO MATURITY

The yield of a bond, also referred to as *current yield*, is the coupon rate, or interest rate divided by the bond price. In the above example, the yield on a bond that cost $878 and paid $80 is:

$$\$80/878 \ = \ 9.1\%$$

The *yield to maturity* (*YTM*) of a bond represents the *internal rate of return* (*IRR*) of the bond. This concept assumes that a bond is purchased at prevailing market prices and is held to maturity. The *YTM* can be calculated by algebraically solving for *i* in the present value formula. This gives the present value of the stream of interest payments and the payment of principal at maturity. The formula for approximating the *YTM* is:

$$YTM = \frac{\text{coupon} + \text{annual appreciation}}{\text{average investment}} = \frac{R + (V - P)/n}{(V + P)/2}$$

Where:

YTM = Yield to Maturity
R = coupon or payment per period
V = par (face) value of bond
n = number of time periods
P = price paid for the bond

For example, consider a $1,000 face value bond with a $35 annual coupon purchased for $900 which matures in 10 years. It has a yield to maturity of 9%.

$$YTM = \frac{35 + [(1,000 - 900)/10]}{(1,000 + 900)/2}$$

$$= \frac{35 + 10}{50}$$

$$= 9\%$$

BOND RATINGS

Bond ratings are a qualitative measure of credit risk performed by independent rating services. This is independent of the interest rate risk associated with bond price fluctuations resulting from interest rate changes. Four prominent firms that perform bond rating services are Standard & Poor's Corporation (S&P), Moody's Investor Service, Duff and Phelps, and Fitch Investor's Service. They perform a formal evaluation of a company's credit history and its ability to repay bond obligations. Ratings are then published that are a measure of risk associated with those bonds. Preferred stocks also have ratings similar to bond ratings.

The rating agencies use a system of letters to indicate their view of a bond's credit rating. The highest rating for a bond is usually AAA, or *Triple A* (see Table 9–1).

A bond is described as having a s*plit rating* if there is a difference between the ratings given to a bond by the different rating agencies. It is rare for a split rating to be more than one grade apart. For example, Moody's may rate a series of bonds at Aaa, while Fitch might rate them AA. Bonds are rated at the time they are issued. This initial rating affects the marketability of the bonds as well as the effective interest payment. The quality of a bond is periodically reviewed by the rating services. The rating effects the marketability and price in the secondary market long after the primary issue. The secondary market is trading that occurs after the initial bond offering.

Table 9–1 Corporate Bond Credit Ratings

Leading Bond Rating Services Explanation of Corporate and Municipal Bond Ratings	Rating Service			
	Fitch	Moody's	S&P	Duff & Phelps
Investment Grade				
Highest Credit Quality Only slightly more risk than U.S. Treasury debt	AAA	Aaa	AAA	1
High Quality Modest Risk	AA+ AA AA–	Aa1 Aa2 Aa3	AA+ AA AA–	2 3 4
Upper Medium Grade Good Credit Quality	A+ A A–	A1 A2 A3	A+ A A–	5 6 7
Medium Grade Adequate Credit Risk	BBB+ BBB BBB–	Baa1 Baa2 Baa3	BBB+ BBB BBB–	8 9 10
Below Investment Grade				
Predominantly Speculative Junk bond territory obligations may be met	BB+ BB BB–	Ba1 Ba2 Ba3	BB+ BB BB–	11 12 13
Speculative—Low Grade Moderate risk of default on obligations when due	B+ B B–	B1 B2 B3	B+ B B–	14 15 16
Highest Speculation High risk of default	CCC CC CC	Caa Ca Ca	CC CC CC	17
Lowest Quality— Interest not being paid	C	C	C	
In Default	DDD DD D	D	D	

Table 9-1 provides a comparison of the nomenclature used for bond ratings. The distinction is shown between ratings for bonds that are *investment grade* and those that are not. This designation usually defines the risk level beyond which institutional investors will not go. Portfolio managers who have special fiduciary obligations, such as those investing for pension funds, will not invest in bonds below investment grade. These below-investment-grade bonds are often called *junk bonds*.

Standard & Poor's may add a plus or minus sign to further define a rating. Moody's will add a 1 such as a Baa1 to indicate highest quality bonds within a particular category. Bond analysts who rate bonds examine a company's financial condition using the same analytical techniques as those used in appraising common stock. The bond ratings have significant implications for bond values and for interest rates on bonds. Table 9-2 indicates the general rates of interest for different classes of bond ratings. Ordinarily, the greater the risk, the lower the price relative to the face value and interest rate. The greater the risk, the lower the rating and the higher the interest rate on the bond.

Table 9-2 Comparison of Bond Interest Rates

Moody's Corporate Bonds	1987	1988	1989
Aaa	9.38%	9.71%	9.26%
Aa	9.68	9.94	9.46
A	9.99	10.24	9.74
Baa	10.58	10.83	10.18
30-Yr Treasuries	8.64%	8.98%	8.45%

Source: *Federal Reserve Bulletin,* September 1990

Typical bond ratings for the utilities/gas pipeline companies, which comprise the more highly leveraged segment of the oil industry, are usually upper medium grade, Moody's A2 or Standard & Poor's A grade. In the early 1980s, the integrated oil companies' bond ratings carried an average rating of Aa1 to Aa3. By 1988, the average rating for integrated oil companies had dropped to A2.

With common stocks, the yield is equal to the annual dividend divided by the stock price. Bonds are seldom purchased at their face or par value. A bond's price and the bond yield always move in opposite directions.

With a bond trading at par, the YTM, current yield, and the coupon rate are equal. If the bond is purchased at a discount or at a premium, the YTM can be less or more than the current yield. These relationships are shown in Table 9-3.

Table 9-3 Example Bond Prices and Yields

$1,000 par value Bond

Coupon	Bond Price	Type of Bond Price	Current Yield	YTM*
$90	$ 900	Discount	10%	10.5%
$90	1,000	Par	9%	9%
$90	1,100	Premium	8.8%	8.4%

*Assumes a 10-year maturity

A bond is identified by the issuing company, the interest rate, and the year of maturity. For example, CompX10½93 is the nomenclature used by financial reporting agencies to identify a bond issued by Company X that pays a 10½% coupon maturing in 1993. Because bonds usually are issued at $1,000 face value, the interest rate of 10.5% is equivalent to a coupon rate of $105 per year, usually paid semiannually.

CALL PROVISIONS

Most bonds are now issued with call options giving the issuer the right to retire a bond before its maturity date. These provisions are similar to the call options associated with preferred stock. These provisions give the issuer flexibility to respond to fluctuations in the level of interest rates. For example, suppose a bond is issued with a 9% coupon during a period of high interest rates which subsequently decline. At the new level of interest rates the same bond could be issued with a 7% coupon. The interest savings could be substantial. The concept of defeasance of debt was discussed in Chapter 4, where new high-interest rate bonds were effectively substituted for old low-interest rate debt. Call provisions typically require the bond to be redeemed at a premium equal to one year's interest. For example, prior to maturity, a 9% coupon bond might be called at $1,090. Due to the similarity between bonds and preferred stock, the valuation techniques are virtually identical.

Preferred Stock

Preferred stock is often called a *hybrid security*. There are many types of preferred stock. Depending on the provisions, options, and call features, the stock can have more or less of the characteristics of debt or equity. From the lender's point of view, preferred stock is considered a class of equity, since preferred stock claims on assets are always junior to debt. Preferred dividends, like bond interest payments, are paid out of operating income before earnings to common shareholders are computed. Therefore, shareholders view most preferred stock as debt. An equity analyst usually treats preferred stock as though it were debt.

This is one of the more philosophical areas in financial theory, and some discussion of just where preferred stock lies is worthwhile. Some preferred stocks carry mandatory redemption requirements and, therefore, are more characteristic of pure debt. They should be treated as such by the analyst. As the level of debt increases in the capital structure, the cost of debt increases, and corporate debt can take on the costly and volatile attributes of equity. This gets a bit complex. The point being that the assets of a company are subject to an entire spectrum of claims, and there is sometimes no clear division between debt and equity.

Table 9–4 shows the spectrum of corporate debt and equity.

Table 9–4 Corporate Capital Structure—Financial Spectrum

PURE DEBT	Lowest Risks Lower Costs	First Mortgage Bonds Senior Secured Bonds Junior Secured Debt Debentures (not collateralized)
QUASI-DEBT HYBRID SECURITIES		Convertible Bonds (usually subordinate) Redeemable Preferred Stock Preferred Stock with fixed maturity or sinking fund requirements
QUASI-EQUITY		Second Preferred (subsequent issue) Cumulative Preferred Income Bond or Adjustment Bond interest not guaranteed Convertible Preferred Noncumulative preferred with no provisions
PURE EQUITY	Highest Risks Higher Costs	for repayment of principal Common Stock

For practical purposes, and particularly for purposes of analyzing the value of common equity, preferred stock is almost always treated as though it were corporate debt. But preferred stock is almost always inferior to other debt. Unlike corporate bonds, failure to pay a preferred stock dividend does not constitute default. Failure to pay required interest and principal on a bond does.

Price appreciation resulting from increased earnings will benefit common shareholders, not bond holders or preferred shareholders. As a result, common stock is more earnings sensitive, while bonds and preferred stock are interest-rate sensitive. Increasing interest rates will decrease the value of bonds and preferred stock, while decreasing interest rates will enhance the value of these fixed-payment instruments.

It is important to estimate market value of preferred stock when trying to arrive at a value of common stock. This is especially true when estimating liquidation value. Because preferred stock is considered from an accounting point of view to be a class of equity, it will sometimes be booked at par value, which can be substantially less than its liquidation value.

The dividend payments of a preferred stock can be considered a perpetuity. Under that assumption, the valuation of preferred stock is:

$$\text{Market Value} = \frac{\text{Annual dividend}}{\text{Market rate of interest}}$$

Assume, for example, a preferred stock that has no conversion features pays a dividend of $5 per share. If the market rate of interest for preferred stocks is 9%, then the value of the preferred stock is $55.55:

$$\text{Market Value} = \frac{\$5}{.09}$$

$$= \$55.55 \text{ per share}$$

When evaluating preferred stock, the key is knowing what the market rate of interest is for preferred stock. This can be determined by examining the dividend-to-price ratio for preferred stocks. Table 9–5 summarizes preferred stock statistics for Standard and Poor's corporate series. The market rate of interest for preferred stock shown in this table for 1989 is around 9%. This is also the market rate of interest for most of the preferred stock in the petroleum industry.

247

Table 9–5 Preferred Stock Ratios

	1987	1988	1989
Dividend/Price Ratio [1] Preferred Stocks	8.37%	9.23%	9.05%
Price/Dividend Multiple [2] Preferred Stocks	11.9	10.8	11.1
Dividend/Price Ratio [3] Common Stocks	3.08%	3.64%	3.45%

[1] Standard and Poor's corporate series based upon sample of 10 issues: four public companies, four industrials, one financial, and one transportation (yield)

Market rate of interest for preferred stocks is equal to the dividend/price ratio (yield)

[2] Multiple is equal to inverse of dividend/price ratio

[3] Standard & Poor's 500 (yield)

Source: *Federal Reserve Bulletin*, September 1990

CUMULATIVE PREFERRED STOCK

Cumulative preferred stock allows dividends to accumulate if they are not paid. If dividends are interrupted, the accumulated unpaid balance must be paid before dividend distributions to common stock can be made. With noncumulative preferred stock, the dividend payment will be lost if the issuer chooses to skip a payment.

CONVERTIBLE PREFERRED

Convertible preferred stock can be converted into common stock at a predetermined exchange ratio. Call options are particularly important when evaluating preferred stocks or bonds. Call provisions outline the call price, time, and how much notice an issuer must give prior to redemption. The most common call provision is a *standard call*. Usually the standard call stipulates that for the first 5–10 years following the issue, the stock or bond may be redeemed by the company at its call price. The call price is often defined as the issue price plus one year's dividend, or coupon, in the case of bonds. The call price would include accrued dividends, if there are any.

Another common type of call provision is the *conventional call*. The conventional call usually states that the company may force redemption at a specified price (or price schedule), plus accrued dividends with 30–60 days' notice. The premium paid for the conventional call is usually higher than for a standard call. But with the conventional call, the issuer is not restricted to a cash redemption and may redeem the preferred with common stock.

Preferred stock typically trades on current yield. The method of calculating the yield on preferred stock is similar to the YTM formula for a bond. The current yield calculation is referred to as the yield-to-call (*YTC*) formula.

Preferred Stock Yield-to-Call Formula

$$YTC = \frac{\text{Annual dividend} - \dfrac{(\text{price} - \text{call price})}{\text{number of years held}}}{\dfrac{(\text{price} + \text{call price})}{2}}$$

Assume, for example, that a preferred issue is selling at $115 per share and pays a $9 cumulative annual dividend. The current yield is 7.8% ($9/$115). The stock is redeemable at $100 in five years. The *YTC*, assuming the stock is redeemed at that time, is 11.16%:

249

$$YTC = \frac{\$9.00 - (115 - 100)/5}{\dfrac{(115 + 100)}{2}}$$

$$= \frac{\$9.00 - 3.00}{107.5}$$

$$= 6/107.5$$

$$= 5.58\%$$

The market value of the preferred stock in the example would be estimated by calculating the present value of the dividend stream (for the five years) as well as the $100 call price. This is similar to estimating the value of a bond.

$$V = R \frac{1 - \left[\dfrac{1}{(1 + i)^n}\right]}{i} + \frac{\$1,000}{(1+i)^n}$$

Where:

V = value of the preferred stock
R = the payment per period (dividend)
n = the number of periods
i = applicable market interest rate

This formula combines the present value formulas for the preferred dividend stream and the payment of the call price at maturity. For example, with a market rate of interest at 9%, an investor should be willing to pay $89.22 for preferred stock paying a $9 annual dividend and carrying a call price of $100 in five years.

$$V = \$9 \frac{1 - \dfrac{1}{(1 + .12)^5}}{.12} + \frac{\$100}{(1 + .12)^5}$$

$$= \$9(3.6) + 1.76 \frac{\$100}{}$$

$$= \$32.4 + \$56.8$$

$$= \$89.22$$

TAX CONSIDERATIONS

Preferred stock has a unique tax feature for corporate holders for whom 70% of preferred dividends are not taxed. Therefore, only corporations should hold preferred stock. The tax effect of preferred stock is governed by the tax rate and the percentage of the preferred dividend that is subject to tax. The calculation is shown by the following formula:

$$\text{After-tax Yield} = R - [R \times (1 - (P \times T))]$$

Where:

R = dividend rate
T = tax rate
P = percentage of dividend subject to tax

Assume a preferred stock dividend rate is 9% and the corporate tax rate is 34%. The after-tax yield is 8.08%.

$$\text{After-tax Yield} = 9\% - \left[9\% \times (1 - (.70 \times .34)) \right]$$

$$= 8.08\%$$

LEGAL AND TAX ENVIRONMENT FOR MERGERS

Legislation drafted over the past 100 years to govern mergers and acquisitions tells quite a story. Corporate raiding is not a new concept. The aggressive nature of many raiders is a timeless characteristic fueled by the potential for vast profits and power. Legislation always seems to be a few steps behind the action, but eventually legal guidelines are formed to try to create a fair and just business environment. In the United States, it started with the Sherman Antitrust Act of 1890.

Laws and Regulatory Agencies

SHERMAN ANTITRUST ACT OF 1890

Federal legislation designed to prevent monopolies and restraint of trade essentially began with the Sherman Antitrust Act. Prior to this, people thought of a trust as a fund managed by a trustee for minors or widows. This legislation prohibited acts or contracts that tended to create monopolies or trusts. Nevertheless, between 1889 and 1904, U.S. industrialists formed 318 corporate combinations similar to Rockefeller's Standard Oil. Created in 1882, it is considered the first of the great trusts. The Standard Oil Trust controlled over 30 subsidiary companies. It was governed by a board of trustees consisting of Rockefeller and seven associates. The subsidiary companies granted their voting stock in return for trust certificates. The trust certificates gave the bearer the right to receive interest payments. The trustees then had the power to set prices and control marketing policies for all of the subsidiary companies. As a corporate device, the trust, or *voting trust*, was abandoned soon after the passage of the Act, but *holding companyies* or *interlocking directorates* took its place. A holding company was a single firm that acquired all, or the majority of, the voting stock of its subsidiaries.

In 1889, the state of New Jersey passed legislation dealing with corporate law that made the holding company structure possible. Standard Oil Company then became Standard Oil of New Jersey. Companies or subsidiaries controlled by holding companies were supposedly independent, but directors and management were controlled by the holding companies. Holding companies created during this era had substantial influence over the timber, flour-milling, meat-packing, sugar, steel, tobacco, cottonseed oil, whiskey, salt, lead, and leather industries. These trusts abused their power. They forced customers to pay secret rebates and manipulated consumers by controlling production and fixing prices.

In 1890, John Sherman and other Republican leaders passed the Sherman Antitrust Act to satisfy the rising public outrage against the trusts. At that time, there was not much of a move to enforce the law. It is ironic that the passage of the Act preceded the first big wave of mergers and acquisitions that spawned so many monopolistic giants. Eventually the Sherman Antitrust Act provided the foundation for the era of trust-busting, which ultimately dissolved Standard Oil in 1911. In that year, the Supreme Court ruled that Standard Oil Company had conspired "to drive others from the field and exclude them from their right to trade." The Court ordered that the company be dissolved.

CLAYTON ANTITRUST ACT OF 1914

In 1914, Congress passed the Federal Trade Commission Act and the Clayton Act in support of the Sherman Act. The Clayton Antitrust Act was passed as an amendment to the Sherman Act to define certain unlawful practices not specifically identified in the Sherman Act. The Clayton Act dealt with some of the flagrant abuses of interlocking directorates. This made it illegal for a person to hold membership on the board of directors of competing companies. It provided further limitations upon holding companies and restraint of trade. Section 7 of the Clayton Act prohibits any merger "where that effect . . . may be to substantially lessen competition" or that may "tend to create a monopoly."

The Robinson-Patman Act, passed in 1936, amended Section 2 of the Clayton Act. The price-discrimination provisions of the Clayton Act were broadly rewritten by the amendment. Another major amendment to the Clayton Act, the Cellar-Kefauver Act of 1950, expanded the scope of Section 7 of the Clayton Act. The most common grounds for antitrust violations under this section of the Clayton Act involve horizontal mergers. Here competition is reduced when competitors combine directly to do business in the same general product or service in the same geographic area. An example of the influence of this legislation is the result of the Mobil-Marathon takeover battle. Mobil had offered $5.1 billion for Marathon in September of 1981. On December 1, 1981, the bid was halted on antitrust grounds. Had this acquisition been contemplated in the mid-1980s, it is unlikely that the injunction would have been rendered against the bid. The politics and attitudes of the times had changed.

Either of the two antitrust authorities, the Justice Department or the Federal Trade Commission (FTC), may terminate a prospective merger. Traditionally, the FTC concentrates on consumer-oriented industries, such as food and beverage or soaps, while the Justice Department concentrates on the structure of basic industries, such as steel and petroleum.

Other grounds for antitrust violations deal with the horizontal merger of competitors in a highly concentrated industry. Horizontal mergers are assessed according to the degree of concentration and the impact of a proposed transaction on the degree of concentration. The Hirshman-Herfindahl Index created in 1982 is used by the Justice Department to measure market power or concentration. Prior to this, the tests of market concentration were less formal. The index is derived by adding the sum of the square of the market share of each producer in a given market. For example, if there were six companies in a market with shares of 25%, 25%, 20%, 15%, 10%, and 5%, the Hirshman-Herfindahl Index would be:

$$(25^2 + 25^2 + 20^2 + 15^2 + 10^2 + 5^2) = 2,000$$

If one of the largest firms with a 25% share were to merge with the smallest firm with a 5% share, then the new concentration would be:

$$(30^2 + 25^2 + 20^2 + 15^2 + 10^2) = 2,250$$

The index, as a result of the merger, would increase by 250. This is a relatively large increase in the index. Table 10–1 outlines the Justice Department's 1984 merger guidelines defining the general thresholds at that time.

Table 10–1 Hirshman-Herfindahl Index Guidelines
(Early 1980s)

Concentration	Hirshman- Herfindahl Index at time of Merger	Increase in HH Index as a result of the merger	Likelihood of Justice Department Challenge
Unconcentrated	0–999	Not Applicable	Extremely unlikely
Moderately Concentrated	1000–1800	Less than 100 More than 100	Unlikely More likely than not
Highly Concentrated	Above 1800	Less than 50 50–100	Unlikely More likely than not
		More than 100	Likely

There have been times when this formula was gospel, but federal enforcement of the antitrust statutes has been lax the last few years. This is perhaps one reason why the states have enacted antitrust legislation similar to the Clayton Act.

STATE ANTITRUST LAWS AND M&A LEGISLATION

During the 1980s, many states began to enact or upgrade antitrust laws, and enforcement was stepped up. Sometimes the best defense a company had was the antitrust laws of the state in which they were incorporated, or where the principal business interests were located. Even where the FTC and Justice Department did not block a proposed transaction, the state attorney generals could impose challenges. While the federal government focuses on the disclosure and antitrust aspects, the state regulatory bodies govern matters of procedure and mechanics of the deals. The Supreme Court has upheld the so-called *second generation* statutes passed by the state legislatures.

The states will sometimes restrict or limit the payment of *greenmail* to a raiding company. The state regulatory process can take up to four to six months.

FEDERAL TRADE COMMISSION ACT OF 1914

This act created the Federal Trade Commission (FTC) and gave it power to conduct investigations and issue orders preventing unfair practices in interstate commerce. The FTC was established with powers complimenting the existing authority of the Justice Department and designed to improve enforcement of the FTC Act and the Clayton Act.

The Commission received wide latitude to create guidelines outlining fair and unfair methods of competition.

SECURITIES ACT OF 1933

The Securities Act of 1933 was the first law enacted by Congress to regulate the securities markets. The legislation was designed to stabilize the securities industry by requiring registration of securities prior to public sale and disclosure of pertinent financial data and other information. The legislation also contained antifraud provisions prohibiting false representations.

SECURITIES AND EXCHANGE ACT OF 1934

In 1934, the Securities and Exchange Commission (SEC) was established as a regulatory body to administer and enforce the Securities Act of 1933 and the Securities Exchange Act of 1934. The SEC would also regulate securities listed on national securities exchanges, as well as over-the-counter markets, by maintaining a continuous disclosure system.

In addition to the Securities Acts of 1933 and 1934, the SEC administrative responsibilities have been expanded by the Public Utility Holding Company Act of 1935, the Trust Indenture Act of 1939, the Investment Company Act of 1940, the Investment Advisors Act of 1940, and the Securities Acts Amendments of 1975. The SEC Act of 1934 applies mostly to tender offers and the response of target companies to the offer. It has a direct bearing on the actions a board of directors must take following an *unsolicited* offer.

The Board of Directors

The board of directors of a target company has a right and a fiduciary obligation to fend off a hostile takeover attempt if the attempt is not in the best interests of the shareholders. If a board decides to put the company up for sale, the board members are charged with the responsibility of maximizing shareholder value.

There are five main forms of unsolicited acquisition efforts:

- tender offers
- exchange offers
- open market accumulation
- proxy contests
- "bear hug" letters

THE WILLIAMS ACT

The Williams Act was enacted in 1968 as a result of the wave of unannounced takeovers in the 1960s. The Williams Act and amendments to the Act now comprise Sections 13 (d) and 14 (d) of the Securities Exchange Act of 1934. This legislation primarily deals with regulations concerning the bidder in a tender offer.

This legislation details specific information which must be disclosed about a tender offer or acquisition of more than 5% of a company's stock. It was developed to protect shareholders and management from sudden takeover attempts. These were known in the early 1960s as *Saturday Night Specials*, where first word of a takeover would be a public tender offer. The legislation also ended what was referred to as the *creeping tender.*

Following are some of the commonly encountered rules of the SEC that deal with tender offers.

Rule 13 (d). The 13 (d) filing is the one most people are familiar with. Any person or entity acquiring direct or beneficial ownership of 5% or more of another corporation's stock must file a statement on Schedule 13 (d) with the SEC within 10 days. The purchaser must also file a 13 (d) with the stock exchange where the target company's shares are listed and with the target company. This statement must detail specific information about the entity or person who has acquired the stock and what their intentions are. This rule is designed to protect against unfair takeover attempts and to keep stockholders and the market, in general, aware of material information that could affect the price of the stock. The filing of a 13 (d) may be the first indication that a substantial block of stock has been acquired. Prior to the 10-day filing deadline following acquisition of over 5% of the stock, the acquirer may purchase additional stock so that at the time of the filing, the acquirer may own substantially more than 5%.

One of the most common complaints from corporate management about the 13 (d) filing is that there is virtually no penalty against a raiding company if it misfiles a 13 (d). A misfiled 13 (d) has either false, misleading, or incomplete information. Virtually the only penalty in the past 10 years for a misfiled 13 (d) is that the document must be amended and refiled. In some takeover actions, numerous 13 (d) forms were submitted and resubmitted. There is a lot of room for better enforcement of this rule.

Rule 13(e)-3. This is called the *going private rule*, and requires that management's offer to independent shareholders be in good faith and constitute fair value as determined by two qualified independent people. These are called *fairness opinions*. Information concerning the nature of the transaction, source of funds, reports, opinions, terms, and conditions are reported to the SEC.

Rule 13(e)-4. This tender offer statement includes information about the offer, source of funds, purpose of the offer, financial information, and other information.

Rule 13 (g). This is an annual filing requirement for companies that have ownership of 5% or more in other companies.

Rule 14 (a). This rule deals with disclosure requirements under a proxy fight.

Rule 14 (d). Tender offer regulations, restrictions, and related disclosure requirements are covered under this rule. At the time a tender offer is made to shareholders, a 14 (d)-1 must be filed with the SEC outlining the nature of the tender offer and other information similar to the 13 (d) filing.

Rule 14(d)-2. This rule deals with the commencement of the tender offer. Usually, the date the offer is first published is considered the commencement date.

Rule 14(d)-4 and 14(d)-6. Specific information about the terms of the offer, the identity of the bidder and the bidder's background, intentions, and source of capital must be disseminated to security holders of the target company. Other 14(d) disclosure requirements include such things as purpose of the offer, financial statements of both target company and acquirer, and any other material information.

Rule 14(d)-5. A stockholder list may be requested by the bidder, and the target may elect to either mail the bidder's tender offer material at the bidder's expense, or furnish the list to the bidder.

RULES CONCERNING THE TARGET COMPANY

Rule 14(e)-2. Within 10 business days, the target company must make a statement that it:

1. recommends acceptance or rejection of the offer
2. remains neutral, or
3. is unable to take a position.

Rule 14(d)-9. The target company recommendations and communications to stockholders must be filed with the SEC, the bidder, and the appropriate stock exchanges on Schedule 14(d)-9, called a *solicitation/ recommendation statement*. It must include reasons for the recommendations or any inability to take a position.

HART-SCOTT-RODINO ACT OF 1976

This Act requires that the Federal Trade Commission and the Justice Department review a proposed transaction in light of federal antitrust laws before consummation of a merger. Prior to the Hart-Scott-Rodino Act (HSR Act), there were no disclosure requirements to the antitrust agencies, nor were the transactions subject to antitrust provisions.

General requirements. A bidder may not purchase 15% (or $15 million) or more of the target company's voting stock unless certain information is filed with the Justice Department and the FTC, and the required waiting periods have been observed. This allows government regulatory agencies time to conduct investigations and block a merger if that is required before consummation.

Waiting Periods. The HSR Act requires a premerger notification (*file and wait*) period of 15 calendar days commencing at the time of filing by the bidder in a cash tender offer, or 30 calendar days for all other types of transactions. If the offer is other than a cash tender offer, the waiting period is 30 days. However, waiting periods may be terminated early at the discretion of the government.

Requests for Additional Information. The government may also request additional information. If the request is made to the bidder, the waiting period can be extended 20 days from the date of compliance with the request. In an all-cash tender offer, the waiting period is extended 10 days.

Target Company. The target company must also file certain information, but any delay in filing or responding to requests for additional information does not extend the waiting period.

Time Periods Governing Tender Offers:
1. The minimum offering period—20 days.
2. The initial period during which shares may be withdrawn—15 business days.
3. Outside date after which shares not purchased may be withdrawn—60 calendar days.
4. Additional withdrawal period after commencement of competing offer by a person other than target company—10 business days.
5. Minimum offering period following an increase in price or any material change in the offer—10 business days.

Early termination. At the discretion of the government, if neither agency intends to take any enforcement action, the waiting periods may be terminated early. Early termination can be particularly important in a hostile tender offer, or in a competitive offer situation where prenotification requirements may otherwise favor a particular party.

Table 10-2 Timing of a Cash Tender Offer

Business Days	Raider	Target Company Board of Directors	Target Company Shareholders
	Raider purchases over 5% of stock has 10 days to file 13(d)[1]		
1	Tender Offer Commences • HSR Filing • File 14(d)-1 with SEC and appropriate stock exchanges • File with state and other regulatory agencies		
10		Must • File Position Statement with SEC • Send shareholders its recommendations regarding offer	
15	Initial HSR waiting period ends[2]		Maximum withdrawal period expires
20			Proration period expires for a partial offer
			Minimum offer period expires[3]

[1]Does not necessarily precede tender offer
[2]HSR waiting period is 15 calendar days for cash tender offer and 30 days for exchange offer
[3]This chronology reflects only the most significant events relating to a transaction

A raider has unlimited time to acquire up to 5% of the target company's stock and prepare a tender offer and strategy. This gives the advantage of preplanning and surprise. A raider has total control over the timing of the offer. Within a 20-business day time period, the target board of directors must:

1. Respond to the offer
2. Develop a defensive strategy
3. Implement that strategy

The board of directors has a fiduciary responsibility to the shareholders to exercise in good faith business judgment in making decisions. In the absence of self-interest, fraud, bad faith, gross overreaching, or abuse of discretion, courts will not interfere with *exercise of business judgment.*

Definition of a Tender Offer. While the federal securities laws do not define a tender offer, the SEC has outlined eight factors that distinguish tender offers from non-tender offer transactions:

1. Active widespread solicitation of public shareholders
2. Solicitation for a substantial percentage of stock
3. The offer to purchase at a premium
4. Terms of the offer are firm—not negotiable
5. Offer contingent on the tender of a fixed minimum number of shares
6. The offer open for a limited time period
7. Offerees subjected to pressure to sell stock
8. Public announcement of a purchasing program preceding or accompaning a rapid accumulation of shares

Tax Environment

There are many considerations that impact the selection of the appropriate accounting method for a corporate merger. The major concern involves the determination of whether a transaction is to be classified as a *pooling of interests* or as a *purchase*. These are the two methods of accounting for mergers.

Most acquisitions during the 1980s were accounted for with the purchase method. The pooling of interests method is subject to rigorous conditions and is less frequently used.

POOLING OF INTERESTS

The pooling of interests method of accounting is employed whenever voting common stock is issued to acquire voting common stock. The purpose of this accounting method is to present two or more previously independent entities as a single entity. With pooling of interests accounting, the resources of both companies are pooled, and the balance sheet values of both companies are added together.

The primary condition of independence for the acquiring compan, is that it can not own more that 10% of the total outstanding voting stock of the acquired company prior to the merger. A transaction can be classified as a pooling of interests when two companies are combined in such a way that:

1. The stockholders of both companies maintain an interest in the combined company
2. The management of both companies continue with the combined entity
3. The resources contributed by each company are reasonably comparable
4. The nature of operations of the companies remains essentially unchanged after the merger.

The philosophy behind the pooling of interests concept is that a mutual advantage should be achieved by combining the resources of two businesses. Unfortunately, the accounting method allowed numerous abuses. Excessive payments for acquisitions could be buried in the balance sheet. For example, with the pooling method the book values of the two companies assets and liabilities are added together. The difference between the new total assets and liabilities is the new *equity* of the merged enterprise. If one company gave up more value than it received, the excess would be charged effectively against equity of the merged enterprise and would never show up in the income statement. Therefore, in order for a transaction to qualify, the requirements are rigorous.

Another characteristic of the pooling method is that the earnings of both companies are included for the full year even if the merger took place at the end of the year. Prior years are restated on a pro forma basis to show how the earnings would have been stated if the merger had occurred earlier.

One characteristic of the pooling method of accounting is that when, through an exchange of shares, a company acquires another company with a lower P/E ratio the combined P/E ratio will always increase. This has inspired many acquisitions.

Table 10–3 demonstrates the impact on consolidated financial statements of the pooling of interests method of accounting for a merger. It is assumed in this case that on the last day of the year, Company B acquires Company A for stock with a market value of $100 million and a par value of $25 million.

PURCHASE METHOD

If a transaction does not qualify for pooling of interests accounting, it must be accounted for as a purchase. The purchase method of accounting for a business combination usually involves cash transactions or whenever assets are acquired. A transaction may be considered a purchase when:

Table 10–3 Consolidation Under the Pooling of Interests Method
($ MILLIONS)

Income Statements	Acquired Company A	Acquiring Company B	Consolidated Statement Pooling of Interests
Net Sales	$200	$500	$700
Less Cost of Sales	150	350	500
Gross Profit	50	150	200
Less Selling Expenses	20	100	120
Net Income (BT)	30	50	80
Less Taxes	10	17	27
Net Income (AT)	$20	$33	$53
Balance Sheets			
Working Capital	$50	$140	$190
Net Fixed Assets	25	50	75
Goodwill	0	0	0
Total Net Assets	$75	$190	$265
Capital			
Common Stock	25	50	75
Retained Earnings	50	140	190
Total Capital	$75	$190	$265

1. Proprietary interests of the stockholders of the nonsurviving entity are terminated
2. Management of the nonsurviving company is terminated
3. The nature of the business of one of the companies is substantially changed
4. There is a large difference in the size of the companies

None of these conditions is considered to be conclusive. The governing factor is determined by the intent of the parties as indicated by the structure of the merger.

The acquired assets are appraised and recorded at their FMV at the time of the acquisition. Goodwill is based on the difference between book value and FMV. In a purchase of assets, if the amount paid exceeds the book value of the net assets, the excess may be handled in one of two ways. It may be treated as goodwill and accounted for as an intangible asset. The other method of handling the payment in excess of book value is to add it to the book value of the PP&E. In either case, it would be amortized over a period of years and deducted from earnings. However, amortization of goodwill is often not tax deductible.

Table 10–4 demonstrates the impact on the consolidated financial statements of the purchase method of accounting for a merger. It is assumed that Company B acquires Company A for $100 million cash on the last day of the year. The acquiring company adds the earnings of the acquired company only from the date of acquisition. There is no addition to earnings in the example because the transaction occurred on the last day of the year for this example.

THE TRANSACTION STRUCTURE

Tax laws allow a corporate merger to be structured as either a taxable transaction or a tax-free transaction. In a taxable transaction, the seller recognizes a gain or a loss on the sale of stock or assets. Depending on the nature of the assets, a gain will be treated as either an ordinary gain or a capital gain.

Table 10–4 Consolidation Under the Purchase Method
($ MILLIONS)

Income Statements	Acquired Company A	Acquiring Company B	Consolidated Statement — Pooling of Interests
Net Sales	$200	$500	$500
Less Cost of Sales	150	350	350
Gross Profit	50	150	150
Less Selling Expenses	20	100	100
Net Income (BT)	30	50	50
Less Taxes	10	17	17
Net Income (AT)	$20	$33	$33

Balance Sheets

Working Capital	$50	$140	$90*
Net Fixed Assets	25	50	75
Goodwill	0	0	25
Total Net Assets	$75	$190	$190

Capital:

Common Stock	$25	$50	$50
Retained Earnings	50	140	140
Total Capital	$75	$190	$190

*$100 million paid to Company A shareholders in "Purchase" (as opposed to "Pooling")

Assets acquired for cash in a taxable transaction will have a new basis equal to the price paid. Depreciation deductions will then be based upon the new basis.

There are many types of taxable transactions. The most common element of taxable transactions is that the proprietary interests held by the selling company or its stockholders are completely, or at least substantially, terminated.

TAX-FREE TRANSACTION

The term "tax-free" is actually a misnomer. Tax code provisions that govern mergers hold the buyer responsible for recapture taxes. The seller must pay taxes for the *boot* and deferred taxes upon sale of equity. The boot is the nonequity portion of the seller's compensation. The proportion of equity to nonequity determines if the transaction will be classed as a Type A, B, or C transaction for tax purposes. The so-called tax-free transactions require that a large portion of the consideration be in the form of equity.

TYPES OF CORPORATE REORGANIZATION

There are seven basic types of corporate reorganization defined by Section 368 of the 1954 Internal Revenue Code. These reorganizations are designated in tax literature according to the subparagraph to which they refer. Thus, a *Type A* reorganization refers to subparagraph *A*, which deals with a statutory merger or consolidation. The three main methods of reorganization are the Types *A*, *B*, and *C*.

Type A Reorganization. The Type A reorganization, or consolidation from two original entities, is essentially a statutory merger in which the acquiring company absorbs another company, and a separate and distinct legal entity is formed. This is usually the most common and most flexible of the tax-free reorganizations as far as the type of consideration (payment) is concerned. Stock (common or preferred, voting or nonvoting) is exchanged for stock.

269

The advantage of the Type A reorganization is that a minimum of 50% in value of the acquisition price must be in the form of stock. The remaining 50% can consist of cash, warrants, or debt securities. The stock-for-stock exchange in such cases is tax free to the shareholders. The exchange of stock for assets may not affect the tax-free status of the merger, but shareholders may be subject to some adverse tax consequences.

In a Type A reorganization, the tax attributes of the disappearing entity will be carried over to the surviving corporation. The purchase method of accounting for a Type A merger would result in the purchase price being allocated among the assets being acquired; therefore, it would not be the appropriate method. The pooling method would be the appropriate accounting method.

Type B Reorganization. A Type B reorganization, often called a stock-for-stock reorganization, is less flexible, and the methods of payment are limited. Type B reorganizations are the second most common means of structuring a deal. Under the Type B reorganization, the only consideration that can be used by the acquiring company is its own voting stock that can include preferred stock or the voting stock of its parent company, but not a combination of both. The acquiring company can only exchange its stock for the stock of the acquired company. Immediately following acquisition, the acquiring company must have control of the acquired company. Control means possession at least 80% of the total combined voting power of all classes of stock entitled to vote and at least 80% of all other classes of stock of the corporation.

In a Type B reorganization, the purchase method of accounting would not be appropriate. Since the consideration consists only of voting stock, the pooling of interests method is the appropriate accounting method for the acquisition.

Type C Reorganization. A Type C reorganization is basically a stock-for-assets exchange and probably the least common type of merger. It is often referred to as a *practical merger* because of the similarity to the Type A exchange. The acquiring company buys the assets of the acquired company outright. The acquiring company is often just a shell, with its only asset being the stock of the acquired corporation. It is usually liquidated after its assets have been acquired.

Type C exchanges differ from Type B exchanges because the acquiring company must purchase substantially all of the target company's assets for stock. The remainder can be purchased for any other form of consideration. In a Type B exchange, once 80% of the stock is acquired, subsequent acquisitions will still qualify as a Type B exchange. In addition, the acquired company must distribute the stock, securities, and other properties it receives, as well as its other properties, pursuant to the plan of reorganization.

Because assets are acquired in a Type C exchange, the purchase method should be used rather than the pooling of interests method of accounting. Table 10-5 summarizes the legal and tax treatment for various types of acquisition strategies.

Table 10–5 Summary of Legal and Tax Treatment of Transactions

		Legal Treatment		New Cost Basis
	Taxable	Acquisition of Stock	Acquisition of Assets	
Asset Acquisition	Yes	No	Yes	Yes
338 Transaction	Yes	Yes	No	Yes
Stock Acquisition	Yes	Yes	No	No
Type A Reorganization	No	Yes	No	No
Type B Reorganization	No	Yes	No	No
Type C Reorganization	No	No	Yes	No

COMMENTARY

O il companies once were headed primarily by geologists and petroleum engineers. Today these companies are being run more frequently by people with financial backgrounds. The financial role has become more complicated and more critical. It has also expanded. Ten years ago, the now-common management positions in investor relations were almost nonexistent. This is a sign of the times.

There are more than 50 million shareholders in the United States alone who either directly or indirectly own about 25% of the public common stock. Any well-balanced stock portfolio should have some oil company stocks. Hopefully, this book has provided helpful information for both financial and nonfinancial professionals as well as interested shareholders and analysts.

An understanding of the basic principles of financial management is critical for all elements of corporate leadership. Nonfinancial managers and personnel need to know how their efforts fit into their company's agenda. Furthermore, financial managers and analysts are better equipped with an understanding of the technical and operational aspects of this industry.

Oil company analysis requires a blend of financial theory and an understanding of the technical aspects that characterize the industry. Knowing how a company compares with its peers can provide additional insight.

Basic fundamentals outlined in this book provide a good foundation. An analyst can go a long way with these fundamentals, common sense, and intuition. There are many ways to evaluate a company with lots of room for creativity. Furthermore, there are nearly always surprises, and reading company financial reports can be interesting. Even casual reading of an annual report will often indicate whether or not management has a defined business plan and a clear vision of its place in the industry. It will also probably indicate whether or not the company is staying on course. Companies that do not chart a course and stay on it invariably have problems.

The rampant industry restructuring that occurred in the 1980s was the result of laws that allowed an atmosphere favorable to corporate raiders and market forces that focused on earnings. With stocks trading at substantial discounts to underlying asset values, raiders were willing to pay relatively heavy premiums for control of these assets. The natural tendency to grow through integration and diversification carried substantial risks. If the market did not respond favorably, and share prices became too undervalued, the companies were vulnerable.

Either these same conditions will reoccur or different conditions will promote the next wave of restructuring activity. Management and professionals must be alert and informed to be able to protect their companies, their shareholders, and their jobs.

The regulatory trend lately has been toward more open disclosure and greater shareholder rights. This should make financial analysis both easier and more interesting. Reporting requirements are substantially greater and more helpful to the analyst than they were even 15 years ago. With the combination of enhanced shareholder rights and increased institutional shareholdings, management will be faced with new dynamics in the realm of corporate control.

The influence of environmental considerations was just emerging 10 years ago, and few people anticipated the huge impact that already is being felt. Particularly in the downstream sector of the oil industry, environmental laws will have a gigantic effect.

Faced with the dynamics of change on many fronts, oil industry professionals and shareholders will benefit by becoming better informed about both financial and operational aspects of the business. I hope this book will help.

—Daniel Johnston

APPENDICES

Appendix 1 • Abbreviations

ASE	American Stock Exchange
ADR	American Depositary Receipt
ADV	Ad Valorem Tax
AMEX	American Stock Exchange
API	American Petroleum Institute
Arb	Arbitrageur
ARPS	Adjustable Rate Preferred Stock
BS	Balance Sheet
B/D	Broker-Dealer
B/CD	Barrels per Calendar Day (refinery: 365 days)
B/SD	Barrels per Stream Day (usually 330 days)
BBL	Barrel (crude or condensate) 42 U.S. Gallons
BCF	Billion Cubic Feet of Gas
BCPD	Barrels of Condensate Per Day
BOE	Barrels of Oil Equivalent (see COE)
BOPD	Barrels of Oil Per Day
BOEPD	Barrels of Oil Equivalent Per Day
BWPD	Barrels of Water Per Day
BTU	British Thermal Unit
CA	Current Assets
CAPM	Capital Asset Pricing Model
CD	Certificate of Deposit
CEO	Chief Executive Officer
CFO	Chief Financial Officer
CIF	Cost, Insurance, and Freight
CME	Chicago Mercantile Exchange
COE	Crude Oil Equivalent (also called BOE)
D&B	Dunn and Bradstreet
DCF	Discounted Cash Flow
DCFM	Discounted Cash Flow Method
DDB	Double Declining Balance Method
DD&A	Depreciation, Depletion, and Amortization

DJIA	Dow Jones Industrial Average
DJTA	Dow Jones Transportation Average
DJUA	Dow Jones Utility Average
EBIT	Earnings Before Interest and Taxes
EBITD	Earnings Before Interest, Taxes, and DD&A
EBITXD	Earnings Before Interest, Taxes, Exploration Expenses, and DD&A
EBO	Employee Buyout
EBO	Equivalent Barrels of Oil (see BOE and COE)
EIA	Energy Information Administration
EMV	Expected Monetary Value
EOR	Enhanced Oil Recovery
EPR	Earnings Price Ratio
EPS	Earnings Per Share
ESOP	Employee Stock Ownership Plan
FASB	Financial Accounting Standards Board
FC	Full Cost Accounting
FIFO	First-in, First-out
FIT	Federal Income Tax
FMV	Fair Market Value
FOB	Free On Board
FY	Fiscal Year
GAAP	Generally Accepted Accounting Principles
GAO	General Accounting Office
G&A	General and Administrative Expenses
G&G	Geological and Geophysical
IDC	Intangible Drilling Costs
IPO	Initial Public Offering
IR	Investor Relations
IRB	Industrial Revenue Bond
IRR	Internal Rate of Return
IRS	Internal Revenue Service
ITC	Investment Tax Credit
LBO	Leveraged Buy Out
L/C	Letter of Credit

LDC	Less Developed Country
LDC	Local Distribution Company
LDC	Long Distance Carrier
L/I	Letter of Intent
LIBOR	London Interbank Offered Rate
LIFO	Last-In, First-Out
LNG	Liquified Natural Gas
LP	Limited Partnership
Ltd	Limited Liability
LPG	Liquid Petroleum Gas
M&A	Mergers and Acquisitions
MBBLS	Thousand Barrels
MBO	Management Buyout
MCFD	Thousand Cubic Feet of gas per Day
MMBBLS	Million Barrels
MMCF	Million Cubic Feet of gas
MSE	Midwest Stock Exchange
NASDAQ	National Association of Securities Dealers Automated Quotation
NAV	Net Asset Value
NGL	Natural Gas Liquids
NOL	Net Operating Loss
NPV	Net Present Value
NRI	Net Revenue Interest
NYFE	New York Futures Exchange
NYM	New York Mercantile Exchange
NYSE	New York Stock Exchange
OCS	Outer Continental Shelf
OPEC	Organization of Petroleum Exporting Countries
OPM	Options Pricing Model
ORI	Overriding Royalty Interest
ORRI	Overriding Royalty Interest
OTC	Over The Counter
P&L	Profit and Loss Statement
PE	Price Earnings Ratio

PFD	Preferred Stock
PLC	(British) Public Limited Company
PR	Public Relations
PSE	Pacific Stock Exchange
PUC	Public Utilities Commission
PUHCA	Public Utilities Holding Company Act
PV	Present Value
PVP	Present Value Profits
R&D	Research and Development
RI	Royalty Interests
RLI	Reserve Life Index
ROA	Return on Assets
ROC	Return on Capital
ROE	Return on Equity
ROI	Return on Investment
RRA	Reserve Recognition Accounting
RT	Royalty Trust
S&P	Standard and Poor's
SE	Shareholders' Equity
SE	Successful-efforts Accounting
SEC	Securities and Exchange Commission
SF	Sinking Fund
TCF	Trillion Cubic Feet of Gas
TLCB	Tax Loss Carry Back
TLCF	Tax Loss Carry Forward
VAT	Value-added Tax
WI	Working Interest
WPT	Windfall Profits Tax
YLD	Yield
YTC	Yield to Call
YTM	Yield to Maturity
$/bbl	Dollars per Barrel
$/BOE	Dollars per Barrel of Oil Equivalent
$/BOPD	Dollars per Barrel of Oil per Day
$/MCF	Dollars per Thousand Cubic Feet of gas
$/MCFD	Dollars per Thousand Cubic Feet of gas per day

Appendix 2
Selected Energy Statistics—United States • 1988

Stripper Oil Wells	454,150	Average Production	2.7 BOPD
Other Wells	158,298	Average Production	44.0 BOPD
Total U.S. Oil Wells	612,448	Average Production	13.3 BOPD
Total Gas Wells	256,004	Average Production	200 MCFD

Average Daily Oil Production	8,140,000 BOPD
Average Daily Gas Production	50,000,000 MCFD
Seismic Crew Count	2,161
Active Drilling Rigs	936

Wells Drilled

Oil	13,582
Gas	8,789
Dry	10,670
Total	33,041

Proved U.S. Reserves

Oil	26,825	MMbbls
Gas	168	TCF
NGL	8,238	MMbbls

Reserve Life Index

Oil	9.5 Years
Gas	10.1 Years

Source: United States Department of Energy—
Energy Information Administration,
American Petroleum Institute,
Independent Petroleum Association of America,
Baker Hughes Rig Count,
Seismic Crew Count Society of Exploration Geophysicists

Appendix 3
Production Statistics for Key Energy States • 1989

	Average Daily Production Rate Per Well		Statewide Average Daily Oil Production	Percent U.S. Production
	Oil BOPD	Gas MCFD	MBOPD	(Rounded)
Alaska	1,400	12,484	1,871	26%
California	21	710	912	13
Colorado	14	135	90	1
Kansas	3	108	148	2
Louisiana	14	333	312	4
Michigan	9	279	49	1
Mississippi	20	575	71	1
Montana	14	46	58	1
New Mexico	10	108	175	3
North Dakota	28	1,463	96	1
Oklahoma	3	198	271	4
Texas	10	267	1,784	25
Utah	22	210	49	1
Wyoming	21	745	247	4
Gulf of Mexico	189	4,070	660	9
Total			7,788	96%
U.S. Average	12	178		

Source: United States Department of Energy,
Energy Information Administration,
World Oil

Appendix 4
Severance and Production Taxes for
Key Energy States • 1990

	OIL (%)	GAS	State Reported Production Taxes as Percentage of Gross O&G Revenues (%)
Alaska	12.5–15	10	10.4
California[1]			6.5
Colorado[2]	2–5	2–5%	1.7
Kansas[2]	8	8%	9.25
Louisiana[2]	12.5	$.07/MCF	2.37
Michigan[2]	4–6.6	5%	5.73
Mississippi	6	6%	6.1
Montana[2]	5	2.65%	13.4
New Mexico[2]	3.75	$.163/MCF	10.9
North Dakota[2]	5	5%	8.65
Oklahoma[2]	7.085	7.085%	6.7
Texas	4.6	7.5%	5.2
Utah[2]	4	4%	2.9
Wyoming	6	6%	6.0

[1]California uses a Mineral Properties Tax of 2 ½ cents per barrel.

[2]There are too many exemptions for and exceptions to the severance taxes to list them all. Most exemptions are for marginal or stripper wells and EOR operations.

Appendix 5
1988 Energy Statistics—Selected Countries

	1988 Daily Oi Production MBOPD	Estimated Reserves 1/1/1989 MMbbls	Producing Oil Wells	Average Rate Per Well BOPD
NORTH AMERICA				
United States	9,814	26,825	616,821	13
Canada	1,378	6,975	39,355	35
Mexico	2,583	53,012	3,704	697
North America Total	13,775	86,812	659,880	18
SOUTH AMERICA				
Argentina	446	2,280	8,822	51
Brazil	576	2,883	5,363	107
Columbia	374	2,196	3,039	123
Ecuador[1]	309	1,155	926	333
Venezuela[1]	1,903	59,794	11,943	160
Other	342	1,390	7,513	46
South America Total	3,950	69,698	37,606	105
AFRICA				
Algeria[1]	1,030	8,400	870	1,184
Egypt	856	4,643	850	1,008
Gabon[1]	158	960	305	518
Libya[1]	1,039	22,380	1,015	1,023
Nigeria[1]	1,514	16,000	1,816	834
Other	902	6,352	1,118	807
Africa Total	5,499	58,735	5,974	920

	1988 Daily Oi Production MBOPD	Estimated Reserves 1/1/1989 MMbbls	Producing Oil Wells	Average Rate Per Well BOPD
MIDDLE EAST				
Iran[1]	1,650	63,000	648	2,546
Iraq[1]	2,740	99,000	652	4,202
Kuwait[1]	1,288	96,030	490	2,628
Saudi Arabia[1]	4,928	254,959	579	8,511
U.A.E.[1]	1,570	56,139	1,133	1,385
Other	1,835	15,680	2,624	700
Middle East Total	14,011	584,808	6,126	2,287
FAR EAST				
Australia—NZ	53	2,639	68	637
Brunei—Malaysia	675	4,579	1,090	620
China	2,740	22,000	36,141	76
India	656	4,464	2,350	279
Indonesia[1]	1,315	8,352	5,883	223
Other	125	785	6,298	20
Far East Total	6,064	42,819	52,630	115
Total OPEC	17,402	688,814	26,434	748
World Total	60,039	923,558	768,154 [2]	77

[1] OPEC Countries
[2] Excludes Eastern Block countries

Source: *World Oil,*
 Oil & Gas Journal,
 United States Department of Energy

Appendix 6
Wholesale Oil & Gas Prices—Total U.S.
1935-1990

Year	Oil $/bbl	Gas $/MCF	Year	Oil $/bbl	Gas $/MCF
1935	0.97	.06	1965	2.86	.16
1936	1.09	.06	1966	2.88	.16
1937	1.17	.05	1967	2.92	.16
1938	1.14	.05	1968	2.94	.16
1939	1.04	.05	1969	3.09	.17
1940	1.02	.05	1970	3.18	.17
1941	1.14	.05	1971	3.39	.18
1942	1.20	.05	1972	3.39	.18
1943	1.20	.05	1973	3.89	.22
1944	1.20	.05	1974	6.87	.30
1945	1.20	.05	1975	7.67	.45
1946	1.39	.05	1976	8.19	.59
1947	1.93	.06	1977	8.57	.80
1948	2.60	.07	1978	9.00	.91
1949	2.54	.06	1979	12.64	1.81
1950	2.51	.07	1980	21.59	1.59
1951	2.53	.07	1981	31.77	1.98
1952	2.53	.08	1982	28.52	2.43
1953	2.68	.09	1983	26.19	2.59
1954	2.78	.10	1984	25.88	2.68
1955	2.77	.10	1985	23.88	2.63
1956	2.79	.11	1986	12.66	1.38
1957	3.09	.11	1987	15.60	1.65
1958	3.01	.12	1988	12.58	1.69
1959	2.90	.13	1989	15.89	1.71
1960	2.88	.14	1990	19.75	1.69
1961	2.89	.15	1991	——	——
1962	2.90	.16	1992	——	——
1963	2.89	.16	1993	——	——
1964	2.88	.15	1994	——	——

Source: Energy Information Administration

Appendix 7
Conversion Factors for Energy

Btu Equivalents: Oil, Gas, Coal, and Electricity

One British Thermal Unit (Btu) is equal to the heat required to raise the temperature of one pound of water (approximately one pint) one degree Fahrenheit at or near its point of maximum density.

One barrel (42 gallons) of crude oil
= 5,800,000 Btus of energy
= 5,614 cubic feet of natural gas
= 0.22 tons of bituminous coal
= 1,700 kw hours of electricity

One cubic foot of natural gas (dry)
= 1,032 Btus of energy
= 0.000178 barrels of oil
= 0.000040 tons of bituminous coal
= 0.30 kw hours of electricity

One short ton (2,000 pounds) of bituminous coal
= 26,200,000 Btus of energy
= 5.42 barrels of oil
= 25,314 cubic feet of natural gas
= 7,679 kw hours of electricity

One kilowatt (kw) hour of electricity
= 3,412 Btus of energy
= 0.000588 barrels of oil
= 3.306 cubic feet of natural gas
= 0.00013 tons of bituminous coal

METRIC CONVERSIONS
One metric ton of crude oil
= 2,204 pounds
= 7–7.5 barrels of oil

One cubic meter of natural gas
= 35.314 cubic feet

One cubic meter of liquid
= 6.2888 barrels

One liter of liquid
= 1.057 quarts

Distance
1 foot	= 0.305 meters
1 meter	= 3.281 feet
1 statute mile	= 1.609 kilometers
	= 0.868 nautical miles
1 nautical mile	= 1.852 kilometers
	= 1.1515 statute miles

Area
1 square mile	= 640 acres = 2.59 square km
	= 59.0 square hectares
1 square kilometer	= 0.368 miles = 100 hectares
	= 247.1 acres
1 acre	= 43560 square feet
	= 0.405 hectares
1 hectare	= 2.471 acres

Volume
1 cubic foot	= 0.028317 cubic meters
1 cubic meter	= 35.514667 cubic feet
1 cubic meter	= 6.2898 barrels
1 U.S. gallon	= 3.7854 liters
1 liter	= 0.2642 U.S. gallons
1 barrel	= 42 gallons = 158.99 liters

Weight
1 short ton	= 0.907185 metric tons
	= 0.892857 long tons
	= 2000 pounds
1 long ton	= 1.01605 metric tons
	= 1.120 short tons
	= 2240 pounds
1 metric ton	= 0.98421 long tons
	= 1.10231 short tons
	= 2204.6 pounds

Appendix 8
Present Value of One-time Payment

$$\text{Present Value of \$1} = \frac{1}{(1+i)^{(n-.5)}}$$

(Midyear discounting)

Period (n)	5%	10%	15%	20%	25%	30%	35%
1	.976	.953	.933	.913	.894	.877	.861
2	.929	.867	.811	.761	.716	.765	.638
3	.885	.788	.705	.634	.572	.519	.472
4	.843	.717	.613	.528	.458	.339	.350
5	.803	.651	.533	.440	.366	.307	.259
6	.765	.592	.464	.367	.293	.236	.192
7	.728	.538	.403	.306	.234	.182	.142
8	.694	.489	.351	.255	.188	.140	.105
9	.661	.445	.305	.212	.150	.108	.078
10	.629	.404	.265	.177	.120	.083	.058
11	.599	.368	.231	.147	.096	.064	.043
12	.571	.334	.200	.123	.077	.049	.032
13	.543	.304	.174	.102	.061	.038	.023
14	.518	.276	.152	.085	.049	.029	.017
15	.493	.251	.132	.071	.039	.022	.013
16	.469	.228	.115	.059	.031	.017	.010
17	.447	.208	.100	.049	.025	.013	.007
18	.426	.189	.087	.041	.020	.010	.005
19	.406	.171	.075	.034	.016	.008	.004
20	.386	.156	.066	.029	.013	.006	.003
21	.368	.142	.057	.024	.010	.005	.002
22	.350	.129	.050	.020	.008	.004	.002
23	.334	.117	.043	.017	.007	.003	.001
24	.318	.106	.037	.014	.005	.002	.001
25	.303	.097	.033	.011	.004	.002	.001

Appendix 9
Present Value of an Annuity

Present Value of an Annuity of $1

(Midyear discounting)

Period	5%	10%	15%	20%	25%	30%	35%
1	.976	.953	.933	.913	.894	.877	.861
2	1.905	1.820	1.743	1.674	1.610	1.552	1.498
3	2.790	2.608	2.448	2.308	2.182	2.071	1.970
4	3.634	3.325	3.062	2.836	2.640	2.470	2.320
5	4.436	3.976	3.595	3.276	3.007	2.777	2.579
6	5.201	4.568	4.058	3.643	3.300	3.013	2.771
7	5.929	5.106	4.462	3.949	3.534	3.195	2.913
8	6.623	5.595	4.812	4.203	3.722	3.335	3.019
9	7.283	6.040	5.117	4.416	3.872	3.442	3.097
10	7.912	6.444	5.382	4.593	3.992	3.525	3.155
11	8.512	6.812	5.613	4.740	4.088	3.589	3.197
12	9.082	7.146	5.813	4.863	4.165	3.637	3.229
13	9.626	7.450	5.987	4.965	4.226	3.675	3.253
14	10.143	7.726	6.139	5.051	4.275	3.704	3.270
15	10.636	7.977	6.271	5.122	4.315	3.726	3.283
16	11.105	8.206	6.385	5.181	4.346	3.743	3.292
17	11.552	8.413	6.485	5.230	4.371	3.757	3.299
18	11.978	8.602	6.572	5.271	4.392	3.767	3.305
19	12.384	8.773	6.647	5.306	4.408	3.775	3.309
20	12.770	8.929	6.712	5.334	4.421	3.781	3.311
21	13.138	9.071	6.769	5.358	4.431	3.785	3.314
22	13.488	9.200	6.819	5.378	4.439	3.789	3.315
23	13.822	9.317	6.862	5.395	4.446	3.791	3.316
24	14.139	9.423	6.899	5.408	4.451	3.794	3.317
25	14.442	9.520	6.932	5.420	4.455	3.795	3.318

Appendix 10
Formulas, Equations, and computations

Formula for the future value of an annuity is:

$$F = P \; \frac{(1 + i)^{n - 1}}{i}$$

Where:

F = future value of an annuity
P = annuity payment
i = rate of interest
n = number of time periods

Present Value Equation for Dividend Stream

$$P = \frac{D(1 + g)}{(1 + i)} + \frac{D(1 + g)^2}{(1 + i)^2} + \cdots + \frac{D(1 + g)^n}{(1 + i)^n}$$

Where:

P = present Value
D = dividend rate at beginning of period
g = growth rate of dividends
i = discount rate or interest rate
n = time periods

McDep Ratio

The McDep Ratio stands for "Market Capitalization (Mc) plus Debt (De) divided by appraised value of Properties (P). The term was coined by oil analyst Kurt Wulff.

Market Capitalization = Stock price times number of shares

Debt   =   Total liabilities
            −   Current assets
            −   50% of deferred taxes
            +   Preferred stock (treated as debt)
            +   50% of deferred capital gains tax*

Property = Appraised value of oil and gas properties, acreage pipe lines, refineries and other assets (excluding current assets).

* The deferred capital gains tax is equal to the difference between book value and appraised equity times the tax rate.

Appraised equity (Property − Debt) is based in part on the estimated deferred capital gains tax which is based on appraised equity. Because of this dependency relationship, the estimate of deferred capital gains tax requires a trial and error approach.

Appendix 11
Natural Gas Products

C1	C2	C3	C4	C5+	Terminology
<— LNG —>					Liquified Natural Gas
		<— LPG —>			Liquified Petroleum Gas
	<- - —— NGL —————>				Natural Gas Liquids
				|<-COND->	Condensate
Meth.	Eth.	Prop.	But.	Pent.+	

Liquified Natural Gas (LNG):

One MCF gas = 43.57 pounds of LNG

One Ton of LNG = 46 MCF gas

C1 = Methane
C2 = Ethane
C3 = Propanes
C4 = Butanes
C5 = Pentane

Appendix 12
Sources of Information for the Energy Industry

American Petroleum Institute
Publications and Distribution Section
1220 L Street N.W.
Washington, DC 20005
(202) 682-8375

National Petroleum News
NPN Fact Book
950 Lee Street
Des Plaines, IL 60016

Independent Petroleum Association of America
1101-16th Street N.W.
Washington, DC 20036

- *United States Petroleum Statistics*
- *Petroleum Independent* Magazine
- The Oil Producing Industry in Your State (*Petroleum Independent*, Sept. Issue)

Twentieth Century Petroleum Statistics
DeGolyer and MacNaughton
One Energy Square
Dallas, TX 75206

Standard & Poor's *Industry Surveys*

Industry Norms and Key Business Ratios
Duns Analytical Services

Federal Reserve Bulletin

Almanac of Business and Industrial Ratios
Prentice Hall, by Leo Troy, Ph.D.

Department of Energy
National Energy Information Center EI-231
Energy Information Administration
Forrestal Building Room 1f-048
Washington, DC 20585

- *Monthly Energy Review*
- *Annual Energy Review*
- *International Oil & Gas Exploration and Development Activities*
- *Annual Outlook for Oil and Gas* DOE/EIA - 0517(90)
- *Costs and Indices for Domestic Oil and Gas Field Equipment and Production Operations*

International Petroleum Encyclopedia
PennWell Publishing Co.
Box 1260
Tulsa, OK 74101

Oil & Gas Journal

- Annual Refining Report (U.S. Refineries)
- Worldwide Report (Refineries Worldwide)

Petroleum Information Resume (Annual Review)
Petroleum Information Corporation—a company of The Dun & Bradstreet Corporation

Appendix 13
Summary of Information Found in the 10-K Report

PART I

Item 1   Business Discussion—General Information
         Corporate Structure and Current Developments
         Segment and Geographic Information
         Key Purchasers/Markets and Competition
         Financing
         Acquisitions
         Exploration and Production

Item 2   Description of Properties
         Acreage
         Drilling Activity
         Producing Wells
         Production Summary
         Unit Sales Prices and Production Costs
         Reserves Summary
         Oil and Gas Regulation

Item 3   Legal Proceedings
Item 4   Submission of Matters to a Vote of Security Holders

PART II

Item 5   Market for the Registrants Common Equity and Related Security
         Holder Matters
Item 6   Selected Financial Data—Quarterly High and Low Stock Trading
         Values
Item 7   Management's Discussion and Analysis of Financial Condition
         and Results of Operations

Item 8   Financial Statements and Supplementary Data
         Auditor's Opinion Letter
         Balance Sheet
         Income Statement
         Statement of Cash Flows
         Footnotes
            1. Sales of Assets—Reorganization
            2. Summary of Significant Accounting Policies
            3. Oil & Gas Acquisitions—Mergers
            4. Oil & Gas Expenditures
            5. Long-term Debt
            6. Other Long-term Liabilities
            7. Employee Benefits
            8. Income Taxes
            9. Stock Options and Warrants
            10. Earnings Per Share
            11. Commitments and Contingencies
            12. Segment Reporting and Major Customers
            13. Related Party Transactions
            14. Quarterly Financial Data
            15. Oil and Gas Data
                (a) Results of Operations
                (b) Costs Incurred and Capitalized Costs
                (c) Standardized Measure of Future Net Cash Flows (SEC
                    Value of Reserves)
                (d) Changes in Standardized Measure

Item 9   Changes in and Disagreements with Accountants on Accounting
         and Financial Disclosure

PART III *

Item 10 Directors and Executive Officers
Item 11 Executive Compensation

Item 12 Security Ownership of Certain Beneficial Owners and Management

Item 13 Certain Relationships and Related Transactions

*Items 11 to 13 are normally *incorporated by reference* to the Proxy Statement.

PART IV

Item 14 Exhibits, Financial Statement Schedules, and Reports on Form 8-K

Schedules

I	Short-term Investments & Marketable Securities
II	Amounts Receivable from Related Parties
III	Condensed Financial Information
IV	Indebtedness of affiliates*
V	Property, Plant, and Equipment (PP&E)
VI	Accumulated Depreciation, Depletion, and Amortization (DD&A) of PP&E
VII	Guarantees of Securities of Other Issuers*
VIII	Valuation of Accounts Receivable and Reserves
IX	Short-term Borrowings
X	Supplementary Income Statement Information
XI	Supplementary Profit and Loss Information*
XII	Income from Dividends (Equity in Affiliates)*
XIII	Other Investments

* Less common schedules.

Schedules may be omitted if they are not considered applicable, or if the information is shown elsewhere in the financial statements or related notes.

GLOSSARY

accelerated depreciation (see **depreciation**)

accrual accounting a method of matching income and expenses during an accounting period for which they are applicable, regardless of the actual date of collection or payment (see **cash basis accounting**)

ad valorem Latin for *according to value*, meaning a tax on goods or property, based upon value rather than quantity or size.

authorized shares the maximum number of shares, either common or preferred, as stated in the corporate charter, that a corporation may issue. A company may issue fewer shares, but issuing more shares requires amendment of the charter with shareholder approval.

American depositary receipt (ADRs) a receipt issued through a U.S. bank, usually for one or more shares in a foreign company. ADRs trade like stock on a U.S. exchange.

arbitrage the practice of exploiting the differences in price (*spread*) of a commodity, stock, or currency that is traded on more than one market. For example, an arbitrageur may simultaneously buy a commodity contract on one exchange and sell a contract for the same commodity on another where the price difference would allow him to lock in a profit. In the merger and acquisition business, the arbitrageurs would look for opportunities to purchase stock in a company being taken over and would sell short the stock of the acquiring company to lock in their profit and limit their risk.

bear market a market characterized by generally falling stock prices. Someone is said to be *bearish* if they have a pessimistic outlook. A *bear* is someone who expects the market to fall.

beta measure of the volatility of a stock relative to either stock market index or to an index based upon a universe of industry-related stocks. If a stock's price tends to follow its industry group up or down in synchronization, the stock will have a beta of 1. Stocks that rise more sharply than the stock market or an industry-related group in a bull market, and fall more sharply in a bear market, will have a beta greater than 1. A low beta stock will exhibit a relatively stable performance during market fluctuations. For example, if every time the market went up 10%, the stock of Company X only went up 7%, the beta for the company, relative to the market, would be 70% (or .7). (see **Capital Asset Pricing Model**)

blue chip stock a term that refers to the common stock of a well-known, established, and reputable company that has a long record of stability and growth. Often-mentioned examples of blue chip stocks include IBM, Exxon, Du Pont, and General Electric.

bond a certificate of indebtedness extending over a period of more than one year from the date of issue. A debt of less than one year is usually called a *note*. A bond is an obligation that usually requires interest payments and must be repaid at a specific time. A non-interest bearing bond is called a *zero coupon* bond.

bond indenture a supplementary agreement to a bond issue that defines the rights, privileges, and limitations of bondholders.

book value (1) the value of the equity of a company. Book value of stock is equal to the equity divided by the number of shares of common stock. Fully diluted book value is equal to the equity less any amount that preferred shareholders are entitled to divided by the number of shares of common stock. (2) Book value of an asset, or group of assets, is equal to the initial cost less DD&A.

boot the nonequity (usually cash) portion of the seller's compensation in an acquisition.

breakup value the money that would be raised if all of a company's operating entities and assets were sold and debt paid.

bull market a market characterized by generally rising stock prices. Someone is said to be *bullish* if they have an optimistic outlook. A *bull* is someone who expects the market to rise.

business judgment rule refers to the fiduciary responsibility of management and directors to shareholders to act in good faith and on an informed basis in what they reasonably and honestly believe to be in the best interests of the company and its stockholders. The rule does not require that directors be correct in making judgments and decisions, but that they exercise their judgment in good faith, after due deliberation, based upon facts available.

call or **call option** the right to buy shares of a stock at a fixed price during a given period of time. Preferred stock or bonds may have call options.

call provisions conditions associated with a bond or preferred stock allowing the issuer to redeem the bonds at a predetermined price (redemption price).

Capital Asset Pricing Model (CAPM) sophisticated model of the relationship between *expected risk* and *expected return*. The model is based upon *expected value* theory and the theory that investors demand higher potential returns for higher risks. The return on an asset or security should be equal to a risk-free return (such as from a short-term Treasury Security) plus a risk premium.

capital gain the difference between the purchase price of an asset and the selling price, if the asset sells for more than the purchase price.

capitalize (1) in an accounting sense, the periodic expensing (amortization) of capital costs, such as through depreciation or depletion. (2) to convert an (anticipated) income stream to a *present value* by dividing by an interest rate, as in the dividend discount model. (3) to record capital outlays as additions to asset value rather than as expenses.

capitalization all money invested in a company including long-term debt (bonds), equity capital (common and preferred stock), retained earnings, and other surplus funds

capitalization rate the rate of interest used to convert a series of future payments into a single present value.

capitalization ratio the percentage of long-term debt, preferred stock, and equity capital to total capital. Also called "Corporate Capital Structure."

cartel a group of businesses or nations that agrees to control prices by regulating production and marketing of a product. A cartel has less control over an industry than a monopoly. *Trust* is also sometimes used for a synonym for cartel.

cash flow (1) in a loose sense, defined as net income plus depreciation, depletion, and amortization, and other noncash expenses. Cash flow is usually synonymous with *cash earnings* and *operating cash flow.* (2) an analysis of all the changes that effect the cash account during an accounting period.

cash basis accounting an accounting method that records revenues and expenses only when money has changed hands.

charter the common term for the certificate of incorporation validated by the state of residence giving legal status to a corporation.

commercial paper short-term promissory notes issued by corporations.

convertible debenture a debenture that is convertible into common stock. The conversion terms are usually based upon price at the option of the debenture owner.

convertible preferred stock a preferred stock that is convertible into common stock. The conversion terms are usually based upon a predetermined price schedule at the option of the preferred stockholders.

cost of capital the minimum rate of return on capital required to compensate debt holders and equity investors for bearing risk. Cost of capital is computed by weighting the after-tax cost of debt and equity according to their relative proportions in the corporate capital structure.

cramdown transactions where shareholders or bondholders are forced to accept certain combinations of securities or provisions.

current assets liquid assets that are readily convertible into cash and assets that are expected to be converted into cash within one year.

Current liabilities debt and other obligations that are due within one year. Current liabilities usually include accounts payable, taxes, wage accruals, and the portion of long-term debt and notes payable within 12 months.

current ratio the ratio of current assets to current liabilities. It is related to working capital, which is equal to current assets less current liabilities.

curtailed production oil or gas production that is producing at a relatively reduced rate due to market or regulatory restraints.

debenture a bond issued without collateral (unsecured).

debt service cash required in a given period, usually one year, for payments of interest and current maturities of principal on outstanding debt. In corporate bond issues, debt service is the annual interest plus annual sinking fund payments.

debt-to-equity ratio (1) total long-term debt divided by common share-holders' equity. This is a measure of financial leverage. (2) total liabilities divided by total shareholders' equity. This shows to what extent owner's equity can cushion creditor's claims in the event of liquidation. (3) long-term debt and preferred stock divided by common stock equity.

deferred charge (or deferred cost) a payment that is carried forward (as an asset) and not recognized as an immediate expense. Examples would be prepaid expenses that provided services, or an insurance premium payment that provided coverage beyond the accounting period in which the payments were made.

defeasance short for in-substance defeasance, a technique whereby a corporation discharges old, low-rate debt without repaying it prior to maturity. The corporation uses newly purchased securities with a lower face value but paying higher interest or having a higher market value. The objective is a cleaner (more debt-free) balance sheet and increased earnings in the amount by which the face amount of the old debt exceeds the cost of the new securities.

depletion (1) economic depletion is the reduction in value of a wasting asset by the removal of minerals. (2) depletion for tax purposes (depletion allowance) deals with the reduction of mineral resources due to removal by production or mining from an oil or gas reservoir or a mineral deposit.

depreciation an accounting convention designed to emulate the cost or expense associated with reduction in value of an asset due to wear and tear, deterioration, or obsolescence over a period of time. Depreciation is a noncash expense. There are several techniques for depreciation of capital costs:
- strait line
- double declining balance
- declining balance
- sum-of-the-years' digits

development well a well drilled within the proved area of an oil or gas reservoir (as indicated by reasonable interpretation of available data) to the depth of a stratigraphic horizon known to be productive.

dilution the effect on book value per share or earnings per share if it is assumed that all convertible securities (bonds and preferred stock) are converted and/or all warrants and stock options are exercised.

dividend cash distribution to stockholders usually on a quarterly basis. Dividends are usually declared by the board of directors based upon earnings.

Dow Jones Averages price weighted average of Dow Jones Industrial Average (DJIA)—30 of the United States' largest industrial companies; Dow Jones Transportations—20 largest transportation companies; and Dow Jones Utilities—15 largest utility companies.

Dow Theory interpretation of overall market trends based on past price performance and trading levels, and notion of market cycles (day to day, two to four weeks, four years).

due diligence generally, the exercise of fiduciary responsibility through use of generally acceptable engineering and/or financial principles (as the case may apply) in carrying out engineering or financial functions. The term is also used more narrowly to describe the care and exercise of business judgment by officers, directors, underwriters, and others in connection with public offerings of securities or mergers and acquisitions.

Dutch auction system in which bidders compete for sale (not acquisition) by lowering price *bid down*. Used sometimes with company creditors who know they may not get 100 cents on the dollar. Creditors will begin to bid down to a level (say 75 cents on the dollar), where an outsider may be willing to purchase the receivable or debt obligation.

earnings the amount of profit realized after deduction of all costs, expenses and taxes. (also referred to as net income and net earnings)

earnout a method of compensating a seller based on some index of future earnings performance. Earnout arrangements allow a means of hedging during periods of volatile prices, especially where a buyer and seller have a big difference of opinion over value or sale price. Earnout arrangements in the oil industry are more common when oil prices are volatile.

equity the residual interest in the assets of an entity, after deducting its liabilities (see stockholders' equity.)

equity capital money raised by issuance of common stock or preferred stock. Corporate capital structure consists of equity and debt capital.

equity method the method of accounting for long-term investments when the investor company exercises significant influence over the other company

exchange offer a transaction in which securities are issued as part of the consideration

ex-dividend the sale of a stock after the *ex-dividend date*, but before the next dividend payment. Stock sold ex-dividend is sold with the understanding that the buyer will not get the next upcoming dividend distribution. (see **ex-dividend date**)

ex-dividend date the date after which a buyer will not receive the next dividend of a stock

expense (1) in a financial sense, a noncapital cost associated most often with operations or production. (2) in accounting, costs incurred in a given accounting period as expenses, and charged against revenues. To *expense* a particular cost is to charge it against income during the accounting period in which it was spent. The opposite would be to *capitalize* the cost and charge it off through some depreciation schedule.

exploratory well a well drilled in an unproved area. This can include: (1) a well in a proved area seeking a new reservoir in a significantly deeper horizon, (2) a well drilled substantially beyond the limits of existing production. Exploratory wells are defined partly by distance or depth away from proved production and by degree of risk associated with the drilling. Exploratory wells involve a higher degree of risk than development wells.

extraordinary items nonrecurring, usually one-time events requiring a separate income statement entry as well as explanation in footnotes. These can include write-off of a segment, sale of a subsidiary, or negative impact of a legal decision.

fairness opinion when certain transactions are undertaken by management that effect independent shareholders, the SEC may require an outside opinion as to the fairness of the price paid to independent shareholders.

fiduciary a person entrusted with the control of assets on behalf of others, or having a duty, created by his position, to act primarily for the benefit of others. Most states have laws governing the actions of fiduciaries. A fiduciary is a person holding a position of confidence; for example, a member of the board of directors of a company.

finding cost the amount of money spent per unit (barrel of oil or mcf of gas) to acquire reserves—includes discoveries, acquisitions and revisions to previous reserve estimates.

fair market value of reserves in the ground often defined as the present value of future net cash flow discounted usually at a specific discount rate. A common usage defines FMV at two-thirds to three-fourths of the present value of future net cash flow discounted at the prime interest rate plus 1–2% points.

first-in, first-out (FIFO) the method of inventory accounting where it is assumed that inventory is used or sold in the chronological order in which it was acquired. The formula is: Inventory at the beginning of period plus purchases during accounting period minus ending inventory equals costs of goods sold. In a period of rising prices, the FIFO (first-in, first-out) method produces higher ending inventory, a lower cost of goods, and a higher gross profit than the LIFO method.

fixed costs expenses a company cannot adjust in response to fluctuations in revenues. These usually include rentals, lease payments, and interest payments.

fixed charge coverage amount of funds that are made available during an accounting period to pay for fixed costs during that period—usually as pretax earnings, plus interest expense and rent compared to the fixed costs.

float (1) the number of shares of common stock available for trading, excluding closely held stock that may not be readily available in the market. (2) Float is also the time lag in the check-clearing process.

fully-diluted earnings per share the earnings per share, assuming conversion of all convertible securities, and exercise of all warrants and options.

funded debt (1) long-term debt raised through the issuance of bonds. (2) a bond issue whose retirement is provided for by a sinking fund.

futures contract a contract to buy or sell a quantity of oil or gas at a specific price on a certain date.

futures market a commodity exchange where futures' contracts are traded.

going concern a term applied to an established business entity that is in the process of operating a profitable business, as opposed to a collection of assets or a business that is going out of business

going concern value the value of a company as an operating entity. Some appraisers will attribute any value above net asset value or liquidation value to going concern value.

going public when a private company decides to raise capital by sale of shares of common stock through a public offering (regulated by the SEC).

goodwill (1) from the perspective of an appraisal, goodwill represents the intangible value of an entity as distinguished from the value of its assets. Goodwill is generally defined as the value of a good reputation, established client base, and/or high-quality management. (2) In an accounting sense, it is the excess of cost over book value of a company in an acquisition. For example, if a company with $100,000 book value was purchased for $120,000, the extra $20,000 would be *booked* as goodwill.

growth stock stock of a company that is expected to increase in market value at a relatively rapid rate. Some definitions of a growth stock are based on a growth rate of, for example, at least 15%. These stocks are often characterized by a high price earnings ratio and low dividend payout ratio.

hurdle rate term used in investment analysis or capital budgeting that means the required rate of return in a discounted cash flow analysis. Projects to be considered viable must at least *meet the hurdle rate.* Investment theory dictates that the hurdle rate should be equal to or greater than the incremental cost of capital.

independent oil company a company that is involved primarily in exploration and production (the upstream sector).

independent producer a loose term that generally refers to an individual or a small company. The term usually implies that the independent is not integrated.

initial public offering (IPO) a company's first offering of shares of common stock to the public.

inside information a legal term for material information that has not been publicized and could influence the value of a company's stock. This type of information is usually known only to company directors, management, and financial advisors.

institutional investor a bank, pension fund, mutual fund, insurance company, university endowment fund, or other institution with a large investment portfolio that invests in the securities markets. Because of the size of their transactions, institutional investors often get special transaction services and pay lower commissions.

institutional investor a bank, insurance company, university, pension fund, or other institution that invests in the securities markets.

insurgent in a proxy battle, the outside party that may be seeking board representation or control through a shareholder proposal or proxy solicitation.

intangibles all intangible assets such as goodwill, patents, trademarks, unamortized debt discounts, and deferred charges.

integrated oil company a company having operations downstream as well as upstream. The term usually implies exploration and production *integrated* with transportation, refining and marketing operations. Typically, the term is used for nonmajor oil companies.

interest coverage ratio income before income tax expense plus interest and debt expense divided by before-tax interest costs.

internal rate of return (IRR) the discount rate that gives a present value of future cash flow from an investment equal to the cost of the investment.

investment bank a firm that underwrites public stock offerings. Investment banks also provide financial advisory services and may help to arrange funding for mergers and acquisitions.

last-in, first-out (LIFO) an inventory accounting method that ties the cost of goods sold to the cost of the most recent purchases. The formula is: cost of goods sold equals beginning inventory plus purchases minus ending inventory. Balance sheet inventories during times of inflation are typically lower than market value of inventories under LIFO accounting. The difference is referred to as LIFO cushion. In contrast to first-in, first-out (FIFO), LIFO produces a higher cost of goods sold during periods of rising prices, resulting in lower gross profit and taxable income.

leverage the relationship of debt and equity is often measured by the debt-to-equity ratio, defined by total long-term debt divided by shareholders' equity. The greater the percentage of debt, the greater the financial leverage.

liquidate the act of selling an asset or security for cash.

liquidity (1) the characteristic of a stock with enough shares outstanding to absorb large transactions of stock without substantially disturbing the price. (2) the ability of an individual or company to convert assets into cash.

London interbank offered rate (LIBOR) the rate that the most creditworthy international banks that deal in Eurodollars will charge each other. Thus, LIBOR is sometimes referred to as *the Eurodollar Rate*. International lending is often based on LIBOR rates; for example, a country may have a loan with interest pegged at *LIBOR plus 1.5%*.

long term debt liabilities that are expected to fall due after 12 months.

major oil company the term *major* refers to the largest integrated oil companies. These companies will often be fully integrated with exploration, production, transportation, refining, petrochemicals, and marketing operations.

market capitalization the market capitalization of a company is equal to the number of shares of common stock times the market price per share.

McDep ratio pseudo acronym that stands for market capitalization plus debt divided by property (see Appendix 10).

mezzanine financing debt financing subordinate to senior debt. Mezzanine financing often will have conversion features that allow equity participation through stock options or warrants.

minority interest the percentage of ownership attributable to minority stockholders who own less than half the shares of a subsidiary. An amount that appears in the stockholders' equity section of a consolidated balance sheet and represents the ownership of a consolidated subsidiary belonging to minority interest holders. On the income statement, the minority's share of income is subtracted to arrive at consolidated net income.

net earnings, net income or **net profit** (see **Earnings**)

net revenue interest the representative oil and gas ownership after deducting royalty claims on the oil and gas production. A *working interest* holder who owns an 80% working interest in a property with a 10% royalty obligation has a 72% net revenue interest.

note a certificate of indebtedness similar to a bond but with a term usually of less than a year.

operating profit (or loss) the difference between business revenues and the associated costs and expenses (COGS and operating expenses) exclusive of interest or other financing expenses, and extraordinary items or ancillary activities. It is synonymous with net operating profit (or loss), operating income (or loss), and net operating income (or loss).

paid-in capital the portion of owners' equity that has been received directly from investors, usually in exchange for common stock (but can include preferred stock). Sometimes it is classified more specifically as *additional paid-in capital* (excess over par value), *paid-in surplus*, or *capital surplus*.

parity price with oil and gas, the price of gas as it compares on a thermal or heating basis (Btu) to oil.

par value an arbitrary value set as the face value of a security. At one time, par value represented the original investment for each share of stock. Per value has more meaning with bonds or preferred stock where interest or dividends are quoted as a percentage of par value.

pink sheets a daily listing of over-the-counter stocks and the broker/dealers that make a market in the stocks. Pink sheet companies are not traded on the NASDAQ.

points (1) With common stock, a point represents the change of one dollar per share in the market price of the stock. (2) With bonds, a point represents a one percent change in bond value relative to face value of the bond. If a bond with a face value of $1,000 drops in market value by $20, it has dropped 2 points. (3) In commercial lending, a point represents one percent of principal charged up front as a fee.

portfolio the aggregate of all assets held by an investor

preferred stock a class of stock that pays dividends at a specified rate and has prior claim on dividends (and/or assets). Preferred stock usually does not carry voting rights.

present value the amount that, if paid today, would be equivalent to a future payment or stream of future payments based upon a specified interest (discount) rate. Present value is the sum of all discounted cash flows from a particular investment.

price/earnings ratio or p/e ratio the relationship of a stock price and the earnings per share defined as the price per share divided by the earnings per share

prime lending rate typically considered the interest rate on short-term loans banks charge to their most stable and credit-worthy customers. The prime rate charged by major lending institutions is closely watched and is considered a benchmark by which other loans are based. For example, a less well-established company may borrow at *prime plus 1%.*

pro forma Latin for *as a matter of form*. A pro forma is a financial projection based upon assumptions and possible events that have not occurred. For example, a financial analyst may create a consolidated balance sheet of two nonrelated companies to see what the combination would look like if the companies had merged. Often a cash flow projection for discounted cash flow analysis is referred to as a pro *forma cash flow.*

prospectus an *offering* statement made available to potential investors. For companies *going public*, the prospectus disclosure requirements are regulated by the SEC.

proved reserves quantities of oil or natural gas that can with reasonable certainty be recovered economically with existing technology.

proxy a written power of attorney given by a stockholder allowing an agent or representative to vote on their behalf at corporate meetings.

proxy fight a means by which shareholders can seek to influence or change a company's board of directors. Proxy fights are becoming more popular and provide an alternate means of gaining control of a company. In a proxy contest, outsiders are referred to as *insurgents.*

put or **put option** the right to sell shares of a given stock at a set exercise price within a fixed time period.

qualified opinion where company auditors make reference in the Auditor's Opinion to an item, event, or issue that may have material negative effect on company financial status.

quick ratio or quick-asset ratio a refinement of the current ratio where only those current assets that can be quickly converted to cash are divided by current liabilities (also referred to as the *acid test*).

rate base in the utility industry, consumer prices governed by a regulatory body will be based upon a fair rate of return on capital invested (rate base), which usually includes the net original cost of plant and equipment. In some instances, it includes allowances for working capital, materials, and supplies.

receivable money owed to a company for services or products sold, also known as accounts receivable.

reserve for contingencies an appropriation of retained earnings set aside (thus not available for dividends) for possible future events such as lawsuits or natural disasters. Other reserve funds or appropriations may be for such things as future plant expansion, for example.

red herring a preliminary draft of a new public stock offering or prospectus that has not been reviewed by the SEC. These must carry a warning in red ink on the cover that the offering has not yet been reviewed by the SEC and may not contain all the information about the issue. It must also state that information may change before the final prospectus is issued.

retained earnings earnings or profits net of dividend payments that have been retained back into the business. Often an important component of stockholders' equity.

reserve replacement ratio the amount of oil and gas discovered in a given period, divided by the amount of production during that period.

risk premium the return over and above the riskless return investors try to obtain as a compensation for the risk born by holding a particular investment.

reverse split (see **stock split**)

sell short the selling of securities or commodities that are not owned by the seller. In effect, the seller borrows the securities in anticipation of a decline in price, and sells them. This is called a *short position*. Ultimately the investor must purchase securities to repay the loan (*cover his position*). If the securities can be purchased for less than the price at which they were borrowed, then the investor makes a profit. If not, the investor has lost money.

senior debt debt instruments that have first claim on a firm's assets (secured debt) or cash flow (unsecured debt).

severance tax a tax on the removal of minerals from the ground usually levied as a percentage of the gross value of the minerals removed. The tax can also be levied on the basis of so many cents per barrel or per million cubic feet of gas.

shareholder proposal a shareholder may make a proposal (limited by cutoff dates) to be presented to management and shareholders at the annual shareholder meeting. Unless excluded under certain provisions of SEC rules, the proposal will be included in the proxy statement.

short sale (see **sell short**)

sinking fund a means of accumulating funds on a regular basis in order to retire debt (or some preferred stocks) with a fixed maturity. Sometimes bonds will have sinking fund provisions.

split (see **stock split**)

spot market an open market for oil or gas where buyers and sellers bid or negotiate on prices in expectation of taking delivery of the product. This is different from the *futures market,* where a contract is usually purchased with no intention of taking physical delivery.

spot price oil or gas prices established in the open *spot market.* It is often considered a leading indicator of price direction and contract prices.

statutory merger a merger in which one of the merged companies survives as a legal entity.

stock dividend a dividend paid out in stock rather than in cash.

stock option a right to purchase or sell a specified number of shares of stock at a specified price within a specific time frame. Also often called an *incentive stock option* because options are often given to officers and employees who can exercise their option by buying the stock at the option price and selling the stock on the open market. This would only be done if the option price was way below market price.

stock split an increase (sometimes decrease) in the number of shares of common stock outstanding, usually by a fixed ratio, of 2:1 or 3:1. The total common equity remains the same. For example, a stock may be trading at $50 per share just prior to a 2:1 stock split. After the split, each shareholder will have twice as many shares trading at $25 per share. Common equity remains the same—no value is created. A decrease in the number of shares, called a *reverse split,* is done sometimes to get share price up to a more manageable trading value. The shareholders in a one-for-two split would have half as many shares, but the par value and market value would double.

stockholders' equity the difference between a company's total assets and total liabilities. Often referred to as *net worth* or book value. Represents the stockholders' ownership in the company.

stripper well a well that produces at a low rate of production. For legal/ tax purposes, a stripper well is a well producing on the average of less than 10 barrels of oil per day, or less than 60 thousand cubic feet of gas per day.

subordinated a descriptive term used for debt securities to establish hierarchy of claims. Subordinated debt implies that there is a debt instrument with a superior claim. A *junior subordinated debenture* would rank below a subordinated debenture.

subsidiary (or **subsidiary company**) a company controlled by a *parent company* through ownership by the parent of more than 50% of the subsidiary's outstanding common stock

success ratio ratio of successful wells to total wells drilled. A distinction is sometimes made between technical success and commercial success for a well. Technical success simply refers to whether or not hydrocarbons have been found, and commercial success refers to whether or not the hydrocarbons found were in commercial quantities or not.

take-or-pay contract a type of contract where specific quantities of gas (usually daily or annual rates) must be paid for, even if delivery is not taken. The purchaser may have the right in following years to take gas that had been paid for but not taken.

technical analysis a method of making investment decisions about a stock based upon market factors such as trading volume and price behavior

tender offer an offer to buy shares in a corporation, usually at a higher price than the share's (then current) trading value. If enough shareholders decide to sell, the company can usually be taken over.

total return total profits received from an investment, usually based upon an annual rate. In a common stock investment, this includes both dividends and price appreciation.

treasury stock common stock that has been reacquired from stockholders by the issuing corporation. Treasury stock may be reissued, retired, or retained indefinitely. It carries no voting rights and receives or accrues no dividends. The creation of treasury stock provides an alternative to paying taxable dividends. Creation of treasury stock enhances the value of remaining shares.

two-bite rule in the face of an unsolicited tender offer, a utility company may be able to reorganize in self-defense, into a holding company structure to gain protection under Section 9(a)(2) of the SEC Act. This is done by transferring utility assets to a subsidiary. The acquisition of the stock by the outsider requires the SEC approval for both entities.

undervalued a term used to express a judgment about the current market price of a security. The term means that the stock has been judged to be trading at a price that does not reflect actual value based on earnings quality, or value of assets represented by the stock.

underwriter general industry term for a company, usually an investment bank, that facilitates the public sale of securities by an issuing company. The process of issuing securities is usually done through sale of the securities to the investment banker (underwriter), who then resells them to the investing public. The term implies that the investment bank is at risk between the time of sale and resale.

volume the total number of shares of a stock that are traded during a given period.

warrant a certification or type of security usually issued together with a bond or with preferred stock. It gives the holder the right to purchase securities at a predetermined price, often higher than market price and usually for a period of a year or more, or may be a perpetual *right*. In contrast, a right that represents the right to buy shares normally has a subscription price at less than market value and usually has a life of two to four weeks.

windfall profits tax federal legislation passed in 1980 to levy a tax on oil company profits that were earned as a result of sharp price increases in the 1970s.

working capital or net working capital current assets minus current liabilities. Working capital represents the minimum amount of cash a company could raise in a sudden liquidation.

working interest the operating interest in an oil or gas property. The working interest holder or holders receive all revenues from oil or gas production out of which are paid royalties, costs, and taxes. In contrast, the *net revenue interest* is the interest after royalty payments.

write-down (or write-off) the company's accounting recognition of the reduction of value of an asset beyond ordinary DD&A. The decline in value is charged against income in the period that the write-down is taken. A write-down is another example of a noncash expense and is usually a nonrecurring charge. DD&A is a systematic means of *writing down* the value of assets.

yield the annual return on investment from dividends (or interest) expressed as a percentage of either original cost or current price.

Merger and Acquisition Jargon

asset play a company whose underlying assets are worth more than what the stock market is willing to pay. (often spoken of in terms of "*the sum of the parts being greater than the whole*")

breakup value the value of a company, assuming the assets were broken out and sold separately.

bear hug a bear hug is an offer that is made directly to the target company's board of directors rather than to the stockholders (as in a tender offer), and is contingent upon the board's approval. If the offer is high enough, sometimes the board will reluctantly feel compelled to accept because of the legal responsibility to act in the best interests of the stockholders. A bear hug is a means of applying pressure on the board and alerting the company's stockholders of an offer in the making. Usually, it indicates a potential underlying hostile strategy such as a tender offer at a lower price.

blank check authorizing the issue of new shares (usually preferred stock) at the discretion of the board of directors, or sometimes at the discretion of top management. The board of directors can use this blank check to issue a special class of stock to a *white squire* to defend the company against takeover.

blank check preferred stock preferred stock that a board may use to initiate a *right* plan or issue a special class of stock to a *white knight* or white squire.

control share cash out some state statutes require a buyer who has acquired a specific controlling percentage of a corporation's stock to pay fair value to outstanding shareholders defined as the highest price paid. These statutes were designed to protect against the abuses of the *two-tiered* takeovers.

creeping tender prior to the Williams Act of 1968, a raider could secretly acquire a substantial stock position before making a tender offer. Also known as a "toe-hold acquisition" resulting from the gradual, incremental acquisition of stock.

crown jewels this refers to the most profitable and desirable assets or subsidiaries of a target company.

crown jewel option the strategy of selling off the crown jewels in order to reduce the attractiveness of the company for takeover.

fair-price provisions (see **shark repellant**)

four-nine position a holding of slightly less than 5% of the outstanding shares of a company to avoid the SEC 13(d) disclosure requirements.

going private the process of buying all of the publicly held stock of a company. The company, therefore, is no longer public and becomes privately held.

golden handcuffs employment agreements, usually with upper level management, that make leaving the firm costly. An example would be lucrative stock option rights conditioned upon specified time of service.

golden handshake a provision in a preliminary acquisition agreement where the target firm agrees to grant the acquiring firm a substantial bonus if the transaction does not take place.

golden parachute the guarantee of a large payment to top management of companies that lose in a takeover. Such agreements provide corporate officers with a payoff if the acquiring company fires them. These bonuses can reach $10 million or more for the chairman of a large company.

greenmail a payment made by a takeover target to a potential acquirer. The payment is usually made to buy back acquired shares at a premium in order to secure an agreement from the bidder to discontinue the acquisition attempt.

grey knight a rescuer who may not be entirely friendly, but may be more acceptable than the raider.

hostile takeover an acquisition that was not acceptable to, or agreed upon by, the target company board of directors.

in play a firm that has been targeted for takeover. Usually the filing of a 13(d) or a tender offer announcement is the beginning of a company's recognition as a takeover candidate.

insurgent in a proxy contest, the outside shareholder or group seeking board representation or control through a proxy fight.

"just say no" defense strategy used in response to a bear hug offer, when the board of directors simply refuse the offer and rely on the existing antitakeover barriers that have been constructed for defense.

junk bonds high-yield, high-risk bonds that are often used to finance takeovers.

leveraged buyout (LBO) the purchase of a company financed usually with debt secured by the acquired firms own assets. A transaction in which a company is purchased with borrowed money, creating a new capital structure that is primarily debt.

lock-up defense a white knight is given the right to purchase unissued (but authorized) shares in the target company. Or in a variation on this theme, a white knight has the right to purchase specific assets should the target company become the subject of a hostile bid.

mezzanine financing debt financing that is subordinate to senior secured debt. Mezzanine financing often has equity conversion features, stock options, or warrants.

pac-man defense a strategy named after the once-popular video game. This defense is where a company turns and tries to swallow its pursuer.

poison pill a defense that makes the takeover so expensive that the predator gives up the quest. The target company, for example, might issue diluting or sacrificial stock conditional upon the success of an unwanted takeover.

poison pill rights plan a plan wherein rights are distributed as a common stock dividend exercisable only if takeover action triggers the rights. *Flip-over* rights give shareholders the right to purchase raiding company stock at half price.

poison-put in the event of a takeover, allows bondholders to put or redeem the bond under certain specified terms. Debt issues with poison-put provisions were created to protect bondholders by providing the option to convert debt to cash or into common stock if there were a *change of control* in the company. Traditionally, acquiring firms have used large amounts of debt to finance acquisitions. The target firm's bonds, after acquisition, are often perceived as having more risk. Rating agencies downgrade the old debt, and the market value of the bonds drop.

proxy contest a means by which shareholders can seek to influence or change a company's board of directors. Proxy fights are becoming more popular and provide an alternate means of gaining control of a company. In a proxy contest, outsiders are referred to as *insurgents*.

raider a hostile outside entity or individual who seeks to acquire or take over other companies.

restructuring defenses may provide a superior alternative to a takeover. The main strategies include:
* crown jewel sales
* spin-offs
* self-tenders or share repurchase programs

Saturday night special was coined in the 1960s when there were a large number of sudden takeover attempts initiated by public tender offers that were often announced over the weekend. The inception of the disclosure requirements of the Williams Act of 1968 brought an end to this tactic.

scorched earth a self-destructive strategy in which a company attempts to discourage takeover by making itself less attractive. This strategy has been implemented by selling off divisions or other assets that a pursuer wanted. A company can also make itself unpalatable by arranging for large loans to come due in the event it is acquired. However, most raiders assume this would occur anyway.

shark repellent any tactic that a company uses (such as changes in a firm's bylaws) to make it difficult for an unwanted suitor to gain control. Among the most common:
1. *Golden parachutes* for management and other severance plans.
2. *Fair-Price Provisions*—require that all shareholders receive the same price. Some require that the price be based upon FMV or highest price paid to any other shareholder during acquisition.
3. Another tactic is to create a staggered board of *directors* in order to make it difficult for a raider to install a majority of directors or to *pack* the board.
4. *Super majority* provisions stipulate the amount of votes required to ratify a takeover bid from a simple majority to two-thirds or three-fourths of the shareholder vote
5. *Safe harbor*—a form of defense where a target company acquires a business in a heavily regulated industry. The licensing and clearance regulations make the target less attractive and provide, in effect, a safe harbor.
6. *Anti/greenmail provisions*

short swing profit a gain made by an insider (which includes anyone who owns more than 10% of the outstanding shares) who holds the stock for less than six months. Short-swing gains must be paid back to the company whose shares were sold.

standstill agreement limits further purchase of target company shares by an acquiring company. May encompass agreement between aggressor and target companies regarding acquisition of stock by aggressor, and halting of legal action by target. Often each company (target and raider) makes concessions.

swipe an unnegotiated offer to purchase a company's stock that is made after management has announced an intention to sell the company. The swipe price is usually higher than the price proposed by management of the target company.

target or **target company** a company that is purchased or is the focus of a hostile or friendly takeover attempt.

two-tier offer an offer for less than all of the shares of a company. Usually the tactical objective in a two-tiered offer is to gain controlling interest of a company with the first tier of the offer. Fair price provisions are designed to protect shareholders who do not tender their shares in the first step of a tender offer. Early use of this tactic was particularly abusive to the second tier shareholders once the raider gained control.

tin parachute the guarantee of a severance plan (broader than the golden parachute) for lower tier employees of companies who lose in a takeover. Such agreements provide employees covered in the plan with a severance package, if termination occurs during or shortly after a change in control.

white knight a corporation that comes to the rescue of a target company, usually at the target's request in a hostile takeover attempt. The white knight provides rescue by agreeing to better terms than those offered by the pursuer, such as a higher price and assurances that executives of the acquired corporation will not be forced out. The opposite of a white knight would be a *black knight*.

white squire a corporation that aids a target company, usually at the target's request, in a hostile takeover attempt by purchasing and holding a large, but not a controlling, block of stock.

INDEX